THE LADY INVESTIGATES
Women Detectives and Spies in Fiction

Having noiselessly opened the safe, Janet took from it the case containing the diamonds, and substituted for it a similar case, on top of which she placed an envelope.

Janet Darling, the Love Detective. Illustration by
E. E. Briscoe from *Forget-Me-Not*, 1909.

THE LADY INVESTIGATES

Women Detectives and Spies in Fiction

PATRICIA CRAIG
and
MARY CADOGAN

Oxford   New York
OXFORD UNIVERSITY PRESS
1986

Oxford University Press, Walton Street, Oxford OX2 6DP

Oxford New York Toronto
Delhi Bombay Calcutta Madras Karachi
Kuala Lumpur Singapore Hong Kong Tokyo
Nairobi Dar es Salaam Cape Town
Melbourne Auckland

and associated companies in
Beirut Berlin Ibadan Nicosia

Oxford is a trade mark of Oxford University Press

First published 1981 by Victor Gollancz
First published as an Oxford University Press paperback 1986

British Library Cataloguing in Publication Data
Craig, Patricia
The lady investigates: women detectives and spies in fiction.
1. Women detectives in literature   2. Detective
and mystery stories, English—History and criticism
I. Title   II. Cadogan, Mary
823'.0872   PR830.W/
ISBN 0-19-281938-0

Library of Congress Cataloging in Publication Data
Craig, Patricia
The lady investigates.
(Oxford paperbacks)
Originally published: New York:
St. Martin's Press, 1981.
Bibliography: p.   Includes index.
1. Detective and mystery stories, English—History and criticism.
2. Spy stories, English—History and criticism. 3. Women detectives in literature.
4. Women spies in literature.
I. Cadogan, Mary.   II. Title.
[PR830.D4C72 1986]   823'.0872'09352042   86-5179
ISBN 0-19-281938-0 (pbk)

Printed in Great Britain by
Richard Clay (The Chaucer Press) Ltd.
Bungay, Suffolk

CONTENTS

ACKNOWLEDGEMENTS

THE AUTHORS and publishers would like to thank the following for permission to reproduce the extracts and illustrations indicated below:

Kenneth Allott and Secker & Warburg Ltd for the quotation on page 113 from *Collected Poems* by Kenneth Allott

Chatto & Windus Ltd and the Literary Estate of Sylvia Townsend Warner for the quotation on page 233 from *The Espalier* by Sylvia Townsend Warner

Faber & Faber Ltd for the quotation on page 164 from *Collected Poems* by W. H. Auden

IPC Magazines Ltd for the illustrations from *Forget-Me-Not* (frontispiece and page 61); from the *Union Jack* (pages 73 and 76); from the *Schoolgirls' Weekly* (pages 116 and 119); and from the *School Friend* (page 124)

The *Evening Standard* for the illustration on page 221

ILLUSTRATIONS

INTRODUCTION

The only above-board grown-up children's stories are detective stories.

Elizabeth Bowen

FOR OVER A hundred years the female detective has existed as a standard character in popular fiction. In 1861, eight years before the publication of John Stuart Mill's *The Subjection of Women*, an imaginary female sleuth was going about her business at Scotland Yard. Later in the century, the success of the Sherlock Holmes stories and the beginnings of a distinctive pattern for the detective theme helped to foster a view of the woman investigator as an effective literary symbol. By 1900, active and engaging young female sleuths were creating an uproar at the Café Royal, setting off gaily to cycle round the world, solving mysteries on the way, and clearing panic-stricken friends and relatives of false charges. Many types that later became outstanding in the hands of a competent author were presented in rudimentary form about this time: the spectacular detective, the philanthropic detective, the travelling detective, the comic detective, the impeccable detective. In America appeared the forerunner of the most celebrated type: the 'elderly busybody' detective. She was created by Anna Katharine Green in 1896, but of course her most striking embodiment is in Agatha Christie's Miss Marple—the most legendary of them all.

Anna Katharine Green (1846–1935), born in Brooklyn, New York, is an important figure in the history of the genre: she was the first woman to write detective fiction, and this places her at the head of a long line of authors which includes Agatha Christie, Dorothy L. Sayers, Mary Roberts Rinehart, Carolyn Wells, Phoebe Atwood Taylor, Ngaio Marsh, Margery Allingham, Josephine Bell, Patricia Highsmith and many others. There is a strong tradition of women writers of detective fiction, which is not at all the same thing as the tradition of women detectives as characters in fiction, though sometimes the two overlap.

The apparent feminism of many of the early stories featuring women sleuths is at odds with the sentimental endings which popular authors often felt obliged to append to their works. However, the general idea behind the use of a female detective is bound to appear progressive, irrespective of how it is worked out. There are many varieties of investigator, but two basic methods of approach are soon discernible. There is the person who succeeds, time and again, because of specialized 'feminine' knowledge which suddenly acquires a new respectability, if only for the duration of the tale; and there is the person who competes with male detectives on equal terms. Both of these contributed something to the evolving feminist ethic, though it is undeniable that the latter was the more radical and far-reaching.

The detective form proper also began with an American, Edgar Allan Poe, whose story 'The Murders in the Rue Morgue' (1841), supplied a basic plot which has been repeated, with endless variations, ever since. As well as Poe, Dickens, Gaboriau and Wilkie Collins have been claimed, with justice, for detective fiction; but it was not until the 1880s that the genre acquired, along with a characteristic atmosphere and narrative pattern, its most significant and enduring hero, Sherlock Holmes. The enormous popularity of the Holmes stories certainly gave an impetus to the detective theme, and tales of crime and criminals began to proliferate. To begin with, these were usually short stories. However, after the First World War, the novel began to come to the fore in both England and America, and with the arrival of authors like Agatha Christie, Dorothy L. Sayers, Anthony Berkeley, S. S. Van Dine and others, the period known as the Golden Age got under way. It was during this time that close rules for detective writing were laid down. In 1928 a Detection Club was founded in England, whose members swore to eschew 'Divine Revelation, Feminine Intuition, Mumbo-Jumbo, Jiggery-Pokery' and other dubious ploys in writing their books. The satisfaction offered by the majority of crime writers at this time was primarily intellectual, with interest centred on the puzzle and not in the characters. 'Locked room' mysteries, 'closed community' murders and country house settings appeared in abundance, and not only middlebrow entertainers but poets and dons joined in the exercise with gusto. This type of novel remained in fashion for a very long time—right up to the 1950s, in fact, when a shift of emphasis, partly a result of increasing realism in all branches

of fiction, occurred. The psychological thriller began to super-
sede the straight detective story, as masters of the new crime
genre like Simenon and Highsmith received due acclaim from
the public. P. D. James, whose first novel appeared in 1962,
marked a tentative return to a more traditional form, but one
which allowed for the realistic approach.

The fortunes of the lady detective, as a literary figure, were
closely bound up with the fortunes of the genre as a whole; it
was naturally during the Golden Age (c. 1925–1940) that the
most formidable women investigators emerged. At all times,
however, the character was adapted to suit many different
purposes and to express a whole range of narrative attitudes.
One of her most interesting incarnations, for example, is the
teenage detective who came on the scene in 1921 but reached
something approaching apotheosis in the person of Nancy Drew.
And at the present time, after all her vicissitudes, the woman
detective seems to be flourishing.

In this study, we have attempted to trace the development
of this significant character from her beginnings in the Victorian
era up to the present, taking examples from both English and
American fiction. Why did so many authors choose to make
their detectives female? We found a number of reasons:
novelty; dramatic effect (making the least-likely-person the
sleuth instead of the culprit); in order to justify an unorthodox
method of detecting; because the figure could be presented
fancifully (which suited the mood of popular fiction up to the
1920s), whimsically or comically (the latter in keeping with the
spirit of light writing of a later era); and because nosiness—a
fundamental requirement of the detective—is often considered a
feminine trait. In literary terms, the woman investigator has
benefited from the narrowing of the gap between detective fiction
and serious fiction (a recent development); in the hands of writers
like P. D. James and Amanda Cross she can take her place among
the most agreeable of contemporary heroines.

We have included special agents in a couple of chapters,
because many of the qualities which make a detective also make
a spy, when wartime conditions exist. As a general rule, these
are less popular with the reading public than the 'straight'
detectives, but they were very much in vogue around the time
of both world wars. In recent years (from the 1960s on) girl
spies have reappeared, transformed into superwomen send-ups

like Modesty Blaise—in other words, marked by increasing fantasy, while the sleuth becomes increasingly plausible and three-dimensional. Certainly the female spy has ceased to have much connection with detecting in the conventional sense. Also, it seemed unfair to omit from *The Lady Investigates* those characters who are not called detectives but actually detect, even if only in a subsidiary role. Wives and helpers are discussed in Chapters IV and X, though we have concentrated on those who take the centre of the stage from time to time.

Naturally it has proved impossible to bring in *every* female investigator; but we have tried to deal with a representative assortment. We hope that the most common types have been included, even if individual sleuths have had to be left out, for reasons of space, unavailability of material, or simply because other examples presented themselves more insistently. One small apology: it has sometimes proved necessary to give away the plots of certain stories, and we hope our readers will already be familiar with these.

We have tried to keep literary judgements to a minimum, since we are dealing with works of such varied quality; those that can stand serious treatment are, we hope, treated seriously. Style is always important; but no one expects evocative prose from Agatha Christie, subtlety of characterization from Baroness Orczy or realism from Carolyn Keene, and it would be pointless to dwell on the absence of these attributes. The detective tradition has many strengths of its own. As a popular art form its principal business is to entertain, but it also provides, willy nilly, very clear pointers to the social attitudes and preoccupations of its time. We have tried to indicate what these were and how they were presented, within this limited but fascinating genre.

As usual, we should like to thank our families and friends for encouragement and support. We are especially indebted to the following for assistance and information: Daniel Kirkpatrick of the St James Press; Michael Cottrill; Barbara Harris; Dorothy Harrison; Regina Glick; George Locke of Ferret Fantasy; the Librarian and staff of the Beckenham Public Library; the Librarian and staff of St John's Park Library, Blackheath, and the librarians of the London Old Boys' Book Club.

PATRICIA CRAIG
MARY CADOGAN

I

PARMA VIOLETS AND PANACHE

Early Lady Detectives in England, 1861–1919

> 'We of the Female Department are dreadfully subservient
> to the men, though don't tell me that women have not ten
> times as much intuition as the blundering and sterner sex.'
> Baroness Orczy, *Lady Molly of Scotland Yard*, 1910

THE TRADITION of women sleuths began in England in 1861
with Mrs Paschal in *The Revelations of a Lady Detective*. This was
first published anonymously, but in subsequent editions was
attributed to W. S. Hayward.* Andrew Forester Junior soon
followed up, producing a nameless crime-solving heroine in *The
Female Detective* (1864). These respectable but convention-defying
ladies are nicely balanced in time, almost midway between the
first fictional detective (Edgar Allan Poe's C. Auguste Dupin in
1841) and the most celebrated (Conan Doyle's Sherlock Holmes,
whose adventures started in *Beeton's Christmas Annual* for 1887).

Both Mrs Paschal and Forester's anonymous lady investigator
took up detective work as an escape from the dreadful alternative of genteel poverty. Like many of the male sleuths who
succeeded them, they had a touch of eccentricity that must have
been refreshing to Victorian readers, who were generally used
to more domesticated heroines. It would, however, be wrong to
suggest that their creation represented a serious expression of
feminism; the stories that featured these two women were
firmly escapist. Mrs Paschal's sleuthing activities began when
she was a widow 'verging on forty'. She did not suffer from
false modesty and was at times frankly conceited, making
declarations about the capacities of her 'vigorous and subtle

---

*Both Ellery Queen (in *Ladies in Crime*) and Michele B. Slung (in *Crime
on Her Mind*) inaccurately state that this book was published under the
pseudonym 'Anonyma'. In fact *Anonyma* was the title of another book
written by W. S. Hayward. There was also some confusion about whether
the first edition was in 1861 or 1864, but the date stamps of the British
Library's copies confirm that 1861 is the date when *The Revelations of a
Lady Detective* first appeared. However, the British Library's catalogue could
be more clear on this point.

brain'. Forester's Female Detective, though more subdued, defended with spirit her participation in a 'despised' calling, remarking realistically that as criminals can come from either sex, so too should their sleuthing opponents. The two ladies were caught up in mysteries involving blackmail, forgery, jewellery thefts, missing wills and mistaken identity that were to become stock ingredients in female-detective fiction for several decades. As well as forming the basis of a genre, however, they anticipated historical fact by having professional associations with the police some twenty years before the force actually began to employ women in any capacity.

Both these female sleuths possessed sufficient histrionic ability to pose when necessary as tradeswomen in order to gain access to evidence that might be concealed in the digs or salons of their suspects. These were untrained amateurs at the acting business; but the theatre soon proved a fertile breeding ground for the female sleuths and spies of English fiction, and the ability to assume different roles was to become an even more important tool of the trade for women detectives than for men. Sherlock Holmes, Sexton Blake and others had no difficulty in altering their distinctive features at will, but their flair for disguise is a pallid affair compared with the dashing metamorphoses of some of the early lady investigators. (Dramatic switches of identity occurred at all levels in the genre, reaching a peak in the girls' papers of the 1920s and 1930s. In these, with hair dye, boot-blacking or schoolroom ink the most down-to-earth fourth-former could successfully transform herself into a gypsy princess or an Eastern adventuress, hood-winking not only her dearest friends but her formidably astute headmistress.)

The early female criminal investigators prided themselves on their ability to tackle situations with panache; but actually they trailed a genteel aura of discreet scent, elegant gowns and earnest tea-cup tête-à-têtes. Their exploits are rarely spiced with authentic danger, and the stories rely heavily on coincidence. From the beginning there was a great deal of emphasis on intuition—or even second sight—as a major instrument of the woman detective, though the early stories provide few practical examples of this. Despite Mrs Paschal's belief in her own brilliance and foreknowledge, her mystery-solving was a laboured stumbling from clue to coincidence, far removed from the process of astute deduction accelerated by inspired hunches

16

that was later to typify the 'whodunit'. This lack of logical elucidation is frustrating for the reader, who needs considerable flexibility to slot easily into the sometimes erratic thought processes of the various authors.

The Victorian lady detectives could be seen as rather romanticized symbols of liberation, but actually their creators were really intent on preserving the status quo. Michele Slung succinctly assesses this ambivalence in the preface to *Crime on her Mind*, her 1976 anthology of stories featuring women investigators. She points out that most of the early lady detectives were abandoned by their authors in mid-career and that they finish off 'not at the Reichenbach Falls but at the matrimonial altar'. This of course reassured their readers that ultimately femininity came before independence. Male detectives could, by public demand, be resurrected from the Reichenbach, but the women sleuths, once sealed in wedlock, were dead to detection for ever. Mrs Paschal, the genre's pioneer, had no problems of this nature, as her career in crime began after her husband's death, at a time in her life when she probably felt too old to consider herself as a candidate for a second marriage. (It is an interesting fact that from the early stories until very recently female investigators appear to have aged prematurely.)

However, the sense of modernity projected by Mrs Paschal is endorsed by the lively appearance of the yellowback first edition—as well as reprinted versions—of her exploits. In each of these the cover picture is colourful and boldly drawn, and every chapter is a separate story. This 'well born and well educated' lady exudes confidence throughout. In a brisk first-person narration she describes her arrival at the 'headquarters of the London Detective Police' in Whitehall. There Colonel Warren, who is head of the Metropolitan Police's Detective Branch, gives her the job of discovering how a certain displaced foreign countess manages to live in such splendid affluence in her Belgravia home. During this briefing Colonel Warren, although a little half-heartedly, backs up Mrs Paschal's estimate of her own worth, and encourages her with the promise 'Your services, if successful, will be handsomely rewarded.' This presumably meant that if an assignment were not satisfactorily carried through she would have to whistle for her fees. At any rate she was better off than many of her successors, who were not paid at all. She explains to readers that Colonel Warren's 'petticoated police' were in fact usually successful. Petticoats is a significant word in her saga in more ways than one; when Mrs Paschal is pursuing her quarry she sometimes shows an admirable lack of regard for undue sartorial modesty:

... I with as much rapidity as possible took off the small crinoline I wore, for I considered that it would very much impede my movements. When I had divested myself of the obnoxious garment and thrown it on the floor, I lowered myself into the hole, and went down the ladder ...

Mrs Paschal then gets shut up in a damp and slimy underground vault where, though only in her petticoats and feeling decidedly parky, she shows no sign of panic but simply 'sighs for a Colt's revolver' and reproaches herself for 'not having taken the precaution of being armed'. (Actually it is doubtful whether she could have blown her way out with small firearms, but she was ever optimistic.) Mrs Paschal shows her mettle on other occasions too: 'I have met people who have turned up their noses at me for being a female detective or thief-taker, as they have thought fit to term me, but I never forgot the insult, and have had my eye upon them, and have caught more than one tripping . . .' Exuberance sustains her even during an eerie adventure entitled 'The Nun, The Will and The Abbess'. In this the modernity cherished by Mrs Paschal is overtaken by a kind of nineteenth-century Gothic grisliness. She enters a bleak Ursuline convent as a novitiate in order to find out what is happening to an eighteen-year-old heiress incarcerated there against her will, who is being tortured by an Abbess with designs on her fortune. The only occasion when the intrepid early investigator succumbs to conventional female weakness is after a skirmish with a nefarious Italian Secret Society, operating in London. Once the harrowing experience is over, she 'showed that [she] was a woman and swooned away' but, let it be noted, only *after* dangerous duty had been done!

Mrs Paschal's immediate successor had rather less flair. Andrew Forester's Female Detective remains unimpressive, partly as a result of her resolute anonymity. 'Who am I?' she asks at the beginning of the book, and goes on to insist that she cannot even give readers a clue about whether she is a widow 'working for her children', or an unmarried woman 'whose only care is for herself'. Nevertheless she is at pains to assure everyone that her professional activities have 'not led towards hard heartedness'. Anonymity is total; even her friends suppose her to be a simple dressmaker. Generally speaking this nameless lady is engaged in melodrama more often than Mrs Paschal. Several of her cases end on a note of irresolution and, in the spirit of the stories in religious tracts of the time, the Female Detective rather patronizingly pushes wrongdoers on to the path of reformation: 'I think he is happy for being in Australia, where they are not so socially particular as in England . . .'

A selection of Sherlock Holmes pastiches published by Ferret Fantasy in 1975 includes two stories featuring a lady detective whose approach to sleuthing is as wholehearted and uncomplicated as Mrs Paschal's. 'The Adventure of the Tomato on the Wall' and 'The Identity of Miss Angelica Vespers' (both by 'Ka') originally appeared in *The Student: a Journal for University Extension Students* in 1894. In these amusing parodies, Mrs Julia Herlock Shomes, who has just become a widow, decides to take up 'the line of Private Enquiry left vacant by her husband'. As a sidekick she recruits Mrs Lucilla Wiggins, whose subservient role is indicated by the fact that she knits, counts her 'dropped stitches' and watches admiringly while Mrs Herlock Shomes cogitates, rakishly smokes cigarettes and expounds upon the crime in question. Like her late spouse, Julia makes instant and detailed analyses of events and situations, but unlike him she is usually wrong. Her first client is almost frightened off by her unflattering diagnosis at the beginning of their first consultation:

> 'I'm sorry to find,' she said very severely as the old man entered, 'that you are in the habit of cheating at cards . . . '
>
> 'I, ma'am,' he cried . . . 'I've never done such a thing in my life . . . if it's the waxed finger ends you've been looking at I'm a cobbler to trade . . .'

Her second client has a similarly daunting reception; Julia demands peremptorily why he is wearing his elder brother's clothes (he isn't, of course) and Lucilla, with uncharacteristic boldness, asks why he is wearing corsets (again, he isn't).

Rather bizarre crime mysteries are cleared up with a great deal of parodied Holmesian verbiage but with little sleuthing skill on the part of Mrs Shomes. Disguise plays an important part in Julia's scheme of things, just as it did for her late husband. In fact the opening of 'The Adventure of the Tomato on the Wall' suggests that the celebrated detective's interest in dressing up went somewhat beyond the line of professional duty:

> ... He told Mrs Shomes very plainly a week after the wedding that he would expect her to be interesting, and to provide some little variety in the menage. It thus came about that Mrs Herlock Shomes used to alter her character two or three times a week. She thought of doing this herself, and Shomes was quite delighted. Sometimes she would be the laundress, and would come attired in a bonnet and shawl and shake her fist in Shomes's face and insist on being paid for a month's ironing in advance; at another time she would be the new cook, and nothing would do but he must give her a quarter's wages. Her favourite dress, however, was a doublet and hose, and in this costume she had been seen by most of her husband's clients, who had not the slightest suspicion that the quiet somewhat retiring page-boy who answered the door was other than he seemed.

There is perhaps a sinister significance about that last disguise. As well as relishing the transformations undertaken by his wife in order to keep their marriage lively, Shomes equally enjoys his own changes of identity. Fortunately Mrs Shomes is able to enter into the spirit of it all: 'Life with him was as interesting and as full of the most delightful unexpectedness as a sixpenny raffle ... I've several times rushed to welcome a man and kissed him, thinking it was Herlock, only to discover afterwards that the creature had committed some terrible crime.'

Another of the Holmes parodies in the Ferret Fantasy collection features a lady with pretensions towards detecting. 'Sherlock Holmes on the Domestic Hearth' was originally published anonymously in 1901 in the *Tatler*. Holmes has happily settled into marriage, though his pedantry and slight stinginess are irksome both to the servants and to Harriette, his wife. She, however, uses her husband's conceit about his sleuthing brilliance to get her own way. One step ahead, she exploits this advantage to have an enormous millinery and dress bill paid without protest.

A lady who, while not a founding sister of the genre, had a more profound effect upon it than any of her predecessors, was Valeria Woodville, the leading character in Wilkie Collins's *The Law and the Lady* (1875). She undertakes the unravelling of a murder mystery in order to prove the innocence of her husband, a motive which was frequently to prompt female sleuths into action. Among the twenty or so women detectives who followed Valeria between 1875 and 1919, there is a large sprinkling of ladies who became investigators solely because they wished to redeem the reputations of their husbands, fathers, brothers or fiancés. In the eyes of their readers this steadfast support for wronged male relatives made their incursions into non-domestic and possibly dubious male preserves respectable—especially if the women in question acted as unpaid enthusiasts rather than career detectives (fees and femininity did not go together in polite society). In some instances the heroine—like Valeria Woodville—would solve only the one crime that was of personal importance to her. Sometimes, however, like Baroness Orczy's *Lady Molly of Scotland Yard* a few decades later, the female forced into sleuthing might first cut her teeth on a series of minor mysteries before, in the final chapter, solving the crime for which her man had been unfairly convicted.

In *The Law and the Lady* Wilkie Collins created an intricate plot and structure which skilfully integrated the separate threads of detection, feminism and horror. The tempo of this very long novel is sharpened by moments of irony and perceptiveness; depth is provided by the heroine's strength of character and her determination to establish the innocence of her husband, who has been acquitted but not completely cleared of poisoning his first wife through a Scottish court's verdict of 'non-proven'. Eustace seems a spineless individual whose charm for Valeria and for women in general, though frequently mentioned in the narrative, is never quite convincing. Before meeting Valeria he has lived uneasily with the Scottish verdict; he keeps his secret from her, and they marry; then, when Valeria discovers what has happened, he simply opts out of the marriage, ostensibly leaving to save her from dishonour, but having in fact thoroughly wrecked her life. Valeria not only reopens and solves the case without her husband's help, but is undeterred by general discouragement. Her dedication affronts critics of 'the new generation' as well as anti-feminists; her clerical uncle is particularly upset by her temerity and insultingly refers to her as a 'lawyer in petticoats', ridiculing her for hoping to succeed where intelligent men have failed. Valeria studies a report of the trial, then interviews witnesses and some of the guests at her husband's home at the time when his wife died. She knows little of the law, but is systematic, with a shrewd understanding of people's behaviour. In fact she is the first woman detective whose investigative exploits are built on step-by-step deduction; she knows when to proceed painstakingly and when to take off and follow a hunch. Her logic and common sense are set off by a brooding, Gothic vein that lies just below the surface of the story and occasionally burgeons. Collins was of course a master of the macabre, and he put his flair for the gruesome to good use in the character of the legless Miserrimus Dexter, a witness at the trial and a friend of Valeria's husband. Severely crippled both in mind and body, Dexter resembles the murky characters in early moral tales for children—at one moment a friendly dwarf, at another the frightening ogre. He is the misfit and outcast whose presence in nineteenth-century stories made readers count their blessings, a European embodiment of Karmic symbols of retribution. Miserrimus alternates between bursts of wild lunacy and a rather despondent friendliness. He is most terrifying when tearing up and down in his invalid chair, out of which he ejects himself suddenly to hop around on his hands like an inverted frog, throwing his body forwards and backwards. To help her husband, Valeria braves all this, and the hideousness of Dexter's house, more than once. His home reflects an 'insatiable relish for horror'; it is adorned with pictures of violent scenes, plaster casts of murderers and a 'hanging shirt' of 'chamois leather' which turns out to be 'the skin of a French Marquis tanned in the Revolution of 'Ninety-Three'.

Despite his inadequacies, of which he is aware in his lucid moments, Dexter presumes to give Valeria some longish lectures on the subject of women's supposed deficiencies. It is not, in his opinion, the attitude of society that holds them back but an 'obstacle in themselves': he explains to Valeria that 'women are incapable of absolutely concentrating their attention on any one occupation, for any given time. Their minds will run on something else—say typically, for the sake of illustration, their sweetheart, or their new bonnet.' It is satisfying, after all this cant, that Valeria catches him out and finds the key to the solution of the murder mystery.

Wilkie Collins was a first-rate thriller writer who could deal capably with melodramatic effects, but subsequent creators of fictional women investigators sensibly left Gothic horrors alone, concentrating on a brisk and energetic approach.

Dorcas Dene was another sleuthing lady largely motivated by devotion to her husband, helping him by becoming the family breadwinner. She first appeared in 1897 in a collection of short stories by George R. Sims called *Dorcas Dene Detective*; a second series of her adventures was published in 1898. Dorcas is introduced as 'a brave and yet womanly woman who, when her artist husband was stricken with blindness . . . had gallantly made the best of her special gifts and opportunities and nobly undertaken a profession which was not only a harassing and exhausting one for a woman, but by no means free from grave personal risks.' She has another male dependent, in the shape of a large brindle bulldog, rather inaptly named Toddlekins; this animal possibly set the fashion for the dogs of enormous size and great intelligence who were to become statutory helpers for teenage girl detectives in the magazines of the 1920s and 1930s. Almost statutory too from the time of Dorcas Dene was the acquisition of a sidekick on the Dr Watson model. An avuncular family friend, known as Mr Saxon, narrates the Dorcas Dene stories, and becomes the detective's regular assistant. Apart from the sentimentality of the introduction just quoted, the stories have a fairly vigorous, forward-looking tone. Like Valeria Woodville, Dorcas is capable of analytical reasoning, and she is also a mistress of disguise, having been an aspiring actress before her marriage.

There is too a good man behind the little woman in the single story about Miss Van Snoop which appeared in the September 1898 issue of the *Harmsworth Magazine*. Nora Van Snoop must have been one of the earliest professional and, one hopes, properly paid lady-detective magazine heroines. At the time when Nora Van Snoop became involved in 'The Stir Outside the Café Royal', the New Woman was a force to be reckoned with, in fiction as well as in fact. Stories of women and girls in challenging situations proliferated, and these usually had career or sporty backgrounds; weekly and monthly papers, as well as books, celebrated the imaginary exploits of lady balloonists and bicyclists, nurses and newshounds. Enterprising authors soon realized that detection provided tougher physical challenges than sports stories and more mental excitement

Miss Van Snoop, drawn by Hal Hurst for the *Harmsworth Magazine*, 1898

than the usual run of career tales.

Clarence Rook, the originator of Miss Van Snoop, was an American who lived for some time in London and wrote several stories about the city's underworld. His female investigator is also an American in London. Her name is significant, as well as being funny. 'To snoop' of course implies something rather meaner than the Oxford Dictionary's definition of 'to enjoy stealthily'; it suggests spying in the nosey-parker sense, not the dignified investigation or deliberations of Sherlock Holmes. Women were already forcing their way into the professions and public life, but it seems that male authors, even when admiring their initiative, wished to imply that detection, except as a temporary measure, was basically unfeminine. However, Hal Hurst's drawings of Miss Van Snoop in the *Harmsworth Magazine* story show an extremely attractive woman. She is actually 'a member of the New York detective force' but this is not disclosed until the end of the story. At first she appears to be an innocent tourist from Detroit, seeing London's sights from a hansom cab; but she suddenly gets out at the Café Royal and proceeds to flout convention by entering the restaurant, unescorted: 'One or two of the men raised their eyebrows; but the girl was quite unconscious, and went on her way to the luncheon-room. "American, you bet!" said one of the loungers. "They'll go anywhere and do anything." '

Nora Van Snoop has spotted a notorious criminal and she picks his pocket in full view of a doorman in order to get the police on the scene; the criminal is taken without a struggle to the police station—although it is Nora who is being arrested. Once there, she identifies her victim as the man who has robbed a Detroit bank and shot its manager—her fiancé. From start to finish Nora has carried out her dangerous task with aplomb, and of course her dead lover is avenged. It is only then that the 'womanliness' so popular with authors of the period took over: '. . . she had earned the luxury of hysterics'; '. . . in half an hour she left the station, and, proceeding to a post-office, cabled her resignation to the head of the detective force in New York.'

Crime had unfortunately robbed Miss Van Snoop of the strong, masculine arms into which lady sleuths, with their duty done, so often retired. Grant Allen's female investigators, Lois Caley and Hilda Wade, were more fortunate in the last chapters of their respective sagas. Miss Caley first appeared in the *Strand Magazine* in May 1898, and Miss Wade in the following March. Grant Allen was a biologist who became a best-selling novelist in 1895 with *The Woman Who Did*. This story has nothing to do with detection but it does have as its heroine an apparently liberated woman. Herminia Barton becomes pregnant by her lover, but is too noble to submit to what she considers the restrictions and hypocrisies of marriage. The narrative tone is heavy, overblown and eulogistic. Herminia is firmly put on a high pedestal 'treading her own ideal world of seraphic harmonies', but she is at the same time diminished as a human being. Though appearing to applaud women who were capable of independent thought and action, Grant Allen was actually reinforcing traditional ideas of feminine inferiority, and Herminia's 'liberation' turns out to be her path to eventual self-destruction. In the author's view, 'deep down in the very roots of the idea of sex we come on that prime antithesis—the male, active and aggressive; the female sedentary, passive and receptive.' His Lois Caley and Hilda Wade seem at first far removed from the 'pure', 'pellucid' (and boring) Herminia Barton; they are characterized by a turn-of-the-century briskness and progressiveness, and their adventures are related with liveliness and occasional wit. However, despite Lois's resolute 'ideal [of] breeziness' and Hilda's awesome intellectual capacities, these ladies are Herminia's sisters under the skin; each is in the ultimate analysis 'woman enough by nature to like being led'.

Lois Caley is that advanced phenomenon of her time, a Girton girl, trained as a political economist. The first episode stresses that in her college days she was 'a tropical hurricane ... a bombshell', a revolutionary 'wielding the advanced weapons of curling tongs and a bicycle'. She is almost penniless but determined not to take up teaching, which seems about all that is respectably available to her. In a businesslike manner, Lois takes stock of herself: 'Nature had endowed me with a profusion of crisp black hair, and plenty of high spirits.' She also mentions her 'large dark eyes' which have 'a bit of a twinkle in them'. With these felicitous attributes, Lois intends to make her way round the world, and she manages to see a great deal of it. Regarding herself rather self-consciously as a modern girl, she rides a camel as a change from her bike, climbs mountains and hunts tigers. The stories contain allusions to rational dress and the new status of women; one indeed makes a prophetic reference to alterations in national status, with Britons eventually having to use the irritating and hateful Continental system of decimalized currency. Lois calls herself a 'consistent socialist' though she soon becomes a commission agent, selling a new and remarkable bicycle on a capitalist basis. One of the charms of travel for her is that by some simple sleuthing she easily outwits scheming foreigners; she also proves the authenticity of a disputed will and restores the honour of an attractive fiancé whom she has acquired on her tour. In the tradition of early romantic detective fiction, her sleuthing aspirations end here.

Lois was not so much a crime investigator as an adventuress in the literal and more wholesome sense of the word. Hilda Wade, her successor, is a less lightweight personality, a fact indicated by her choice of profession: she is a nurse. (There is a strong nursing strain in the female detective genre, and Hilda seems to be the first of the ministering-angel investigators.) Her real name is Maisie Yorke-Bannerman, but she adopts a pseudonym while striving to establish the innocence of her dead father, who was wrongly condemned as a murderer. 'Hilda Wade' is somehow more fitting for a girl involved in the down-to-earth business of detection, but Hilda's approach is not an entirely practical one. She despises the police force for its reliance on 'clumsy clues'; she works largely through her capacity to harness 'the deepest feminine gift—intuition', plus the bonus of a photographic memory and 'a mesmeric kind of glance that seems to go right through' pretty well everyone, from the besotted male admirer who narrates the stories, to criminals and even passing acquaintances like railway booking clerks. This of course sometimes makes it difficult for Miss Wade to cover her tracks; once seen, the hypnotic, hunch-pursuing Hilda is not easily forgotten. Like Lois Caley, Miss Wade has globe-trotting tendencies. The process of establishing her father's innocence takes her to South Africa, Rhodesia, India and remote regions of Tibet. She also suffers shipwreck for three days and nights when returning to England.

On occasions Hilda seems close to the saintly Herminia. Possibly Grant Allen felt that his more modern heroines were moving too far away from what he considered essentially female sedentariness. Hilda brings a touch of religious fervour to her nursing and detective work; she is not one of those mundane mystery-solvers given to peering at small objects through a spyglass, but instead takes on a 'far-away air' as her 'liquid and lustrous eyes look out upon infinity'. Inner tension at these moments is indicated by her habit of pulling flowers apart, or of shredding blades of grass. Hilda Wade is primarily remembered because, after the untimely death of her creator, the last chapters of her saga were written for the *Strand* by Arthur Conan Doyle. The nursing sleuth goes out on a high note, her task fulfilled, warmly clasping hands with Hubert (the steadfastly admiring narrator) and promising to marry him. Just before this, Conan Doyle gives Hilda's story its only moment of understatement. Hubert remarks in splendid throwaway style during their stay in Africa that: 'The Matabele revolt gave Hilda a prejudice against Rhodesia. I will confess that I shared it. I may be hard to please but it somehow sets me against a country when one comes home from a ride to find all the other occupants of the house one lives in massacred.'

Baroness Orczy's Lady Molly, who appeared in 1910, is another member of that indefatigable band of women who took up detection in order to vindicate the honour of their men. Lady Molly's husband, Captain Hubert de Mazareen, is unjustly serving a life sentence for murder. This detective has strong affinities with Hilda Wade, and indeed Baroness Orczy seems to share Grant Allen's idealized but double-edged fantasy images of the female sex—at least so long as the women concerned come from the upper classes. Girls (even more than men) of the lower orders are firmly and frequently slapped down in *Lady Molly of Scotland Yard*. These, in the narrative view, are imbued with the 'highly irritating characteristics of their class'. These characteristics are not always clearly defined but excessive sentimentality is one of them. However, this is more often a quality of the pseudo-progressive but actually mawkish atmosphere that hovers around Lady Molly throughout the book. Adulation surrounds her like an overdrenching with cloying scent; it is inspired in everyone who crosses her path. The 'entire [police] force' are 'invariably deferential' towards her; a highborn French woman, speaking of Lady Molly, reflects that '. . . a true-hearted Englishwoman is the finest product of God's earth, after all's said and done', and Mary Granard, who is Lady Molly's sleuthing sidekick, simply cannot keep her admiration in check: her chief is '. . . the woman I loved best in all the world . . . You see, she could do anything she liked with the men, and I, of course, was her slave.' Happily, however, it is not a case of love's old sweet thong. Lady Molly is on the whole condescending but considerate towards her assistant. Their relationship throws up some feminine variants of the Holmesian misquotation 'Elementary my dear Watson!':

'I don't understand,' I gasped, bewildered.

'No, and you won't until we get there,' Lady Molly replied, running up to me and kissing me in her pretty, engaging way.

Mary Granard chronicles Lady Molly's exploits, and she is one lower-class character who knows her place in Baroness Orczy's scheme of things—before becoming Lady Molly's assistant in detection she was her maid. Mary constantly praises 'my dear Lady's' beauty and charm and brains and style—also of course 'the marvellous intuition, of a woman who, in my opinion, is the most wonderful psychologist of her time'. The stories don't give much hard evidence of this flair for mental activity, and there is little or no logical elucidation; almost everything is achieved by fanciful feminine charm and extremely predictable hunch-playing.

Lady Molly is adept at disguise, and frequently fools Mary as well as those who are not familiar with her appearance. Baroness Orczy is less convincing with Lady Molly's impersonations than with those equally improbable aliases assumed a few years earlier by her most celebrated creation, Sir Percy Blakeney, the Scarlet Pimpernel. With Lady Molly, the author seems to have been trying to produce another aristocratic, enigmatic, efficient and adventurous righter-of-wrongs, but everything that worked with Sir Percy seems to have misfired with Lady Molly; the Scarlet Pimpernel had the advantage of being masculine and therefore easier to cast in a dashing role, within the framework of popular romance. Lady Molly's attempts to appear enigmatic are simply arch; pretending indifference to an assignment which she really cherishes, she comes across as a self-indulgent *poseuse*.

Although Lady Molly is supposed to be a strong character and an embodiment of progress, the tone of the book is often curiously archaic. Criminals are sometimes referred to as 'miscreants' with 'fell purposes', and foreigners—and that sometimes includes the Scots—as well as the native 'peasantry' take some bashings; so too do trade unions and socialist clubs, which are loosely equated with 'the ever-growing tyranny of the Mafia'. Censure of this nature of course reflected fears that lay beneath the smooth veneer of Edwardian society. Generally speaking, Baroness Orczy was more at ease when describing the surface security and splendours than the partially obscured conflicts. There *are* some superficial excursions into artisan poverty and squalour, and the Lady Molly stories flirt with feminism, although this is of the woolly, romanticized variety and bears no relation to any of the organized suffragist movements of the time. Mood and local colour are strongest at the level of genteel affluence, with Lady Molly 'graceful and elegant in her beautiful directoire gown', or, accompanied by Mary Granard, retiring to a Lyons teashop in Regent Street for toasted muffins after a matinée performance of *Trilby*. The text is also occasionally enlivened by atmospheric whiffs of Russian leather and parma violets, so that, despite their limitations as detective fiction, the Lady Molly stories retain a certain vintage charm for readers of today.

Like several other early women detectives Lady Molly solves a series of separate mysteries, and her real reason for taking up detection is revealed only at the end. The finale follows the woman-saves-her-man formula. It is left to Mary Granard to explain that, as soon as Lady Molly was 'once more united with the man who so ardently worshipped and trusted her', she gave up her connection with the police. Mary signs off by describing herself as 'ever faithful'. Presumably with Lady Molly's happiness restored and her sleuthing at an end, Mary will revert to her original position as lady's maid—a daunting thought in the context of her career but one which Baroness Orczy considered unworthy of mention; Mary Granard was after all not from the classes who were supposed to concern themselves with ambition.

Mary is the most openly adoring of all the chronicler-assistants. Others are more restrained about the detectives with whom they worked, but admiration is still generally the keynote. Florence Cusack is the lady investigator in four stories by L. T. Meade and Robert Eustace which appeared in the *Harmsworth Magazine* between April 1899 and October 1900. Miss Cusack calls on a Dr Lonsdale for help with her cases, and he is the narrator of each episode. His similarity to Dr Watson is obvious, though his admiration for Florence seems avuncular and a little less awe-ridden than Watson's for Holmes. Miss Cusack is unlike many of her sisters in detection in that she is not explicitly out to clear some tarnished male reputation; she does, however, imply to Dr Lonsdale in the first adventure ('Mr Bovey's Unexpected Will') that she has no choice about the unusual profession in which she is involved. She is 'under a promise' that she must fulfil. Dr Lonsdale never manages to get to the bottom of this little mystery. According to his description she has an abundance of energy, money and beauty. Like several of the early sleuths she has physical advantages—raven-black hair (blonde or auburn tresses and detecting did not then seem to go together), marvellous eyes and a good complexion. She is, in Dr Lonsdale's view 'the most acute and . . . successful Lady Detective in the whole of London . . . a power in the police courts, and highly respected by every detective in Scotland Yard.' Plot and character development improve as the series proceeds, and in the last story, 'The Outside Ledge: A Cablegram Mystery', Florence unravels the problem of a stocks and shares information leak with keen logical deduction. Messages are being carried from one building to another by a cat which follows a trail along a high narrow ledge; the animal is attracted by the smell of valerian which someone has sprinkled there. Florence not only puts her sense of smell to good use, but also the long fur boa which is featured in Victor Venner's illustrations for this story. Reaching out of a window she drags her boa along the ledge and, sniffing it, establishes that valerian has been put down to bring the cat along. The authors are fastidious enough to make it clear to readers that after solving the mystery Florence flicked her boa 'slowly backwards and forwards to remove the taint of the valerian' before putting it around her neck again.

Miss Cusack's intuition is finely developed, but not quite to the clairvoyant level reached by other female sleuths. In fact she emerges as one of the most engaging heroines of L. T. Meade's numerous novels and short stories. Possibly Robert Eustace's collaboration helped to inject vigour into the narrative style, which is crisper and less sentimental than in Meade's solo efforts. (Another successful woman character resulting from this literary partnership was the criminal in *The Sorceress of the Strand*, 1903.) Florence is one of the few lady detectives who seem simply to have faded away in harness; for her, the personal and romantic mystery vaguely hinted at in the first story is not resolved in the last in the customary lovers' embrace followed by renunciation of a career in detection.

Another female investigator who proceeds by analytical reasoning rather than impulse is Loveday Brooke. Chronologically she precedes some of the crime-solvers already mentioned; *The Experiences of Loveday Brooke, Lady Detective* by Catherine L. Pirkis was published in 1894. Loveday is more of a loner than many female investigators; there is no Watsonian colleague to chronicle or assist with her cases. Nor does she take up detection to redeem the reputation of a maligned male relative. Her motivation is poverty—the most basic of all career-prodders. Loveday is sharp-witted, but deceptively demure; she wears black, 'Quaker-like' clothes and in this respect is a forerunner of the American 'mind nurse' detective Millicent Newberry (see Chapter II) who favours grey and also presents herself primly. Loveday is resolutely nondescript— 'not tall ... not short ... not dark ... not fair ... neither handsome nor ugly.' She starts each case with her mind 'a perfect blank' and her one quirk seems to be a strange habit, when she is reflecting, 'of dropping her eyelids over her eyes till only a line of eyeball showed'.

Hagar Stanley is as vivid as Loveday is self-effacing. At the start of Fergus Hume's *Hagar of the Pawn-Shop* (1898) she appears in a dark red garment and a short black cloak with a scarlet handkerchief 'carelessly twisted round her magnificent black hair' (another brainy sleuthing brunette). Hagar's exotic 'Eastern' beauty of face is 'of the Romany type'. She has left her tribe because she does not want to marry the man chosen for her by the gypsy king. Jacob Dix, to whom she is remotely related, grudgingly takes her in as unpaid drudge in his home and as assistant in his dingy pawn-shop. He dies conveniently early in the saga, and Hagar keeps the business going until Jacob's wandering son turns up to claim it. Hagar is a fairly robust character but, with an unrealistic high-mindedness that springs from the religious tract type of story, she refuses a salary throughout this period, and keeps only just on the right side of the breadline. In each chapter Hagar solves a separate mystery of which the focus is an object brought in for pawning —an early edition of Dante, a jade idol, an amber and diamond necklace, a silver teapot, a Persian ring, etc. Characters are often as highly charged as these objects, and Hagar herself is colourful in action as well as appearance. She boxes the ears of a man who refers to her as 'that Jezebel', and when a police officer tells her she is too good to be a woman she retorts that she is 'not bad enough to be a man'. Her assistant Bolker is luridly impish and deformed, and there are larger than life foreigners like mysterious Chinese and a 'passionate little Tuscan'.

Hagar works on her own, though there *is* a man in her life. Handsome Eustace Lorn is one of her first customers, but only on the last page of the book is it recorded that Hagar has 'come to her own'—she has then just married Eustace and they are happily embarking on a life of caravan domesticity and itinerant bookselling. At this point Hagar predictably turns her back on detection: 'I am Mrs Lorn now, and Hagar of the Pawn-Shop, with all her adventures, is a phantom of the past.' She probably set the fashion for a touch of the bizarre in the field of twentieth-century female sleuthing, although there is often a Victorian heaviness of tone in the stories.

McDonnell Bodkin's Dora Myrl began with an exuberant type of independence that suggests a leap into the modern crime story genre, but this was not sustained; despite her initial promise, Dora was doomed to extinction as a detective when marriage and motherhood caught up with her. She had to 'get her man' in the marital sense, not only to fit in with readers' notions of where a woman's permanent place should be, but perhaps to avoid a clash in popularity and sales markets with one of Bodkin's previously established characters, the male investigator, Paul Beck. In *Dora Myrl, the Lady Detective* (1900) the heroine works on her own as a professional consultant; in *The Capture of Paul Beck* (1909) the author's two detectives are at first opponents and then lovers. Once wedded, Dora is not allowed to carry on in the role of partner or even assistant to her husband; she does however have the consolation prize of producing an offspring, Paul Junior, who follows in his parents' ferreting footsteps as *Young Beck; a Chip off the Old Block* (1912).

The first meeting of Bodkin's two celebrated detectives takes place about half way through *The Capture of Paul Beck* and Paul's professional coolness immediately 'delighted the expert soul of Dora'. Her admiration for 'the greatest detective alive' is not diminished by the fact that they are on opposite sides. She slips quickly enough into the role of subservient female, although she pursues her part of the case with integrity, and at least tries to maintain a façade of independence—for her, like other Edwardian heroines, one expression of this is highspeed bicycling. Both Dora and Paul are considerably skilled at disguising themselves. Dora has the added advantage of being able to blush and tremble at will, but even so she rarely takes Paul in for long. When she *does* outwit him she apologizes afterwards and he forgives her magnanimously from the unassailability of his deeper knowledge and longer experience (he is twice her age): ' "Vexed!" he exclaimed heartily. "Why should I be? I'd have done the same to you if I were bright enough. All's fair in love and war." ' In the critical stages of their professional skirmishing he wins all the tricks, quickly seeing through her disguise as 'a prim, natty little old maid, with spectacles and a false front'.

Dora has a down-to-earth attitude to her work; she knows that many people consider it unsavoury—'The peelers themselves are ashamed of it oftentimes'—but she generally gets on stolidly with the job in hand, saving her more high-flown feeling for the contemplation of Paul's achievements and attractions. She always carries 'a small revolver' and she can pick a lock with one of her hairpins. Although they start as opponents, she and Paul move more closely together as they discover certain affinities; in true *Boy's Own Paper* fashion, for example, each relishes a cold shower to start the day. They also in the end work together to solve the mystery, so that Dora does not suffer total professional defeat from Paul: ' "Dora", he whispered [she is 'sobbing unrestrainedly' at the time] "why worry so much over this miserable business? You lost one game; you'll win the next." ' She *does* win the next game, in the narrative view, by 'capturing' Paul as a husband—but it is not of course stated that he too has 'won' by knocking out her professional opposition.

Some of the pulp magazines produced their own versions of the lady detective in brisk and inventive stories that were sandwiched uneasily between 'charming love romances' like *A Mid-June Bride* or *The Torments of Tessa*. In 1910 Lord Northcliffe's penny weekly, *Golden Stories*, launched Edith Dexter, the Mill-Girl Detective. (No author's name was given, and her adventures were ostensibly related by 'her friend Nancy Lee'.) Edith is unusual in that she frequently comes up against industrial mysteries, although she also deals with the usual run of jewellery thefts and missing-will-mysteries that were the customary lot of the female sleuth. She remained a leading light in the paper over a long period, and graduated quickly from amateur to professional status. She brought about a reversal of one of the usual man/woman relationships in popular fiction by enlisting her brother as her assistant.

Edith was in fact a slightly more progressive development of a previous girl detective in the Northcliffe papers. *Forget-Me-Not*, another penny weekly, had featured Janet Darling, the Love Detective, from 1909. Janet was described as 'the Girl Detective who will only help lovers'. The process of soothing the path to nuptial bliss for various couples rather limited her scope as a sleuth, but her appearance in *Forget-Me-Not*, an unashamed love-story paper, underlined the appeal of the Lady Detective image at that time. Each of Janet Darling's exploits was headed by a piece of high-flown doggerel:

> Her face was like a flower,
> And her Heart for all could feel,
> Truth and Beauty were her dower,
> But her Nerves were nerves of Steel.

She slots more naturally into the romance story genre than into the mainstream of detective fiction.

In the detective context, the Edwardian 'new Woman' flavour was soon eclipsed by the challenges of the First World War. Women took over tough men's jobs, and in doing so proved their ability to use brains as well as brawn. The popular magazines began to cast women from all types of background in roles where they could use intelligence and initiative; some of these heroines unravelled mysteries, either professionally or as amateurs doing their bit for their country. Their sleuthing methods were very simple and they tended to get involved with petty crime rather than espionage. The leading characters were generally young, adventurous and nubile. Lord Northcliffe's *Penny Pictorial* ran 'A Series of Romances Resulting from the Vast Changes in the Spheres of Women'; these stories were written by E. Almaz Stout and attractively illustrated by Leonard Shields, who was to become a major artist for the popular Amalgamated Press girls' papers of the 1920s and 1930s. The *Penny Pictorial* adventures follow a formula: each starts with an incredulous male expressing amazement that

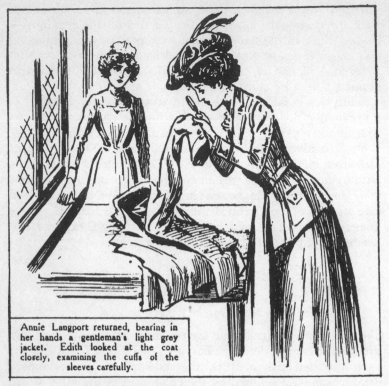

Annie Langport returned, bearing in her hands a gentleman's light grey jacket. Edith looked at the coat closely, examining the cuffs of the sleeves carefully.

Edith Dexter; an illustration from *Golden Stories*, 1911

some slip of a girl can cope as a van driver, postwoman, bank clerk or whatever. The heroine of course proves not only that she can hold down the job but that, as a spin-off, she is easily a match for the wage-snatcher, bank-robber or black-marketeer. There is always some logical deduction, but the girls get by on guts as much as through their sleuthing capacities. They always look fetching, they are 'made of true British fibre', and know that they mustn't faint into the arms of the hero until the criminals or saboteurs have been caught.

But not all the popular magazines presented their heroines so briskly and agreeably. Nostalgia for Edwardian or late-Victorian 'womanliness' is apparent in the slightly off-key motherly character of Kira Polly. She plays the name part in

'Mrs Judas', a short story by James Oppenheim in Cassell's *The Story-teller* of April 1916. Kira is a detective, and her professionalism is to some extent equated with hardness of heart; this reflected lingering disapproval of the woman who took on a man's job. The story starts excitingly: Kira is alone in her London flat when 'She had the strange sensation of waiting for sudden death. Then suddenly a shock went through her, and she sat up. There were two definite steps; a hand parted the curtains; and Levine stepped through.' Ray Levine is the man whom she had brought to justice some years earlier after he had stolen six thousand pounds for Flo ('that wicked woman') with whom he was infatuated. At the time, Kira was 'making love' to Levine, but having him condemned and sentenced for embezzlement was not an act of jealousy on her part: she merely wanted justice to be done—but he of course saw things differently: 'Detective, eh? And catch a man with a kiss! Well, Ki, I hate just one thing, and that's treachery. When I get out—so help me—I'll put a bullet through your heart, Mrs Judas.' Levine has come for his revenge, and Kira shows some skill in persuasion and in staging events which in the end erase his bitterness. Logic is her ally, and she is one female detective who does *not* abandon her career in the last paragraph of the story. Instead, 'she gave Ray one motherly kiss . . . and went to make the coffee'. The story's weakness is that there is so much womanliness and motherliness influencing the action that even at the end the reader doesn't quite understand whether Kira is reinstated as Levine's lover, or has become a surrogate mum. At any rate 'Mrs Judas' was one of the last of the Edwardian-style lady detectives.

What the early female sleuth stories lacked in pace and suspense they made up for with colourful touches and moments of sometimes unintentional humour. In spite of their failings they laid the foundations of an enduring genre, creating prototypes which could later be refurbished according to the changing tastes of the succeeding decades.

II

THE VILLAIN OF THE VILLA

Early Women Detectives in America

They search'd the forest by lanternlight,
They search'd by dawn of day,
At noon they found the bramble-brake
And the pit where her body lay.

William Allingham, 'The Ballad of Squire Curtis'

EARLY DETECTIVE FICTION is sensation fiction with the focus
of interest shifted from the victim or intended victim to the
disinterested onlooker, who is also the investigator. The 'secret'
is the identity of the murderer; it's a practical matter, not an
emotional one, though the genre was slow to shed its emotional
colouring: entertainment for the reading public consisted in
strong sensations.

The first woman to write detective fiction was an American,
Anna Katharine Green (1846–1935), whose *Leavenworth Case*
was published in 1878. The hero of this novel is a New York
police detective, lower-middle-class in origin, named Ebenezar
Gryce. Some years later Mr Gryce acquired, in Miss Amelia
Butterworth, a female unofficial assistant. Miss Butterworth is
an elderly, well-bred spinster with an endearing capacity for
self-deception. 'I am not an inquisitive woman,' is the opening
statement of *That Affair Next Door* (1897); the qualifying 'but'
provides an immediate contradiction. In fact Miss Butterworth
is at that instant peering out of her bedroom window to see
what her neighbours are up to, and she is fortunate enough to
witness the prelude to a murder. On the following morning the
body of a young woman is discovered in the house next door,
battered out of recognition by a heavy article of furniture which
has fallen on it. Even the resolute Miss Butterworth is almost
overcome by the sight: 'I felt a sensation of sickness which in
another moment might have ended in my fainting also, if I had
not realized that it would never do for me to lose my wits in the
presence of a man who had none too many of his own' (she is

referring to the slow-moving policeman whom she has persuaded to enter the house).

When Mr Gryce arrives on the scene she doesn't hesitate to assure him that 'my presence here is due to the anxious interest I always take in my neighbours'; he, of course, is a wily old cynic who is not deceived. A contest of wits ensues between the celebrated detective and the inquisitive maiden lady. 'Outwitted by a woman!' Mr Gryce declares in the end. 'Well, it's a new experience for me ... I'm seventy-seven, but I'm not too old to learn. Proceed, Miss Butterworth.' Before this moment of gratification Miss Butterworth has been subjected to a measure of belittlement: 'meddlesome old maid!' is a term she can hardly be expected to relish. She is an unusual amateur detective who wears a bonnet and 'puffs', takes a poor view of levity and cannot venture into the street at night without feeling 'some secret qualms lest my conduct savoured of impropriety'. When Mr Gryce is incautious enough to joke, 'We shall have you on the force, yet,' she crushes him with the rebuke, 'I am Miss Butterworth ... and any interest I may take in this matter is due to my sense of justice.'

The trick of parodying weaknesses by the simple expedient of letting the narrator deny them is a common way of creating a mood of humorous sympathy for inoffensive foibles. Miss Butterworth is the forerunner of all the old-maid detectives whose nosiness suddenly finds a respectable outlet. She is astute and persistent once the 'fever of investigation' has taken hold of her. Her first success is to find the murder weapon (a hatpin); she also perceives that the dead woman's hat has been worn only once, since it contains a single pin-prick. 'The deuce!' exclaims Mr Gryce. 'Women's eyes for women's matters ...!' Miss Butterworth and Mr Gryce between them get the investigation moving in the right direction, but the identity of the murderer comes as a shock to the spinster sleuth when it's revealed. She is right to assert, '*I* do not believe Howard killed his wife with a hat-pin', but she fails to spot the real villain of the episode. This is a most plausible and agreeable gentleman named Randolph Stone, who has slaughtered the wife of Howard Van Burnam as the result of a mistake in the dark—he thought she was his own. He is about to commit bigamy when his deserted spouse appears. The solution of the crime rests with this betrayed young woman, Olive Randolph, who behaves

throughout in the overwrought manner of a Victorian heroine
—' "Known, known, all known," was her moan.'

The author makes the most of Olive's agitations and troubles,
and the girl is allowed to get her own back on her murderous
husband with the maximum of dramatic effect. She doesn't
disclose her knowledge to the police in a downright or ordinary
manner; instead she arranges a theatrical assignation: 'Two
weeks from tonight as the clock strikes eight. Be wherever I may
chance to be at that hour, and see on whose arm I lay my hand.
It will be that of the man who killed Mrs Van Burnam.' She has
it in mind to stage a melodramatic denunciation: at Mr Stone's
wedding she appears as the second bride. 'Does he not recognize
the only woman with whom he dare face God and man at the
altar?' He does, and the effect on his appearance is described
without understatement: 'No lost spirit from the pit could have
shown a more hideous commingling of the most terrible
passions known to man.' All this is a long way from the spirit of
careful deduction which activated Miss Butterworth throughout. It is as if the author suddenly decided that the technical
procedure of investigating a crime needed a richer embellishment.

Unfortunately the gothic excesses are given freer rein in the
second Miss Butterworth novel, in which the murderer has no
rational motive at all: he is simply a lunatic. *Lost Man's Lane*
(1898) begins with a visit from Mr Gryce to Miss Butterworth.
When the narrator declares, 'Last night the tempter had his
way with me,' she is referring not to an unseemly passion but
rather fancifully to her failure to resist the impulse towards
detecting. A series of disappearances have taken place in a certain
lane in a country town; at this very spot, in a decaying mansion,
live the children of Miss Butterworth's old school friend
Anthea Knollys, a lady who is supposed to have died abroad.
Miss Butterworth realizes that she has neglected her duty
towards the Knollys family for far too long: 'I found myself
packing my trunk before I knew it.' The children, a couple of
agitated young women and a loutish brother, give her a somewhat unusual reception. All is not as it should be at the Knollys
mansion, and Miss Butterworth is disturbed by alarming noises
in the night. William Knollys, the uncouth brother, is revealed
as 'a man with a secret passion for vivisection'. Miss Butterworth
is the horrified witness to a funeral procession at midnight. Has

William's hobby got out of hand? Is this the secret of Lost Man's Lane? No, it is merely the burial of an erring parent who has died after being brought into the house disguised as a phantom. 'Stop your desecrating hand!' cries Lucetta Knollys in an access of emotion. 'This is the grave—the grave, sirs, of our mother!'

The spinster detective has displayed considerable fortitude and ingenuity in getting to the bottom of the disturbing atmosphere which prevails in the Knollys' home, but she hasn't solved the mystery of the disappearing vagabonds. For that it's necessary for Lucetta Knollys to lend a hand, which she does by staging another of those significant rendezvous: 'Tonight at twilight, when the sun is setting, meet me at the great tree just where the road turns. Not a minute sooner, not an hour later. I will be calmer then . . .' This is a rudimentary form of the climactic gathering of later detective fiction when the murderer's identity is disclosed.

Once again, Miss Butterworth has been taken in by the bland social manner of a villain—picturesquely named Obadiah Trohm, and not quite responsible for his actions. His secret passion is not vivisection but incarceration. ' "Six!" he shrieked. "Six! and room for two more! Oh, it's a merry life I lead!" ' A spring hidden in a well-curb works 'the deadly mechanism' which uncovers 'a dreadful cavern' in the lawn. The solution to the crime shows how far the detective story then was from the rational framework of plausible motivation and its consequences, with the sequence simply reversed: the effects presented and the cause then traced. Anna Katharine Green fell under the spell of the charnel atmosphere, and this led her to insert into the narrative all kinds of naïve gothic flourishes. But for all that, Miss Butterworth is a person of common sense whose tart observations may be relished even by a modern reader: 'While I am not lacking, I hope, in many of the fine feminine qualities which link me to my sex, [she declares], I have but few of that sex's weaknesses and none of its instinctive reliance upon others which leads it so often to neglect its own resources.' The tone of coy asperity is Miss Butterworth's most notable characteristic.

'A woman's kind heart stands in the way of her proper judgement of criminals', reflects Mr Gryce; but he is soon disabused of this sentimental notion. The frail and decorative women in these cases, presented as emotional victims, still possess the special knowledge which enables them to turn the tables on their seducers or persecutors, and ultimately they screw up sufficient resolution to use it. Mental stress of course makes them ill and interesting: 'Do you think her delicate frame can stand it?' The situation is always desperate, and when the author fails to tone down her own response to it, bathos results. There's a farcical moment in *Lost Man's Lane* when Lucetta Knollys describes to Miss Butterworth the problems caused for herself and her brother and sister by the inconvenient return of their dying mother. They were trying to make arrangements, she says, for the invalid's comfort, but 'Alas! We did not foresee what would happen the very next morning— I mean the arrival of your telegram, to be followed so soon by yourself.'

Miss Butterworth was not the first woman detective to appear in America. Harry Rockwood's *Clarice Dyke, the Female Detective* was in print in 1883 (the date of the first edition is not known). The heroine is a detective's wife who assists her husband: 'more than once had she rendered him substantial aid in the ferreting out of mysterious crimes.' This situation had become familiar by the 1930s, when numerous fictional husband/wife partnerships were in existence (see Chapter IV). Laura Keen, 'the Queen of Detectives', made an appearance in the *New York Detective Library* in 1892 in somewhat melodramatic circumstances, complete with exotic foreign companions, two pistols and a bowie knife. She belongs in the yellow-penny-dreadful tradition.

Anna Katharine Green went on to create another woman sleuth, Violet Strange (*The Golden Slipper and Other Problems*, 1915), younger than Miss Butterworth and more high-flown in her behaviour: 'one of her idiosyncrasies is a theoretical dislike of her work.' She is a fastidious young woman who doesn't acknowledge curiosity as a motive, humorously or otherwise; once her interest is aroused, however, 'nothing will hold her back'. One of her attributes is a lofty soul, which is hardly an asset in the low business of detecting. Intellectual stimulus is necessary, as an incentive and a justification, and under its pressure the young detective performs remarkable feats of elucidation. 'It's hard to associate intellectuality with such quaintness of expression', observes one of her clients who is about to be surprised. Of course no woman detective is going to look the part in a quintessentially masculine profession; if a female sleuth is not deceptively silly or frivolous or schoolmarmish or bustling in appearance, she will be disarmingly attractive.

Violet Strange's cases, which are chronicled in one volume only, are less detective tales than little instances of moral weakness and reparation; the author's talent for devising logical solutions to a crime is more apparent in her fulllength novels. Indeed it turns out that the girl has attached herself to a detective agency for the purpose of earning money to help an outcast sister—no heroine of pulp fiction could have had a nobler objective.

Hugh C. Weir's *Miss Madelyn Mack, Detective* (1914) is a more interesting example of the genre. Madelyn Mack is a spectacular sleuth who uses a magnifying glass and makes deductions in the manner of Sherlock Holmes:

'. . . Does the second story veranda extend along the entire side of the house?' [she asks]

I think we both stared at her.

'The second story veranda?' repeated Mr Van Sutton. 'I thought you told me that you had never been to my home.'

Madelyn snapped her fingers with a suggestion of impatience. 'I knew there *must* be such a veranda! There could be no other way—'

The stories are more exuberant and skilful, and much better constructed than Anna Katharine Green's, but they owe a great deal to the original model devised by Conan Doyle, whose influence extends not only to the structural device of using a confidant-narrator, but also to the detective's habit of falling back on drugs when things are going badly or when she feels in need of artificial stimulation. 'You've been taking those horrid cola-berries again!' announces Miss Nora Noraker, the newspaper woman who records the cases. We can imagine the tone— concerned and outraged—for Miss Noraker presents herself as an ordinary, impressionable young woman, privileged to watch the gestures and inspirations of genius. She disapproves of drugtaking, but has to accept it as a facet of Miss Mack's flamboyant, wilful personality.

The background details of Madelyn Mack's career are recounted in the opening story: 'the college girl confronted suddenly with the necessity of earning her own living; the epidemic of mysterious "shoplifting" cases chronicled in the newspaper she was studying for employment advertisements . . .' The New York department store owners who refused her a place on their detective staff were made to look silly when the girl undertook the case as a freelance and solved it, but even when she's rich and famous she is plagued by rude policemen, who call her a petticoat detective. Of course they are forced in the end to eat their words: this is the drift of the stories. Miss Mack's performance is always impressive, not to say flashy: ' "Are you a woman or a wizard?" gasped Adolph Van Sutton.'

The detective in action displays a technique of instantaneous deduction which mystifies everyone around her and entertains the reader—sheer bewilderment always has a comic effect:

'I have only one question to ask, Jenkins.' [says Madelyn Mack]
'Yes, Madam!'
'I wish to know whether Mr Endicott ordered a tray of ashes brought up to his room last night?'
Jenkins' eyes widened and his hands dropped to his sides. 'A tray of ashes?' he stammered.

The laconic detective doesn't waste time on explanations, at least until her assumptions have been verified. ' "Nora," she said, without turning, "will you kindly walk six steps to your right?" ' The function of humdrum Nora is to marvel and applaud, but her appreciative nature gets its proper reward—a husband—in the final episode. Twenty-five-year-old Madelyn Mack, of course, is never a candidate for marriage: sheer brilliance has placed her right outside the usual experiences of life. Celebrity on this scale has to be its own reward. Miss Mack is quite literally matchless.

Madelyn's 'first rule of guidance' is 'to remember always that nothing is trivial—in crime.' The fact that petticoats rustle alerts her to the solution in one case of murder. 'Cinderella's Slipper' (the title of another story) is a red herring. The criminals are all men, and the usual motive is a burning necessity to keep some transgression from coming to light. 'The motive of—fear!' is the crucial one which Madelyn Mack appends to a list compiled by the possessor of 'a trained legal mind'. 'Eliminating the field of sordid passion and insanity', remarks Senator Burroughs, 'I divide the motives of the murderer under three heads—robbery, jealousy and revenge . . .' Of course sordid passion and insanity are beneath the notice of the highbrow sleuth, who is principally concerned with the intellectual aspect of the puzzle. Certainly Miss Mack approaches her crimes in a spirit of disinterested curiosity, though she's not lacking in conventional virtues. 'It needs a woman to take care of a woman!' she declares at one point, when a suspect is overcome.

There is nothing homely or disarming about Madelyn Mack, who falls within the tradition of the highly strung, dramatic and omnipotent sleuth which reached a point of culmination in Philo Vance, the suave New York detective created in 1926 by 'S. S. Van Dine'. Weir's stories are often absurd and melodramatic ('My hysterical warning saved her from the fangs of Dr Lester Randolph's hidden cobra,' Nora Noraker recalls in a moment of gratification), but their formal construction has saved them from the worse failings of diffuseness and sentimentality. Madelyn Mack is a good example of the 'exceptional woman' in popular fiction, subject to no inhibiting social pressures and free, as well, from covert narrative disapproval. The fact that she's a woman gives her no special unexpected advantage (no one is rude enough to remark, 'Women's eyes for women's matters', as Mr Gryce said to Miss Butterworth); she is merely professionally adept.

Arthur B. Reeve's eponymous heroine (*Constance Dunlap: Woman Detective*, 1916) on the other hand, is an amateur sleuth, an ex-criminal suddenly overtaken by the philanthropic impulse to save others caught in the downward spiral of events which follows on wrongdoing. She herself is one of 'the Forgers' of the book's opening chapter ('conscience was dulled in Constance') and this perhaps gives her a degree of insight into the intricacies of the criminal disposition. Her husband's suicide ('he had done it for her') is the dramatic event that brings about her reformation, though she goes on embezzling for some time after his death. 'I am afraid I am a crook at heart,' says Constance. She's wrong, of course; in this series it is the unpleasant detective Drummond who is the crook at heart.

The inversion of roles, which might have added sharpness or irony to the narrative, in fact produces weakness and confusion. The author's underlying point, if he intended to make one, about relative culpability, is lost in the awful emotionalism and flatness of the stories. Constance relies rather heavily on 'that thing you detectives scorn—a woman's intuition,' but she also employs pseudo-scientific implements like a 'detectascope' and the two extremes provide further disjunction. Altogether, she's a hybrid character—not strong enough to make the theme of social redemption credible, not stylized enough to pass for a recognizable literary figure, however crude in outline. And for a present-day reader the tales are, quite simply, old-fashioned and dull.

Constance Dunlap embarks on her tasks as a kind of un-official social worker, but even the professional investigator sometimes had a glorified idea of her calling. 'I might be called a mind-nurse, perhaps . . . I help people who are in trouble; they often come to me . . . I am a detective,' states Millicent Newberry, without the least sense of incongruity. The detective as psychiatrist was then a fairly novel concept, and one which these stories entirely fail to justify. It's easy to envisage the lady at the moment of this declaration—smug, plump and senten-tious—but less easy to separate the core of the plots—the straightforward detecting—from the inept social comment, light romantic flourishes and sentimental notions which have seeped into it.

Millicent Newberry, who first appears in *The Green Jacket* (Jeanette Lee, 1917) is a small woman who dresses in grey; this preference remains constant and takes the place of characteriza-tion. The author, never sure of what sort of fiction she's writing, and without a clear image of her central character, dithers between opposing forms of presentation. The detective is either a middle-aged, stout, grey-haired woman, or a proper recipient for romantic advances: 'She was like a picture, he thought, a beautiful shining picture with a little sadness underneath the glow of light.' She assumes each of these guises when it suits the mood of the narrative.

An irrational conviction which proved correct has brought Miss Newberry into the field of detecting. It's enough for her to glimpse a woman on a streetcar to know that she has committed murder. This piece of clairvoyance has secured for the young

Millicent Newberry a job with Tom Corbin's detective agency, but when her employer fails to allow her a completely free hand the impetuous lady sets up on her own. Ten years later, when *The Green Jacket* opens, she is sitting in her office interviewing her ex-employer, who has come to beg for her assistance: he's having trouble with one of his cases. But Millicent will undertake nothing unless it's agreed (in writing) that she shall have the right to determine the punishment of the offender. 'It isn't common sense to go on catching folks and locking them up for ever, or even for a little while . . .' 'Folks' indicates the Pollyanna-type mentality of the heroine. 'Sentimental bosh!' snorts Tom Corbin, echoing for once the view of the reader. But the calm, omniscient 'mind-nurse' has her way.

These stories represent a very low ebb in popular writing, far removed in style and structure from classic or serious detective fiction. The 'use' of a woman as arbiter in criminal matters is to underline the traditional humanity of the sex. Mr Gryce's belief that 'a woman's kind heart stands in the way of her proper judgement of criminals' is simply adapted to define the one as the source of the other: the kind heart is the crucial organ. Unlike Madelyn Mack, that 'conspicuous . . . success in a man's profession', Millicent Newberry operates within specifically designated feminine areas. The usual case she is called in to tackle is one 'a man can't handle—not quite so well as a woman . . . My men are too quick or too clumsy or something . . .' She's the 'intuitive' sleuth taken to an extreme:

> '. . . But sometimes I think it is as hard to catch a thief—as to paint a picture, or write a poem!' she said laughingly.
> '. . . I had not thought of it like that . . . I thought you measured foot-tracks and used a microscope and took away pieces of dust to analyse . . .'

Whichever procedure is followed, it has no grounding in reality; Millicent Newberry is a sleuth who has strayed out of the field of sentimental fiction, and she has imported with her all the conventional trappings of the genre. 'Hush! . . . Your nerves are unstrung . . .' says Milly to one of her clients. We've seen that she prefers the flowery expression 'mind-nurse' (not even 'mind-doctor') to plain 'detective'. And the flair for investigating, the ability to amass and examine facts and draw a sensible conclusion, is turned into a quasi-mystical exercise:

'Only by the intuition that guides all creative life and work did she know she was coming close to a moment when she must yield herself—and at the same time must guide with steady hand, forces more powerful than herself to a successful issue . . .' There is an unlikely cosmic flavour about this brand of detecting—the detective has made herself a cross between a psychiatric social worker and a medium.

The Millicent Newberry novels (*The Green Jacket* and its sequels *The Mysterious Office*, 1922 and *Dead Right*, 1925) need not be taken seriously of course, but they have a certain interest for the literary historian in so far as they indicate various distortions to which the concept of a woman detective was subjected. First we have the woman whose plans for the betterment of society are in conflict with the masculine, pragmatic approach exemplified by Tom Corbin (naturally there are intimations of a romance between the two: this is another of the novels' side issues). Millicent adopts a posture of feminine obstinacy in the face of arguments about the need to 'protect' society; her duty, as she sees it, is to 'cure' the criminal. The author has made her detective female simply to provide a 'feminine' viewpoint on social ills. Then, she has only to abandon herself to unspecified forces to get at the truth of any event. The detective pattern in the books is tenuous and muddled; Millicent stands for a very facile idea of moral goodness, and it is this that shapes the content, not the complex of interrelated facts and fabrications that came to characterize the detective story.

Millicent Newberry is too indeterminate a creation to be considered representative of any particular brand of woman sleuth, but several features attributed to her at one point or another are reproduced in Patricia Wentworth's Miss Silver (see Chapter IX); the English author was less given to equivocation, and fixed these qualities in a permanent form. (Patricia Wentworth, too, for all her shortcomings as a writer, had an excellent grasp of the mechanics of plotting.) Miss Newberry, like Miss Silver, is 'a lady from the top of her hair to the tip of her well-shod feet'; she also exudes the kind of sympathy that inspires the troubled to confide in her. She's the first of the knitting detectives,* moreover, and Jeanette Lee

---

* An earlier knitter, not exactly a detective, is Mrs Lucilla Wiggins, the 'Watson' figure in the cases of Mrs Herlock Shomes, described in Chapter 1.

really devises for this activity a full range of symbolic implications. At one point the detective is described as 'a little grey spider' spinning her 'web of gold'. The knitting reflects, in a literal way, the progress of the case ('She looked down at her knitting. The zig-zag lines were almost together. They were closing in . . . When Partridge owned up, the rest would be simple knitting . . .') but it's also a means to record information: 'Do you mean to say—everything I have told you is knit in there?' Miss Newberry's eccentric method of shorthand results in garments decorated with 'a curious pattern'. Tom Corbin is more accurate than he knows when he expresses the traditional discomfort of the bluff person confronted with finicky work: 'Corbin fidgeted a little. "Funny thing—knitting!" he said.' And of course it has an even more fundamental symbolic relation to the text: it is not the only thing about the books that is soft and woolly.

The true detective framework took some time to evolve, and a number of dead ends are discernible along the way. The adaptation of other forms of fiction to accommodate the detective theme generally proved unsuccessful, but sometimes these contributed motifs which became part of the classic structure. The isolated mansion of the gothic tale, for instance, was a suitable location for the group of suspects. The entire field of operation in the detective novel was marked out by the sensationalists—both English and American—of the 1860s, whose books made 'crime and violence domestic, modern and suburban'.* The romantic thriller provided the heroine threatened by malign possibilities. When the author's greatest interest is in the characters, the detective story resembles the novel of social relations, with the action focused by a single dramatic circumstance: a murder. At the other extreme is the novel that sets out to document the procedure of investigation; the literary hazards here are mechanical writing and narrative sterility, as many critics have pointed out: the dull puzzle which is hardly worth solving because the characters arouse no one's interest.

The early creators of women detectives, both in England and America, were naturally more interested in character than in the humdrum documentation of police work, but character in its less subtle, larger-than-life manifestations—indeed, the

* Elaine Showalter, *A Literature of Their Own* (1977).

quainter the better. There's a sense in which the use of a female sleuth actually hindered development in the genre: if the figure was presented as an oddity or treated as a gimmick this interfered with straightforward detecting. Fanciful treatment of the theme was almost inevitable at the time, when few women detectives actually existed and those that did were considered dubious in social terms. Miss Butterworth refers in her narrative to 'a woman in the service of the police [who] . . . may not meet with your approval': a gulf was fixed between the intelligent amateur seeking the 'truth', free to produce startling effects to entertain the reader, and the woman actually employed in a very limited clerical capacity. Male detectives, of course, never caused amazement in the beholder because they were doing it at all. They weren't handicapped with a bonnet and puffs to minimize the effectiveness of their actions.

Female sleuths, up to about the mid-1920s, were either not taken altogether seriously by their creators, or they were taken very seriously indeed. Both these approaches were tried by Anna Katharine Green, and the former was the more successful. Miss Butterworth, as Michele Slung has remarked in *Crime on Her Mind*, was 'the prototype of the elderly busybody female sleuth', a type that reached its final embodiment in Miss Marple, the only woman detective—and an amateur at that—that the non-specialist has heard of. The characteristic English female detective, indeed, is a refined white-haired old lady; while in America she is a sprightly young woman with her living to earn. The types are not invariable, of course, but they occur sufficiently often to make the point worth noting. It is also interesting that the origins of each can be traced back to the other country; early English sleuths on the whole were young and active, like Florence Cusack and Dora Myrl. In England, the arrival of Agatha Christie and Dorothy L. Sayers, in 1920 and 1923 respectively, marked the beginning of an era of ingenuity and sophistication in the detective story; comparable developments in America took place slightly later, but by 1929, with the appearance of Ellery Queen, Dashiell Hammett, Mignon Eberhart and others, the genre was soundly established and its products had acquired a certain literary standing. The gender of the woman detective was not necessarily regarded as a colourful detail to be piled on top of the other more outré elements of the plot, but could be presented as a circumstance which is taken for granted. Odd ideas about the role and behaviour of the female sleuth persisted, as we shall see; but as a general rule these were expressed outside the mainstream of detective fiction.

III

THE LADY IS A VAMP

Women Spies of the First World War

Shame on you! Shame on you! Oh, fie, fie!
Olga Polowski, you beautiful spy!

Music Hall Song

BY THE END of the first decade of the twentieth century, women detectives on both sides of the Atlantic could, at least in fiction, command respect. Female spies, however, were synonymous with seduction, ruthlessness and betrayal, and were therefore far less popular. During the First World War women began to be commended for taking up many forms of work which only a year or two earlier would have been considered unfeminine, and the fictional woman spy then started to come into her own and comply with the mood of patriotic determination; she was gradually to push out the frontiers of female sleuthing, and to help to modernize the image of the 'lady detective'. The special agents became vivid symbols of independence, but their attitudes were more rebellious and their exploits more bizarre than those of the detectives. There was a touch of bravura about their clothes, coiffures and perfumes, as Plummer, a master-crook in the Sexton Blake saga, finds out when he first meets Vali Mata-Vali:

She was dressed in a jacket and harem pantaloons of heavy silk . . . her hair was black as a moonless night. . . . Plummer was an expert in scents and he knew her elusive waft at once as that very rare and extremely expensive essence known as 'Moi-même'.

(In fact, many a fictional female spy, despite her calculation and cunning, has ruined a dashing disguise and given herself away by failing to acknowledge that a male opponent might become familiar with the perfume to which she is addicted. Like Vali Mata-Vali, Irma Paterson in the Bulldog Drummond canon is a dark and dominant beauty, adept as a crook and as a spy. Her passion for Guerlain's 'Vol de Nuit'—which is, surprisingly, the same perfume as that favoured by Drummond's impeccably English wife, Phyllis—betrays her to Sapper's heavyweight hero on more than one occasion.)

Vali Mata-Vali is described as a 'devilishly beautiful' actress/dancer from French Indo-China, and she first appeared in the 1920s. She owed more than just part of her exotic name to the notorious Mata Hari, who was shot for espionage against the Allies. (For decades, the myth and tarnished glamour of Mata Hari continued to set the pattern for fictional women spies. By 1964, when realism had more or less overtaken the espionage story, Arthur Marshall in *Girls will be Girls* was able to cut Mata Hari down to size with his customary wit: 'Priestess, dancer, lady? . . . We now know the answers and they are "never, certainly not, and, alas, no." ') Whatever the facts of her career, Mata Hari became a symbol of vampish betrayal and of the woman (usually a foreigner) who sells her services to the highest bidder. In fiction this was likely to be the Kaiser, or perhaps a gang of fiendishly cunning orientals planning to take over the world. Fortunately for the Allies, however, even the most intimidating Teutonic adventuress could usually be tamed and brought over to our side by the attentions of an upstanding Englishman. This gratifying fact is demonstrated in Marthe McKenna's *My Master Spy* (1935) when Clive Granville captivates Galie Fhel, a luscious German agent:

> Weakly and in a submissive voice she spoke, her eyes seeking his in the darkened room . . . 'I care not for the command, and it matters not who you are—who Admiral Von Kramann thinks you are,' and her arm lifted and fell in a hopeless gesture. 'I love you . . . My whole life is a sham—all this—' sweeping an expressive slender hand around her, 'false as the false glitter of tinsel.'

In a study of early espionage stories, one of the first questions which arises is 'When is a spy not a spy?' The answer of course is 'When she is British.' In this connection, appropriate distinctions are made between espionage and counter-espionage activities. English women operating behind the German lines were invariably thought of as serving their country, while

German women living in Britain and helping the Central Powers seemed in the popular view despicable, demoniacal and sexually corrupt. These contrasting images were reinforced by the personality differences of Nurse Edith Cavell and Mata Hari. Although it is questionable whether either could be described as a spy in the conventional sense, both were indicted and executed for espionage and there is no doubt that Nurse Cavell behaved with a dignity and selflessness that were not part of Mata Hari's make-up. Mata Hari has been surrounded by so much retrospective fantasy that although her existence was real enough she has almost become a fictional character. There are lurid anecdotes relating to her habit of appearing nude 'in an effort at wholesale enticement' when she was about to be arrested, and about her bathing daily in milk and dancing naked in her cell. She did suffer the ultimate irony of the promiscuous female spy: part of the evidence that condemned her was her contraceptive injection fluid containing oxycyanide of mercury, which the French authorities thought was secret ink. Sam Waagenaar's *The Murder of Mata Hari* (1964) is an intriguing attempt to sift facts from fiction, and he suggests that she was punished as much for her vanity and promiscuity as for espionage: apparently German secret service records never confirmed that Mata Hari was one of their agents. Waagenaar builds up a picture of a vain, gullible and histrionic woman anxious 'at all costs . . . to prove that she was important, that she could be of use'. Her reply to her French interrogator was unequivocal, naïve and, apparently, frank:

I love officers. I have loved them all my life . . . It is my greatest pleasure to sleep with them . . . and moreover I like to make comparisons between the various nationalities. I swear that the relations I have had with the officers you mention were inspired by nothing but the feeling and sentiments which I have just described to you.

Edith Cavell, whose crime against the German state was to smuggle Allied soldiers out of occupied Belgium, provided a less flamboyant but more morally worthy prototype for authors of spy stories. Curiously, she seems to be as much the end result of late Victorian and Edwardian fictional projections as an influence on the espionage stories that came after her. In

"'OU ARE INTERESTED IN DIPLOMACY, LADY ANSTISS. MAY I PRESENT TO YOU OUR LATEST
ARRIVAL?' SAID THE AMERICAN MINISTER."

An illustration by Fred Pegram for the *Harmsworth
Magazine*, 1898

Volume 1 of the *Harmsworth Magazine* (1898/99) there are one or two stories about discreet young women of education, integrity and resource who become involved in unpaid and extremely patriotic 'diplomacy'. (Spying was then an even dirtier word than during the First World War.) In 'How The Minister's Notes Were Recovered' by Beatrice Heron-Maxwell, Lady Anstiss, 'the most beautiful girl in Brussels', helps a young diplomat to retrieve 'some important notes' accidentally sent by the US Minister to the wrong man. The story starts on a slightly feminist note—'Women move the levers nowadays, though men make 'em'—but ends with Lady Anstiss figuratively in the young diplomat's protective arms, and readers appreciating that espionage is not really a suitable exercise for a woman, though a fearfully successful wooing mechanism for a male diplomat. In the same volume appears 'London's Latest Lion' by Gilbert Doyle, subtitled 'An Empire Maker's Love Story'. Again, diplomacy, simple deduction and courtship are inextricably fused: the female protagonist this time is Miss Olive Grahame, a demure governess employed by the Earl of Kenwell; she manages to outwit the foreign schemer Count Morlot, whose guile and Gallic gallantry are really no match for her wits, or for the courage and courtesy of the British Empire Builder, who of course woos and wins the governess.

C. N. and A. M. Williamson, the English husband and American wife who co-authored a series of lively Edwardian romances, made espionage a more dashing though still respectable business in *Love and the Spy* (1908). The heroine is an actress and, therefore, slightly socially suspect; Maxine de Renzie suffers the further handicap of not being Anglo-Saxon—she is Polish by birth—although she has been active in the British secret service for some years. She is an attractive character—beautiful, cultivated, quick-witted and far-seeing in the game of plot and counterplot. Although Maxine does not work directly for her own country, she is still motivated by patriotism rather than avarice, as she uses the money she earns from the British government to help impoverished Poland. Madame de Renzie is well set up with the traditional tools of the woman spy—histrionic ability, the capacity to keep a secret when necessary, and of course sexual appeal. The Williamsons create vignettes that are both witty and touching—the slightly exotic continental female spy trying to make advances to the restrained

Englishman; the actress/spy who has enjoyed success and adulation but is fed up with both professions. Maxine de Renzie, although involved in fairly stereotyped manœuvres of diplomatic theft and retrieval, is an unusually three-dimensional character for the period, who manages to suggest integrity without smugness.

Like her, several other women spies in fiction before the First World War worked for governments other than their own. These ladies were usually motivated by passion for a foreign national. Female characters were not the strong point of William Le Queux, and in *England's Peril* (1889) Lady Casterton rather unconvincingly uses an explosive cigar to murder her husband, who has been campaigning about Britain's inadequate defence preparations. Lady Casterton betrays husband and country because she is in love with the head of the French Secret Service. Though of French extraction, Le Queux did not experience conflicts of loyalty of this nature in his own life, and intense patriotism for Britain was the keynote of his highly charged but rather turgid novels of political intrigue, which began to appear in the 1890s. His stories stressed Britain's unreadiness for war, and firmly plumped for France as her enemy.

A few years after *England's Peril* a less successful English traitoress—also influenced by a foreign lover—crops up in another book that forecasts war and the invasion of Britain. *The Coming Conquest of England* (1904) was written in German by August Niemann. J. H. Freese's English version appeared soon after Erskine Childers's *The Riddle of the Sands*, and it was of course Childers's persuasive account of espionage and intrigue that established Germany as Britain's potential enemy in the popular imagination; Lord Northcliffe's network of newspapers and boys' magazines, and a spate of spy novels by other writers took up this theme.

As *The Coming Conquest of England* is written from the German viewpoint, it is the aggressiveness of Britain that is condemned. The English heroine Edith Irwin feels let down both by her decadent army officer husband and the British establishment. She has cause, for her gambling spouse ungallantly sells her off to a randy maharajah in order to pay his debts, and the highups of the British Army in India, to whom she appeals for protection, are prepared to sacrifice her honour for the maharajah's goodwill. Edith is rescued by Hermann Heideck, a German who hates the British but nevertheless falls for the exploited Edith. In order to shorten the war, Edith passes vital information to Heideck about British naval plans; he is so disgusted by her spying that he renounces her. But he is of course prepared to use the material received to further the interests of the Fatherland. Abandoned by both Germany and England, Edith is driven to suicide. The moral of the story, which is riddled with political ploy and counterploy, seems to be that spying is a reasonable job for a man but deplorable for a woman.

This attitude was certainly modified later by the exigencies of the First World War, but there remained an edge of disapproval for women spies that was not applied to men in espionage. Even Bernard Newman, the author of 128 successful spy stories, who had worked in counter-espionage during the war, seemed dubious about the women in his profession. Writing critically of factual memoirs of some of these ladies, he refers to 'the saccharine reminiscences of these virgin sirens', making the point, presumably, that women agents could actually succeed only if they used promiscuity as a major tool of their trade. However, in his novel *Lady Doctor, Woman Spy* (1937) he comments that '. . . Until the moment of the Armistice the Secret War went on—a veritable war of women, since the majority of the volunteer agents in occupied France and Belgium were women.' He commends the real-life espionage work of Louise de Bettignies and Gabrielle Petit, who directed many of these operations, and he also has a grudging respect for a prostitute named Regina, through whom he organized 'a series of listening posts in the Amiens brothels' in 1917. She had a range of attributes that were helpful in spying, not the least of which was her ability to blink messages accurately in Morse code. Her flair for this kind of signalling is mentioned in an autobiographical piece by Newman in the *Edgar Wallace Mystery Magazine* of July 1965.

Whether or not Marthe McKenna was one of the women agents-turned-author whose attitudes to sex and spying were so unpalatable to Newman, she worked with success in espionage during the war, and then went on to produce several bestselling books about her experiences. Like Bernard Newman, she too was able to write anti-Nazi spy stories when the First World War began to lose its appeal as a fictional subject.

Marthe McKenna (née Knockaert) was Belgian, and when her country was overrun by the Kaiser's armies she spied for the Allies while pursuing nursing duties at a German military hospital in Roulers. In *I Was a Spy* (1933) she describes her activities, which included the prising out of information from German officers without the sacrifice of her virtue. Field-Marshal Earl Haig mentioned her in a dispatch for 'gallant and distinguished service in the field'; Winston Churchill described her as 'brave, wise, virtuous and patriotic' and wrote in a foreword to *I Was a Spy*: 'She fulfilled in every respect the conditions which make the terrible profession of a spy dignified and honourable.' Despite the authenticity of her experiences, some of her early spy stories now seem inflated and unreal.

Mrs McKenna fictionalized some of her own espionage activities in her novel *A Spy Was Born* (1935). A Belgian nursing sister recruits a young German officer, whom she is nursing, as an agent for the Allies. He is Fusilier Paul Orthwald from Bavaria and, true to literary traditions, not a brute like some of his fellow officers who hail from Prussia. Paul's defection to the Allied cause is largely due to the barbarous behaviour of his friend Victor (a Prussian, of course) who rapes a young girl in Belgium and—to complete the picture of depravity—has her crippled, hunchbacked brother sent to a concentration camp. (It is interesting that this novel, which is set in the First World War, has portents of several of the hideous realities of Hitler's war—'sturmtruppers', 'concentration camps', the idea of 'subject races' and so on.) Marthe McKenna, as a nursing-sister spy operating in Belgium, possibly struck echoes of Nurse Cavell in the minds of many readers: each was seen as an embodiment of dedicated self-sacrifice, a symbol of one of women's traditional wartime roles.

Mata Hari, of course, became the epitome of seductive betrayal, the other extreme of behaviour associated with women in time of war. In *Lady Doctor, Woman Spy* Bernard Newman writes of Anna Lessing, a German spy whose ruthlessness, sexual arrogance and exploitation of men and women went far beyond Mata Hari's. The mysterious Lady Doctor (no one seems to know how she came to be called this) was a real-life spy, but Newman has fictionalized her adventures. She was, apparently, the result of an illicit union between a German officer and a Slav woman. Once involved in espionage, she received instructions in the art of disguise from a well-known Berlin actress, and became adept at assuming a variety of roles, from pig-tailed Swiss schoolgirl to English scoutmistress. In the latter character she persuaded a member of her scout pack to carry out a spying exercise at a tank demonstration given for King George V in a field closed to the public. The scout made a drawing of the newfangled contraption which was sent to the German High Command who, apparently, didn't take it seriously. Anna's flirtation with scouting did not make her an admirer of 'B.P.' since later, when she was in charge of training agents at the German School of Espionage in Antwerp, Newman has her giving this advice to her students:

> You have been given a copy of this book *Adventures as a Spy* by Baden-Powell, the boy-scout man. Don't copy him—he was an amateur. Look at these pictures of butterflies he is so proud of! If they had come under my notice I would have flung him into jail—those wing markings are not known in any butterfly in the world.

Lady Doctor, Woman Spy emphasizes Anna's professionalism; she was an excellent linguist and had an understanding of the technicalities of military and industrial equipment. She could also record important information in her sketches and in pieces of knitting (shades of Madame Defarge!). She was also skilled at hiding secret papers, when she crossed the frontier, concealing them under the fall of her breasts where they were secured with strips of sticking plaster. If she caught women suspected of working for the Allies, she stripped them naked, combed out their hair, looked under arms and breasts and into their ears, and even poked a finger up their noses in her search for con-cealed messages and information. Her well-developed eye and ear for detail were put to use in other settings. She claimed that she could gain more information from a social gathering than anyone else in espionage or counter-espionage. Newman writes that at a ball just before an offensive was launched on the eastern front: 'Anna identified every division which was to comprise the Second Army of Samsov without stepping outside the ball-room of the Hotel Bristol at Warsaw.'

Lady Doctor, Woman Spy is, as the author stresses, a work of fiction, but there is no doubt that Anna Lessing's colourful

It was a drama of real life.

Ballroom Espionage again: an illustration to a William Le Queux story in *Forget-Me-Not*, 1916

activities in espionage invited embellishment. German agents of either sex were of course not likely to be presented by British writers as genial characters, and perhaps the least savoury to emerge in the fiction of the First World War is Dr Adolf Grundt ('Clubfoot'). This spymaster and confidant of the Kaiser was a law unto himself, with powers as draconian as those of the German Emperor. He was created by the war correspondent Valentine Williams in *The Man With the Club-foot* (1921); the novel was an immediate success and Williams continued to produce spy stories. Clubfoot was too dramatic a character to be allowed to disappear, even when the First World War had begun to recede from memory, and Williams resurrected him in occasional books throughout the 1920s and 1930s. One of these was *The Crouching Beast* (1928), written in the first person with an English heroine as the narrator. Her name is Olivia Dunbar. Realism is leavened by romance (while on the run Olivia is efficiently wooed by British agent Nigel Druce) and, despite touches of melodrama, the story comes across with lively conviction. It lacks the recriminating tone that characterized many novels set in the First World War; Olivia's narration is shot through with a slightly rueful, self-aware humour, and there is a general sense of style and slickness. The setting is Germany during the weeks leading up to the war. Olivia, who is working as secretary to an American/German authoress in a small garrison town, gives temporary refuge to a British MI5 agent escaping from the fortress prison. He is soon recaptured and shot, but has entrusted to her a cloak-and-dagger mission— the retrieval of a sealed envelope from the gramophone cabinet in a Berlin opera singer's apartment. This contains information that will alert the British Government to the imminence of German mobilization. Olivia is just a nice unassuming English girl, her sense of adventure appearing to have been satisfied once she had put behind her the vegetating routine of life in a 'dreary typing job' in London. However, she is the daughter of a distinguished soldier, and blood will out: 'It would be more prudent, I know, to wash my hands of the whole affair . . . But Daddy, sprung from a long line of Empire builders, always bade me avoid the easy thing . . .'

Loyalty to the imperial tradition quickly thrusts Olivia into a battle of wills with Clubfoot, who is not only well endowed with cunning and cruelty but has the advantage of disconcerting his opponents by his unprepossessing appearance. Certainly Olivia is rather daunted at their first meeting:

He was one of the most hirsute individuals I had ever seen. There were pads of black hair on his projecting cheek-bones, and little tufts at his nostrils, and a velvety thatch darkened the backs of his large and spade-like hands . . . He was a massively built person, with curiously long arms and an amazingly broad shoulder span . . . there was more than a suggestion of some gigantic man-ape about him.

And, of course, there is his club foot and crouching mien to complete the picture of a power-mad fanatic, warped within and without. Olivia eventually falls into Clubfoot's unchivalrous and clomping clutches; she is reduced to using a 'woman's weapon', but seductive wheedling gets her nowhere with the 'beast', who merely crows, ' "Corporal punishment, I believe, is still in force for unruly prisoners. For women as well as for men." His shoulders shook in a spasm of silent mirth. "And you are a very unruly person . . ." '

Olivia is rescued by Nigel Druce, the British spy she ultimately marries, and their success, like that of many heroes and heroines of British Intelligence up against implacable Prussians, springs from the efficiency of their physical reflexes in face of danger as much as from their powers of deduction. The book ends on a nice note. Nigel is awarded the DSO but, as his Secret Service Chief explains to Olivia, 'Since I can't get you a DSO, much as you deserved it, I've asked Cartier's to send you along a bangle.'

There is little of the luxury Cartier touch about Somerset Maugham's espionage stories. These are collected in *Ashenden: or The British Agent* (1928), and were based on Maugham's experiences in Intelligence during the war. The book is considered a milestone in the history of spy fiction for its detailed realism and its movement away from the romantic melodrama and social glossiness that Le Queux had earlier established as the pattern. As Eric Ambler has pointed out, Maugham's is the first fictionalized account of the life of a secret agent 'by a writer of stature with first-hand knowledge' of the subject. Ashenden was the original anti-hero of counter-espionage and 'his official existence was as orderly and monotonous as a City clerk's'. His sifting and sleuthing are done in a mood of callousness, irritation or detachment, and interspersed with periods of boredom or nervousness. Women agents do not feature prominently in the stories, although there is one archetypal dark and voluptuous vamp who worms secrets out of the 'chattering, hideous and fantastic' Hairless Mexican in a lovemaking session, and then has her throat cut. A female spy who fits better into Ashenden's low-toned and slightly seedy world is Giulia Lazzari, a blowsy Spanish dancer involved in working for the Central Powers through her Indian lover Chandra, who is one of their agents. Giulia's activities against the Allies are mere fleabites, but Ashenden intends to use her as bait for the capture of Chandra. As they wait in a French hotel near the Swiss border Ashenden turns into a virtual jailer; his distaste for the whole exercise—and for her—is plain:

> She was far from young, she might have been thirty-five, and her skin was lined and sallow. . . She had at the moment no make-up on and she looked haggard. There was nothing beautiful about her but her magnificent eyes. She was big, and Ashenden thought she must be too big to dance gracefully; it might be that in Spanish costume she was a bold and flaunting figure, but there, in the train, shabbily dressed, there was nothing to explain the Indian's infatuation.

Ashenden, in the uneven duel of wits in which he eventually persuades Giulia to write letters that bring Chandra across the border, is further repelled by the feminine intimacies of her life with which he has had to become acquainted: her dressing-table is littered with toilet things that were 'cheap and tawdry and none too clean. There were little shabby pots of rouge and cold-cream and little bottles of black for the eyebrows and eye-lashes. The hairpins were horrid and greasy. The room was untidy and the air was heavy with the smell of cheap scent.' She is the sort of woman who forces her feet into shoes that are too small, and is too illiterate to write the letters to her lover that Ashenden wants to dictate. His response to her is one of irritation rather than pity, especially when, to save Chandra, she offers herself to the British agent: ' "Don't be absurd," said Ashenden. "Do you think I want to become your lover? Come, come, you must be serious . . ." '

There is nothing low-key about the female German agent in John Buchan's *Greenmantle* (1916). Richard Hannay, who could retain his equilibrium in the face of death, torture, hypnotism and even the denial of his life-supporting cold baths, is thrown distinctly off balance by Hilda von Einem. This Teuton 'she-devil' working for German Intelligence plans to use Green-mantle, a prophet of the blood of Mahommed, to inflame 'the hordes of Islam' against the British. When Greenmantle sud-denly dies she is undeterred, and simply arranges a substitution. The unlikely candidate chosen as the phoney seer is Hannay's chum Sandy Arbuthnot; it has alas to be recorded that he lacks sufficient mettle to resist the blandishments of 'that bedlamite woman'. Hilda von Einem, 'a known man-eater and murderess', has not only cast Sandy in the role of revolutionary leader but—perhaps more fiendishly—she fancies him. His American friend Blenkiron is forced to 'indulge in a torrent of blasphemy' (which amounts to condemning 'this God-darned stuff') when Sandy admits to being fired by her madness. Hannay and Blenkiron, of course, manage to put Sandy back on the rails, but they too have to be ever-watchful of the Teuton temptress: 'with her bright hair and the exquisite oval of her face she looked like some destroying force of a Norse legend.' She also has an inscrutable smile, devouring eyes and 'a bosom that rose and fell in a kind of sigh'.

With Blenkiron, Hilda is like a 'rattle-snake with a bird'. When she turns her attentions to Hannay, he admits, 'The woman frightens me into fits.' It's worse, however, to be ignored by her: 'I hated her instinctively, hated her intensely, but I longed to arouse her interest. To be valued coldly by those eyes was an offence to my manhood . . .' Richard Hannay is pretty uneasy in the presence of any woman, and as the tension of the plot builds up so too does his love/hatred of Hilda: 'Mad and bad she might be, but she was also great.' In fact before the end of the story she has become the embodiment of that 'craze of the new fatted Germany', that notion 'invented by a sportsman called Nietzsche.' According to Hannay & Co., 'Men have a sense of humour which stops short of the final absurdity. There never has been and there never could be a real superman . . . But there is a super-woman, and her name's Hilda von Einem.' (Joan of Arc, whom he greatly admires, would usually perhaps be Hannay's more likely choice as super-woman, but Hilda as the demon-queen of German espionage has obviously played havoc with his judgement.) It is obvious that with this build-up of implicit sexual tension, some blood-letting in the Buchan tradition is called for; this comes near the end of *Greenmantle* when, after being holed up somewhere near the Euphrates by Turkish troops, Hannay, Blenkiron and Sandy have the thrill of taking part in a Cossack charge against the enemy. Hilda of course has to die so that feminine temptations are satisfactorily exorcised.

If Hilda von Einem represented Buchan's image of a female destroyer in the Mata Hari mould, another of his women who dabbles in political intrigue is definitely closer to Edith Cavell, the preserver. In *The Three Hostages* (1924) Hannay's wife Mary joins him in foiling Medina and other ruthless characters who are out to undermine and overthrow the western democracies. Medina is after more than this—in fact he wants not only material power but 'control of human souls'. When the story opens Hannay has been sufficiently mellowed by marriage and fatherhood to take the occasional self-indulgent *hot* bath. By page 48 however, circumstances have become so challenging that he needs his cold plunge again rather desperately: 'I awoke to a gorgeous spring morning, and ran down to the lake for my bath. I felt that I wanted all the freshening and screwing up I could get, and when I dressed after an icy plunge I was ready for all comers.' But he is not quite able to cope unassisted with Medina's machinations. Mary's maternal nature is affronted by the abduction of a small boy as one of Medina's three hostages. She offers to help, but Hannay is uncertain about what she can do; Mary then shows her mettle. Hannay's investigations take him to a London dancing club which seems to attract all his *bêtes noires*. Against the background of ugly music and garish décor he sees 'fat Jews and blue-black dagos', the college boys 'who imagined they were seeing life', and, most repugnant of all, 'puffy Latins, whose clothes fitted them too well, and who were sometimes as heavily made up as the women'. One of these is dancing with a female who is 'hideously and sparsely dressed' with hair 'too bright to be natural'. Suddenly Hannay realizes, with 'a shock that nearly sent me through the window', that 'in this painted dancer I recognized the wife of my bosom and the mother of Peter John'. Mary has proved once again to be 'such a thorough sportsman that she wouldn't take any soft option'. She takes control again towards the end of the book at a key point in the plot. The boy hostage David Warcliff has been rescued, but through hypnosis his mind is still in thrall to Medina. Sandy Arbuthnot storms, and Hannay appeals abortively to Medina to release the child; Mary's maternal impulses make her strong—this is one of the moments when she realizes that British decency is really not enough:

'You have destroyed a soul,' she said, 'and you refuse to repair the wrong. I am going to destroy your body, and

nothing will ever repair it . . . You are a desperate man . . .
but I am far more desperate. There is nothing on earth that
can stand between me and the saving of this child . . . You
may live a long time, but you will have to live in seclusion.
No woman will ever cast eyes on you except to shudder.
People will point at you and say "There goes the man who
was maimed by a woman—because of the soul of a child."
. . . Then from her black silk reticule she took a little oddly-
shaped green bottle. She held it in her hand as if it had been
a jewel . . . 'This is the elixir of death in life, Mr. Medina . . .
It will burn flesh and bone into shapes of hideousness . . .'

Medina of course capitulates under this threat of disfiguration
by acid, and he restores David's mind:

Mary leaned back . . . 'I hope I'm not going to faint,' she said.
'Give me the green bottle, please.'
'For Heaven's sake!' I cried.
'Silly!' she said. 'It's only eau-de-cologne.'

The Three Hostages, written soon after the First World War,
described the threats to the stability of society, all over the
world, posed by anarchists and bolsheviks and power-crazed
individuals. This theme was also taken up by E. Phillips
Oppenheim in *Miss Brown of X.Y.O.* (1927). Oppenheim had
been writing tales of secret diplomacy since 1898, producing
about 115 novels as well as numerous short stories. His style,
even in the 1920s and 1930s, remained Edwardian, and his
approach to espionage was romantic, élitist and melodramatic.
His characters are stereotypes, and those who fail to conform
with his old-fashioned concepts of social acceptability are
patronized or parodied in a somewhat heavy-handed way.
There is, however, an element of appeal in his books now
because of their period atmosphere and detail.

Miss Brown of X.Y.O. is full of communist agitators—
synonymous in this novel with 'anarchist blackguards'—who
make their presence felt in Trades Union offices, in Parliament,
at night clubs and restaurants, and even at parties given by
'white' Russian refugee aristocrats. According to Oppenheim,
these intruders are financed by Soviet Russia to act as professional disrupters of society, but they are not too efficient in
either a physical or a psychological sense. In fact they don't do

much more than make highly charged gestures and speeches in the tradition of the big-hatted, black-cloaked, bomb-throwing anarchist spies of the children's comic papers. The heroine, Miss Edith Brown, stumbles into this world of international intrigue by accident. In the Oppenheim context she passes for a restrained and subtle figure, so controlled and genteel that she is always on the brink of being downright boring to the reader. At the opening of the story Edith (symbolically, in view of her misty-mindedness) is totally engulfed in a murky London fog. She is a freelance typist who has 'suffered all her life from an unprobed spirit of romance', and the exciting world of Oppenheim's brand of espionage is about to overtake her. Lurching through the pea-souper and clutching her portable, Edith comes to rest on the front steps of an impressive house in Kensington; the door is suddenly opened by a servant with 'an honest face' who, surprisingly, asks this perfect stranger from the streets if she will come inside and do some important work for 'a gentleman'. Perhaps even more surprisingly, Edith agrees without a moment's hesitation, and proceeds to take down in shorthand the immensely significant and confidential notes about the structure of an international communist spy network which her unexpected employer dictates. The whole exercise is so hazardous that the gentleman, Colonel Dessiter, is forced shortly afterwards to feign death in order to avoid assassination by the anarchists. Edith, however, gamely struggles on with her typing jobs, although she becomes a target for the communists, who are prepared to go to extremes to prevent her from transcribing her notes. In spite of the danger that she is in, and the fact that her own background is very ordinary, Edith is never intimidated by even the most powerful of these enemies, and she deals frankly with Pennington, the communist MP who was at Winchester and Oxford, and is considered to have a brilliant political future:

> Miss Brown glanced at his perfectly fitting clothes, his neat jewellery, his air of almost elderly foppishness.
> 'One learns a great deal through coming into the world sometimes,' she murmured. 'I have read some of your speeches in the Sunday papers, and I pictured you always with a flannel shirt and a red tie, beating the air with an unclean fist.'

Edith soon gets on to the full-time strength of X.Y.O., which is of course part of the Intelligence Service. She falls in love with her boss Colonel Dessiter, but before they retire to country house married bliss they gambol together through their espionage assignments—their 'world of romance and tragedy and wonder'—like a couple of schoolkids. Edith says about spying 'I felt rather a sneak,' and Dessiter throws her an encouraging 'Well done, Miss Brown,' when she produces a clean transcript, or says something that he agrees with. They are not the only infantile characters in the book: a newly appointed Prime Minister, after only two minutes' acquaintance with Edith, decides that she has all the qualities necessary in a premier's wife and proposes on the spot. Fortunately for England, Edith rejects him.

Oppenheim produced several other female spies who were more exotic than Miss Brown and just as unconvincing. Women characters were usually the weakest links in stories by men of action about men of action, and this applies to the girls in Sapper's Bulldog Drummond saga and to W. E. Johns's Biggles adventures. Johns's attempt at a female spy (and a lover for Biggles) is worthy of mention as in a sense she is the only fictional agent who combines the attributes of Mata Hari and Edith Cavell. Marie Janis started life in a short story, 'Affaire de Coeur' (1918), as an exotic enemy spy who nearly gets Biggles shot: he is besotted with her, and drops behind the German lines messages which contain valuable information about Allied positions; he thinks he is dropping notes to Marie's aged father. She does not crop up again until *Biggles Looks Back* (1964); she is then a prisoner of the communists in Bohemia but has, apparently, followed up her Secret Service career with a spell in nursing. In *Biggles Looks Back* it is obvious that life has very much toned down the frothy First World War blonde whose 'Please Beegles' was almost enough to make the hero crash an aeroplane. (Even then she was not the most subtle or efficient of spies; from her French farmhouse hideout she was supposed to keep in touch with her German HQ by carrier pigeon, but unfortunately, 'the first night Marie was there the pigeon was killed by a cat'.) By 1964 she has settled into a kind of long-suffering dignity, and is deferential to Biggles and his ex-opponent Von Stalhein. The two men co-operate to get her out of communist clutches, and she is content to let them do all the planning and pushing. The passion that has kept her virginal and has made Biggles (by sublimation) into an expert espionage agent and aviator is now transmuted into an asexual triangular chumminess; Marie settles into the domesticity of a Hampshire cottage, and Biggles and Von Stalhein run down regularly at weekends to visit her and chat about the stirring old wartime days. Though not the most enterprising of fictional women spies, Biggles's old flame must at least be one of the longest survivors.

IV

SPOUSES, SECRETARIES AND
SPARRING PARTNERS

Auxiliary Women Detectives from 1913 to the 1970s

'. . . Darling, I do think you're marvellous!' smiled Steve.
'So do I, by Timothy!' placidly declared her husband.
Francis Durbridge, *Paul Temple and the Front Page Men*

As WELL AS the fully fledged women sleuths, there were on
both sides of the Atlantic many female auxiliaries. To some
extent their position in fiction reflected changing social attitudes
in real life; women were demanding more involvement in
challenging spheres of activity but, limited by experience rather
than understanding, they were generally cast in the role of
helpers to enterprising males. In the stories, few of these
auxiliaries had ambitions to become detectives in their own
right; several were drawn into crime-solving by helping their
professional-investigator husbands, lovers, brothers or fathers.
Others kicked off as criminals but eventually became assistants
to the super-sleuths with whom they had previously skirmished.
There were also the secretaries of a few famous detectives who
branched out from the straight and narrow paths of shorthand-
typing into the more exciting avenues of active fieldwork with
their bosses.

One of the earliest and most competent of these auxiliary
detectives was Mademoiselle Yvonne Cartier of the Sexton
Blake stories. (Blake was created by Harry Blyth for Harmsworth's halfpenny *Marvel* in 1893. The character was later taken
over by other writers and his adventures went on appearing for
several decades in many periodicals including the *Union Jack*,
the *Detective Weekly*, the *Penny Popular* and the *Sexton Blake
Library*. It is probable that more words of fiction have been
published about him than any other character in the English
language.) At first Sexton Blake worked alone; then in 1904 he
acquired a teenage boy assistant, Tinker; and Yvonne Cartier,
the creation of G. H. Teed, came into the saga in 1913. Although
the stories appeared in what were nominally boys' papers, the

arrival of Yvonne underlined the fact that many adults were also addicted to the Sexton Blake mysteries. Tinker is obviously a character with whom boy readers could identify; Yvonne, however, is an adventuress who brings a note of romance into the bracing all-boys-together world of Blake and Tinker—and Pedro, their big and masculine bloodhound. (Their Baker Street apartment is in fact shared by a woman, but Mrs Bardell the housekeeper, with her constant malapropisms, is very much on the safe side of middle age.)

Yvonne comes from Australia and although girls from that country are rather more celebrated in light fiction for earthiness than glamour, she is nothing if not exotic. Her name, and the fact that even after years in England she is still frequently addressed as 'Mademoiselle', suggest a streak of the romantically 'foreign' in her make-up. Though not quite Edwardian, Yvonne has some of the legendary elegance of that period. As she remained active in the series until the end of 1926, however, her image became streamlined into something more in keeping with the type of progressiveness projected by popular magazines, with a background of jazz and cocktails, smart apartments and fast cars. The fourteen years during which she held sway covered the First World War, and took in many social changes, including of course the real beginnings of women's emancipation. But despite being in a sense the first of the modern female detectives, Yvonne retains a slightly old-world, gracious flavour. This is communicated through the illustrations from the beginning to the end of her saga, whether she is riding astride (but skirted) and cracking a stockwhip in a 'Val' picture of 1913, drawn by Eric Parker in 1924 as she grapples with a murderous Chinaman or (in a 1939 *Detective Weekly* reprint) depicted as a platinum blonde in elegant slacks. (Yvonne departed from the Victorian tradition of brunette women detectives and had hair that was described as golden or 'burnished-bronze'.) Whether she is on the side of the law or working against it, Yvonne is one of the most adept of crime operators. She is sufficiently quick-thinking to outwit Blake and, naturally, to discomfit the plodders from the Yard; 'she ranked with the greatest scientists of the day', being a dab hand at physics and chemistry, and she conducts her excursions into crime with 'mathematical precision'. With all this added to the usual female detective flair for disguise and a 'perfect'

A dainty figure in white could be descried leaning negligently against the wall. It was Yvonne.

Yvonne Cartier, the adventuress-detective who enjoyed popularity in the Sexton Blake stories in the *Union Jack* for a decade and a half. She was the model on which several of Blake's later female helpers were based.

knowledge of 'Arab languages and customs . . . and Egyptology' (Blake & Co. spend a lot of time in the Near and Far East) she is a force to be reckoned with. Yvonne also owns a yacht, the *Fleur de Lys*, complete with a loyal crew that is almost always at her disposal.

Despite the extraordinarily colourful adventures in which she plays such a prominent part, Yvonne is a credible and satisfactory character in comparison with many of the cardboard cluetracers who preceded her in late-Victorian and Edwardian magazines. In her are combined glamour and dependability, astuteness and niceness. She's fairly emancipated as well; and in this sense it is appropriate that she came on the scene in 1913, when the campaign for female suffrage was at the height of its militancy, and very much in the public eye. Yvonne possesses the kind of determination in the face of heavy odds that might have made her a good suffragette. However, she is never directly involved in political affairs, but remains throughout the series a persuasive embodiment of the type of woman who is extremely active in her own interests.

Her impact upon readers at the time is perhaps best summed up in an incident from one of the earliest stories in 1913. This is low-toned but realistic compared with some of the more fanciful events initiated by Yvonne, and it shows how it was then considered outlandish for a woman, especially if unaccompanied, to drive a car. A fawning London jeweller who bows low as Yvonne climbs into 'a large red motor' outside his premises, 'almost forgot his pose in astonishment as she entered the driver's seat and took the wheel'.

Yvonne's career falls into two main sections. She is at first intent on a campaign of vengeance against a group of powerful enemies, and this sets her against the law. Then—after an idealistic involvement with a 'socialistic' Pacific Island community—she becomes a Consultant, which means in fact that she works in co-operation with Sexton Blake in tackling crime and bringing the perpetrators to justice. The first story, 'Beyond Reach of the Law', sub-headed 'A Woman's Revenge', sets the tone of the Yvonne/Blake relationship. Yvonne is then in her early twenties, and she and her widowed mother have been defrauded by business associates of the Australian goldmine left by Yvonne's father. When her mother dies of grief, Yvonne swears revenge; she quickly gathers together a small group of helpers (all men) although she is pretty well penniless, and has sufficient strength of character to make it understood that 'I am the sole head, and . . my word is law.' Yvonne stops at nothing to disgrace her enemies, and Blake is employed to uncover her crimes. The action, now switched to London, is enhanced by the strong period atmosphere. There are large hats, heavy veils, long dresses in abundance, and city street scenes with classic incidents like this: ' "Follow that taxi!" [Tinker] gasped, as he threw open the door. "A half-sovereign over your fare if you keep it in sight." ' Blake first realizes that he is up against 'a great and scientific mind' when Yvonne, after shadowing him, nips into the empty house next door to Blake's apartment and 'in a few moments' transforms herself into an elderly nun, then beards the detective in his consulting room to extract £10 from him for seaside holidays for deprived children! Her efficiency in disguise is again illustrated shortly afterwards. Yvonne kidnaps Tinker—'Heavens, what will the guv'nor say when I tell him I was foiled by a woman?'—and then with a brown wig and a few touches to her face she manages to become 'a perfect reproduction' of Blake's boy assistant. She kidnaps both Tinker and Blake twice in this first story, and so it is not surprising that the detective begins to mutter 'What a wonderful woman! . . . What a pity! What a brilliant mind, and what a detective she would make!'

Blake could actually have mastered Yvonne on their first encounter but, although his life is threatened, he doesn't fire his revolver because his adversary is a woman. This chivalry, however, finds no echo in Yvonne. With the baseness (according to fictional traditions) of the female she adds insult to the physical injury that she has inflicted upon him. She stands over Blake with her 'tangle of gold-bronze hair . . . tantalizingly illuminated . . . above a white, gleaming skin' and the detective passes into unconsciousness 'to the sound of a silvery, mocking laugh'. All this of course is the perfect preamble to romance. While Blake is wondering how he can recruit Yvonne to the cause of law and order, she finds 'her pulses throbbing with . . . exquisite pain' and offers him a personal partnership as well as a professional one. Blake is attracted to the exotic Yvonne but declines her offer because his 'duty lies in stamping out crime, not promoting it'. Gradually, however, after she has knocked out all her enemies and escaped from a bleak moorland prison,

"If you had a chance to run straight, would you take it?" demanded Blake. Nirvana leaned across and caught her brother's hand. "Yes — yes, he would!" she said earnestly.

Sexton Blake's female adversaries frequently became his allies: a drawing by Eric Parker for a 1925 *Union Jack*

Yvonne begins to work with Blake. There are moments when, in gratitude for some act of investigation or daring on her part, Blake 'seizes both her hands and gazes down into her eyes', but passion is always quickly pushed aside by platonic camaraderie and the unceasing demands of the war against crime.

G. H. Teed was up against one of the basic problems of the writer of a long-running series: he had to keep the romantic interest alive, and at the time (especially in a paper read largely by juveniles) this could not be done by harping on extra-marital relationships. Domesticity was no alternative, as it would have meant the kiss of death to the image of dashing detection. So Yvonne simply had to fade away without explanation. Teed made a carbon copy of her for the *Detective Weekly* during the 1930s with Roxane Harfield, but it was only in the last paragraph of what was intended to be the final book in the mainstream saga that a girl managed to get Sexton Blake, after over 70 years of chastity, to propose (see page 90). Teed's stories were memorable on many counts, and Yvonne set new standards for the female detective. For most of her career she was Blake's auxiliary, but she comes across with greater force than many of her forerunners.

Yvonne's natural successor is another character from one of Northcliffe's detective papers. Eileen Dare came into the *Nelson Lee Library* in 1916 as 'Nelson Lee's Lady Assistant' in stories by E. S. Brooks. (She was well named. 'Eileen' suggests femininity of the unfluffy, dependable kind and 'Dare' obviously implies courage and panache. It was a favoured surname for girl detectives and 'adventuresses' and possibly Eileen was the first of them to have it. Soon afterwards, in 1919, Marie Connor Leighton produced *Lucille Dare, Detective* on this side of the Atlantic, and Mignon Eberhart in America came up with *The Cases of Susan Dare* in the mid-1930s. After the Second World War, when Frank Hampson was planning the cover strip for the new children's magazine *Eagle*, he considered creating a Dorothy Dare, Detective. She never got off the launching pad but Dan Dare, Pilot of the Future, has kept the name going to this day in a spate of revivals.)

Like Yvonne, Eileen first grappled with crime in order to avenge herself on a group of tricksters, 'the Combine' who had disgraced and 'morally murdered' her father by having him falsely convicted of spying for Germany. Eileen's campaign of vengeance runs over several issues, just as Yvonne's did, but because she gets more help from Nelson Lee than Yvonne got from Blake, Eileen does not so frequently have to contravene the law. She seems a very modern heroine. Although she is at times subjected to some 'perils of Pauline' situations her responses are always lively. For example, trapped by her enemies at the top of a blazing building, she thinks nothing of taking a several-storeyed leap to safety; shut in a cellar with

Thames water rapidly rising above her waist she doesn't give in to panic, but merely remarks 'Oh, what a state my costume will be in!' In a less hazardous but still tricky moment she demonstrates her agility: though frequently described as 'dainty' —which presumably also means small—Eileen has no difficulty, when the need arises, in shinning up a six-foot wall in spite of her fashionably long but cumbersome skirt.

Eileen has a touch of the Modesty Blaise talent for equipping herself with extreme efficiency for her bizarre tasks. She possesses 'a little hidden pocket' which always contains 'a tiny, silver-plated revolver'. Like Modesty too she is 'as strong—or stronger—than many men', as we learn when she 'half carries' an injured man several yards from a woodland clearing to her car. Eileen is also 'as clever as ten Scotland Yard detectives put together'. Fortunately her competence doesn't seem to undermine her femininity. Both Nelson Lee and his boy assistant Nipper are very taken with her. Nipper hero-worships the girl, but with Lee there is a strong suggestion that a romance will develop. (It doesn't, however, because Eileen rescues a handsome Royal Flying Corps officer from the burning wreckage of his plane and they soon become engaged.) When Nipper pronounces Eileen 'a ripper', Lee responds 'Miss Eileen is a girl in a thousand. And, although she is a girl, I value her opinion highly, and should never hesitate to take her advice.' However, it is usually Eileen who is on the receiving end of advice from Nelson Lee. He is, of course, older and more experienced, and although she does a great deal on her own initiative, Eileen, for all her brilliance and her moments of mischief, keeps well within the bounds of feminine propriety:

'Nipper speaks as though I were the detective-in-chief, and you were my assistant', laughed Eileen. 'They are not really my cases at all. Sometimes I have brought certain information to you, Mr Lee, but I generally take my instructions from you, and do exactly as you suggest.'

Among the instructions and admonitions that Eileen receives from Nelson Lee is one to tell 'no falsehoods of course'—though she is permitted sometimes to cloud the truth by the dropping of devious hints, or by shifting the emphasis about events in order to outwit her foes of the Combine. The avoidance of a direct lie, of course, was part of Lord Northcliffe's rigid code of ethics for his juvenile papers, and E. S. Brooks in common with many other writers applied this edict on many occasions. Eileen's sleuthing was sometimes subtle, but she also depended a great deal on twists of fate, and in particular on her adversaries' tendency to suffer accidents. For instance, a nurse in the pay of Eileen's enemies has to come off a case after catching her foot in a rug outside the sickroom and stumbling badly; Eileen is then conveniently substituted. In another story, a character fractures his skull not once but twice, losing his memory on the first occasion and regaining it on the second. Eileen also relies heavily on the villains of the piece collapsing psychologically as soon as she confronts them with possible exposure and arrest.

In spite of her striking beauty, which is frequently remarked in the narrative, Eileen can almost instantly take on the likeness of an old, wizened, yellow-faced gipsy pedlar or, with a wig and pince-nez, turn herself into a middle-aged matron. In the matter of disguise she has some advantages over Nelson Lee; her investigative exploits took place at a period when a woman could fairly easily escape recognition without even assuming fancy dress or make-up, and Eileen frequently sports a hat with a face-hiding veil: 'A veil is a really splendid disguise for a woman, for it is impossible to clearly see the features through one.'

Although an auxiliary Eileen was, according to Nelson Lee, 'shaped superbly for detective work'. She was shaped superbly for other things too—'simply a young goddess of girlish freshness and health'. Her crime-solving skills are frequently described, perhaps for the benefit of new readers as the *Nelson Lee* was a weekly paper. There are also impressive lists of 'all the smaller accomplishments of life' that 'came to her naturally': 'She could ride, drive, swim, run like a deer, and her daring and sense of judgement were astonishing. She could play the piano, the violin, she could sing and dance—and do all infinitely better than nine girls out of ten.' Eileen also could write shorthand outlines which were as perfect as those in any manual. With all these things working for her, it seems surprising that Eileen Dare's career was shorter than Yvonne Cartier's. She was retired from the saga in 1917, as soon as she had found her 'perfect specimen of English manhood'. Rather confusingly, she came back in a one-issue story twelve years later to help Nelson Lee solve a mystery, and was still single, merely— according to Nipper—'one of the guv'nor's best friends', and 'the most famous lady detective in the world'.

Wife auxiliaries generally survived longer than the 'adventuresses'. A domestic background to detection was acceptable to readers as long as it was established from the beginning. It was not then a case of home and hearth toning down crime and excitement, as it would be if a detective was 'married off' during the course of the stories. Usually the woman in a partnership of this nature would want to burst out of domestic confines into adventure. Some wives were unwilling for their husbands or themselves to become involved—but, in most instances, once embarked on mystery-solving they couldn't get enough of it. Agatha Christie's Prudence ('Tuppence') Beresford never showed any sign of reluctance to engage in adventures. In fact her somewhat naïve eagerness to undertake perilous assignments in association with her husband Tommy strikes us now as rather unreal and irritating. The Beresfords' exploits began in the early 1920s and ended in 1973 with *Postern of Fate*. At the start of the series, Tommy is young and also intelligent, while Tuppence's resolute brightness suggests the drawing-room comedy ingenue. In middle age the couple tackle a Fifth Column mystery in *N. or M.?* (1941). They come out of retirement in 1968 as a grey-haired and still devoted pair in *By the Pricking of my Thumbs*, at which time Tuppence, despite having brought two children to maturity, seems only a little less kittenish about the whole business of crime than she was in the 1920s. For the purpose of the plots, Tuppence's fluffiness, like that of her American successors Mrs Pamela North and Mrs Desdemona Meadows, turns out to be deceptive. She frequently ferrets out the key clue in whatever case she and Tommy are investigating, though she is also the classic female fool of popular fiction, who rushes in where intelligent men are too prudent to tread.

Partners in Crime (1929), like all the Beresford stories, begins with Tuppence feeling restless in domesticity and longing for something exciting to happen. She thinks with regret of the period during the First World War when she and Tommy did some Secret Service work 'chasing German spies'. Tommy is still working for Intelligence but only as a backroom boy. Suddenly, they are asked to take on an intriguing counter-espionage job, for which they use the cover of a detective agency, and as 'Blunt's Brilliant Detectives' they deal successfully with a series of separate mysteries from counterfeiting to murder. Tuppence is self-congratulatory: 'On the whole, jolly good! We're *very* clever, I think.' In fact, however, they seem to have been playing a series of games, and this is highlighted by their adoption of the methods and mannerisms of different sleuthing celebrities, including Sherlock Holmes, Bulldog Drummond, Father Brown, The Old Man in the Corner and (some self-advertisement on the part of the author) Monsieur Poirot. Of all the husband-and-wife detection teams, Tommy and Tuppence come nearest to representing an equal partnership. They take the initiative by turns and Tuppence is as quick off the mark as her spouse:

> 'Come on,' said Tuppence with determination. [They have been refused admittance to a nursing home where they suspect that a missing lady is held against her will.]
> 'What are you going to do?'
> 'I'm going to climb over the wall . . .'

Tuppence of course never admits her physical limitations, but fortunately she possesses the kind of resilience and powers of restoration enjoyed by slapstick cartoon characters like Donald Duck. As Albert (the Beresford's general factotum who stays the course of the series) confides to Tommy: 'I don't believe anybody could put the Missus out for good and all. You know what she is, sir, just like one of those rubber bones you buy for little dorgs—guaranteed indestructible.' By the time *Partners in Crime* comes to its final paragraphs, however, something has occurred that *does* put 'the Missus out' of crime investigating for some years to come. Tuppence explains to the surprised—but rather relieved—Tommy that she now has some-thing better to do: 'I'm talking . . . of Our Baby. Wives don't whisper nowadays. They shout. OUR BABY! Tommy, isn't everything marvellous?'

The 'baby' turns out to be twins, who rapidly reach maturity because only twelve years later, in *N. or M.?*, they are adult, off their parents' hands and doing their bit for the war effort.

Derek is in the RAF and Deborah, following her father's example, is doing something 'very confidential'. Tommy and Tuppence resent the fact that they have been categorized as too old for war work. (Tommy, who was supposed to be thirty-two in *Partners in Crime*, has now jumped to forty-six, with his wife not far behind.) Their state of inactivity does not last for long, of course: Tommy is given a counter-espionage assignment and Tuppence soon winkles her way into it. Incognito, and ostensibly unrelated, they settle into a seaside boarding house which Intelligence suspects to be the headquarters of 'the whole of the Fifth Column in this country'. This is one of the best of the Beresford stories, with a convincing build-up of suspense and a great deal of witty dialogue. Agatha Christie exploits to the full the effects of the comically claustrophobic boarding house atmosphere. The long-term residents are mostly colourful and well-drawn characters who offer the Beresfords plenty of scope for speculation about the identity of the Fifth Columnists.

There is always a certain hit or miss element in the Tommy and Tuppence stories, and on several occasions in *N. or M.?* Tuppence is careless enough to drop her cover. She is posing as Mrs Blenkensop, a dowdy, fussy and inept widow, but she suddenly finds herself addressing a self-pitying refugee with a very Tuppence-like reproving briskness. She is supposed to be an inexperienced knitter but one of the residents soon spots her 'just racing along' with a khaki balaclava. Tuppence is not entirely at ease in the world of espionage. She quickly becomes attached to people and begins to feel 'a bit of a cad, you know' for spying on the inmates of the boarding house. Her maternal instincts are affronted too when she realizes that she *may* be the instrument for bringing about the arrest and eventual execution of two rather attractive young people: 'Soft, she told herself, middle-aged and soft! That's what she was!'

With the solution of the Fifth Column mystery Tuppence is able to retire to her home and nurse her finer feelings. She is, however, in her usual state of disenchantment with the domestic routine at the beginning of *By the Pricking of my Thumbs*, and indulges in an outburst of characteristic naïveté which expresses her yearning for something exciting to happen. She and Tommy have just agreed to visit an aunt who is in an old people's home.

'We might be in a railway accident on the way there,' said Tuppence, brightening up a little.

'Why on earth do you want to be in a railway accident?'

'Well I don't really, of course. It was just—'

'Just what?'

'Well, it would be an adventure of some kind, wouldn't it? . . .'

In this book Tuppence takes the leading role and moves into a village of the type already familiar to readers of Agatha Christie. Sutton Chancellor, where Tuppence goes on the trail of a lady missing from an old people's home, makes a cosy setting for a crime. The Conservative Ladies' Union, jam-making, flower-arranging, 'the vicar's health, . . . unfortunate differences between the churchwardens' and so on provide a splendid cover-up for macabre happenings; 'ghosts . . . absentee owners and landlords . . . a house that nobody wants or loves', with a few child murders thrown in. Despite the emphasis on drama and danger, *By the Pricking of my Thumbs* is believable and ingenious. Unfortunately there is less control in *Postern of Fate* (1973), the last story to feature the Beresfords. In this Tommy and Tuppence are stereotyped to the point of dullness, and the events are absurd and bizarre.

The Beresford books spanned half a century, but in the '60s and '70s there is a looking back to the chintzy, tweedy certainties of an earlier fictional tradition. The exploits of an American husband-and-wife team, the Lockridges' Jeremy and Pamela North, began in 1937, but there is about them a slick, throwaway style that presages the affluent though uneasy social atmosphere of today. *Mr and Mrs North* is the most staid of the stories; it is a series of domestic vignettes and not a book about detection. *Death Takes a Bow* (1943) was, however, like the succeeding novels, firmly subtitled 'A Mr and Mrs North Mystery'. Jerry is a publisher, and the trappings of the literary world are well used in this book and in *Murder Within Murder* (1946). In each the setting is New York; the main and secondary plots are tightly structured and the dialogue is succinct. Occasionally, though, there is a toppling over into facetiousness, especially when Pam's scattiness gets out of hand. The outwardly feather-brained but essentially shrewd and intuitive 'little woman' is of course a dangerous property for any writer to handle. Pamela North, like Tuppence, is determined to share her husband's sleuthing activities, and his resistance to her involvement is understandable. Her help is sometimes, to say the least, a mixed blessing. It is often difficult to believe that any intelligence exists beneath the naïve veneer. Statements like 'It isn't very nice in here . . . It never is,' which she makes 'thoughtfully' when visiting the morgue, have an imbecile ring. It seems unlikely that such a character will be able to take a prominent part in the unravelling of the crimes the Norths stumble into—but of course Pam's efforts are always essential to the solutions.

Just as the action of the plot frequently hiccoughs around Pamela, so do her own efforts to achieve clarity of thought: 'Bill Weigand [the police lieutenant who works in association with the Norths] turned Pam's last few remarks over in his head, decided that they looked much the same upside down as right side up . . .' As Jeremy says of one of Pam's ideas, 'That isn't a theory, it's a leap out of the dark, into the dark.' In spite of all this Pam somehow contrives to be an engaging character, and the books are consistently amusing. Appropriately, they are written by husband and wife Richard and Frances Lockridge.

In *Death Takes a Bow* and *Murder Within Murder* there are some interesting sidelights on attitudes to the ageing process in women. In England and America during the 1930s and 1940s women, especially if unmarried or widowed, seem to have aged even more quickly in detective stories than in romantic fiction —where a woman's usefulness to the plot generally tended to fizzle out well before she was thirty. Miss Gipson in *Murder Within Murder* is a literary researcher who becomes a murder victim; she is supposed to be fifty, but in the novel she seems quite elderly. There is another example of premature deterioration in *Death Takes a Bow*: ' "Quite a dame," Mullins said. "Quite an old dame." Not so old, Weigand told him. Thirty-five at a guess. "A very precise person," Weigand said.'

The frothiest of all the wife-assistants must be Margaret Manners's Desdemona ('Squeakie') Meadow. 'Squeakie's First Case' was published in *Ellery Queen's Mystery Magazine* in May, 1943. The heroine is married to a newspaperman named David Meadows, and like Pamela North she tags along, taking the initiative if she can, when her husband is involved in criminal investigations. Squeakie goes in for wild and seemingly irrelevant crazes—in this story, witchcraft and the occult—which in the end, of course, help with the solution of the case. Squeakie seems more prone to conscious affectation than Tuppence or Pamela, and her cutie-pie persona is at odds with the logical way in which she eventually puts her finger—or as her husband would say, 'her little pink thumb'—on the murderer.

With Dashiell Hammett we are, of course, considering the work of a far more sophisticated novelist who was not dealing in stereotypes. In *The Thin Man* (1932) Nora Charles comes across as the most agreeable of the sidekick spouses. She is married to Nick, a hard-bitten private eye, retired, but drawn into the solving of a murder mystery. The story is told in a terse first-person narrative and it swings robustly along from the opening, mood-setting sentence: 'I was leaning against the bar in a speakeasy on Fifty-second Street, waiting for Nora to finish her Christmas shopping, when a girl got up from the table where she had been sitting with three other people and came over to me.' Dashiell Hammett writes with the directness of newspaper reporting, and a series of sudden or violent events is linked by the comments of the main participants. There are few conventional descriptive passages, and this 'repartee of crime and conversation' produces a tremendous sense of pace, naturalism and immediacy.

Nora is in a sense Nick's 'feed' rather than his active partner in detection. She asks the questions that enable him to give answers and information to make the plot hang together, and sparks off responses in him that further the crime-solving process. The action takes place in New York; Nick, Nora and their dog ('a Schnauzer and not a cross between a Scottie and an Irish terrier') live in an apartment at the Normandie. Theirs is a world of room service, centrally heated labour-saving apartments and, in spite of Prohibition, scotch-and-soda at any hour of the day or night. In the early 1930s this way of life seemed quintessentially American, and a fascinating contrast with English ideas of domesticity.

The dialogue bristles with the gutsy jargon of cops and dicks which now has a vintage appeal. Dashiell Hammett does not pull his punches, and violence is described without euphemism, but although the approach is hard-boiled the book has plenty of warmth and wit. Nora's femininity doesn't depend on frills and freaky dumbness and is conveyed simply in an exchange of glances with Nick, or in the banter between them:

> We found a table. Nora said 'She's pretty.'
> 'If you like them like that.'
> She grinned at me. 'You got types?'
> 'Only you, darling—lanky brunettes with wicked jaws.'

Nora doesn't do much sleuthing on her own account; when she tries to elucidate the facts of the case she is not particularly successful. As a sounding board for Nick's ideas, though, she is just right, and this role makes sense—for of course it is Nick who is the professional career detective, and not Nora. The series of films based on *The Thin Man* were modified and embellished for the visual medium, but Myrna Loy, the actress who took the part of Nora, managed to communicate the essence of her slick but sympathetic personality.

Another sophisticated husband-and-wife duo are Paul Temple and Steve, created by Francis Durbridge. The couple enjoyed great popularity as radio characters in the 1930s and later decades, and their adventures have also been televised. The first book, *Send for Paul Temple*, was published in 1938 and the novels continued into the 1970s. *Paul Temple and the Front Page Men* appeared in 1939, and was a novelized adaptation of a cliff-hanging serial broadcast by the BBC the previous year. Paul and Steve lead a glamorous existence: he is a bestselling novelist and she's a successful journalist. Home is a Mayfair flat—'We've got to live somewhere, and one might as well start married life in the best possible surroundings. Besides, I adore seeing Steve in a riding habit, and living so near the Row encourages her'—and they also own a Tudor manor near Evesham. Steve doesn't have to worry overmuch about the shopping and the washing up as they have an 'elderly man-servant', Pryce. On the whole Steve's purpose is to look good— 'I've just bought a new gown from Molyneux'—and to provide a relaxing ambience for Paul between his hectic bursts of crime-solving. Generally she is reluctant for him to get involved in the dangers of detective work, but of course Paul does, and early in most of the stories Steve's 'reportorial' instincts are aroused, so that she too joins in the sleuthing process. There is not a great deal of painstaking slogging in the Temples' approach to crime.

They dash around in sleek cars following up their inspired hunches, pace is all-important and, one feels, their elegance is rarely sullied by grime and gore. However, the stories are extremely readable, and they do have some neat twists of plot. In *Paul Temple and the Front Page Men*, for instance, Steve the exemplary auxiliary turns out in the end to be an even more successful novelist than Paul; unknown to him she is the anonymous author of a thriller called *The Front Page Men* which has swept the country—and incidentally encouraged some unsavoury individuals to band together and adopt the criminal techniques of Steve's fictitious gang.

Radio presentation was largely responsible for the success of the Doctor Morelle stories by Ernest Dudley. He and his fusty secretary-cum-assistant, Miss Frayle (whose Christian name was never revealed), were household favourites. Week after week listeners tried to spot the clue (usually the criminal's mistake) that enabled the brilliant but bullying psychiatrist to unravel the mystery. Miss Frayle was not so much an auxiliary as a doormat, the stooge whom Morelle nastily scores off again and again with his (so-called) 'sardonic shafts of humour'. The radio medium, with vocal subtleties injected into the doctor's part by actor Dennis Arundale, made the episodes inoffensive and frequently amusing. Translated into print, however, they seem pretentious, formula-ridden and unfunny. Rather surprisingly, the books continued to be published from 1943 until the 1960s. The tone of the series is set in the opening chapter of the first book, *Meet Dr Morelle*. In this the detective is rude to several people, and particularly of course to poor Miss Frayle. He also tries to intimidate members of the working class by throwing long words as well as his weight around: he 'ascertains furthermore', invites suspects to 'partake of a cigarette', smells with his 'olfactory organ', and so on. He flays Miss Frayle with his tongue and harasses her with his 'hypnotic' powers. When she does what she is told, he torments her for lacking initiative; if she departs from the doormat role she is still subjected to rebuke:

'It would appear no one unknown to you made use of the lift?' [Morelle asks of the hall-porter]

'No.' The answer was definite.

'How about the stairs?' Miss Frayle said. 'Mightn't somebody have—'

The Doctor's voice was like a whip-lash. 'I am not in-capable of conducting my own interrogation, Miss Frayle.'

She mumbled an apology, blushing and fiddling with her spectacles.

She spends a lot of time 'goggling' at Morelle's supposed super-intelligence. 'Goggle', relating to Miss Frayle, is as obtrusive in the text as the word 'sardonic' applied to with Dr Morelle.

Fortunately the secretaries of other detectives were better treated. Della Street, who works for Erle Stanley Gardner's Perry Mason is constantly encouraged and applauded by her 'chief'. Their relationship is easygoing and affectionate, and they are both enthusiastic as far as their work is concerned. The criminal lawyer is not above asking his secretary's advice, and she is never overawed by him. New Perry Mason books con-tinued to appear from 1935 until the 1970s, and of course the television series, which ran for nine years, enhanced the appeal of the sleuthing lawyer and his attractive secretary. Della (played on TV by Barbara Hale) has affinities with the typical Holly-wood career-girl of the 1930s, all wise-cracking efficiency on the surface and kindness underneath. She is maternally solicitous of Perry's welfare, always trying to make him eat and rest properly, but when he has to extend himself to resolve a case she goes along with him wholeheartedly, even if it means having to face physical danger. The private and professional rapport the pair enjoy is described in *The Case of the Silent Partner* (1940): 'Between them existed that rare companionship which is the outgrowth of two congenial people devoting themselves to a common cause. When the going got rough, they were able to function with the perfect co-ordination of a well-trained foot-ball team.' In the same book Perry speaks warmly of 'some fast thinking and some good detective work' done off her own bat by Della. In their exploits there are times when he feels that Della should be protected, or kept out of some particularly un-savoury incident but, in the tradition of the intrepid female auxiliary, she will have none of this: ' "I don't want to be kept in the clear," she said impatiently. "How many times must I tell you that I'm part of the organization? If you take chances, I want to take chances." ' The relationship between the criminal lawyer and his secretary is never defined in detail; a strong mutual attraction is evident but they appear to maintain separate ménages throughout the series. When Perry greets Della at the start of each office day he is apparently really seeing her then for the first time since the evening before. On the last page of *The Case of the Silent Partner* he suggests appointing her his 'legal guardian' if she'll take the job but, with a well-tuned sense of Perry's probable limitations as a husband, she declines. A few years later, in *The Case of the Moth-eaten Mink* (1952), they are still keeping their sexual awareness of each other under the surface—but it is nevertheless apparent to the reader:

> Morris Alburg in the door, watching them, said, 'The way you talk with your eyes,' and shrugged his shoulders.
> 'Mr Mason gets tired of talking with his voice, Morris,' Della Street said, slightly embarrassed.

In *The Case of the Bigamous Spouse* (1967) they are as usual thrown together in situations of danger and intimacy, but they still control their feelings. Perry doesn't go much farther than getting a metaphorical kick out of Della's legs:

> She squirmed out from under the steering wheel, slid along the seat, giving Mason a tantalizing flash of beautiful legs, then stood on the sidewalk shaking her skirt.
> 'Okay, Chief, let's go.'

There are frequent sessions in which Perry has to brief Della against the clock, with the police—or the criminal—on their tail, and her ability to assimilate information and to take rapid action is summed up by her terse and characteristic 'On my way!' Della seems to be Perry's perfect secretary/assistant on most counts; she drives as well as she takes dictation and types; she puts clients at ease and the police off the scent, and of course she always looks good. With her strong, but pleasant and unbossy personality, she has some similarities with Nora Charles, and the badinage between her and Perry Mason at times echoes the succinctness of the dialogue in *The Thin Man*. In view of the prolific nature of the series and the speed with which the stories came off Erle Stanley Gardner's dictating machine they are surprising lively and inventive. Occasionally Della enjoys cutting her 'chief' down to size when he appears to be showing off. (Her kind of teasing would have shaken the miserable Dr Morelle to his carping core.) The essentially cool Perry is in fact on one occasion sufficiently provoked to declare: 'You're too big to spank . . . and too valuable to fire, but if you'll kindly tell me what's the idea . . .' All the stories could, one feels, end with the conventional romantic clinch—but they don't, because the relationship has to be 'continued in our next'. There is, however, frequently a touch of sentiment in the finale. *The Case of the Bigamous Spouse*, for example, ends with Perry explaining that sometimes in the interests of justice,

'. . . You have to take it on the chin once in a while—or at least be ready to.'

'Ready, able and willing, is the legal expression,' Della Street said, and her eyes as she looked at Perry Mason showed the depth of her feeling.

This survey of female sidekicks comes full circle with another look at the Sexton Blake saga. In 1913 the sleuthing hero of the *Union Jack* was associated with Yvonne the Adventuress; by the 1960s this character was nothing more than a memory and Blake's current lady assistant was 'tall and honey-blonde Paula Dane', his efficient and attractive secretary. (Blake, by the way, has not grown older. His ageing process seems to have stuck somewhere in the early forties.) Paula was originated by W. Howard Baker in *Frightened Lady*, a Sexton Blake story of 1956. The Amalgamated Press finally dropped the Blake series in 1963, ending the Sexton Blake Library with *The Last Tiger*, another adventure by the same author. The series went out on a high note, as Paula and Blake get caught up in the suspense and intrigue of foiling a fearsome group of technologically adept Japanese survivors from the Second World War, who plan to take over the world from their Pacific Island hideout. After surviving all these trials and terrors, it is not surprising that Blake weakens sufficiently in the last paragraph to propose ('I think we might risk it—don't you?') and that Paula, undaunted by the down-to-earth nature of this offer of marriage, should accept. As the series had come to an end, marital bliss could safely take over from sleuthing excitement. (The Blake stories *were* revived for a few years by another publisher but the detective's domestic status presented no problem—the engagement was simply ignored!)

The actions and aspirations of these auxiliaries, from Yvonne Cartier to Paula Dane, have added colour and charm to the sleuthing scene for over half a century. The lady helpers were a strange assortment; they embodied conflicting images, suggesting female independence of thought at one level but, at another, being nudged beyond supportive roles to the point of subservience. This kind of see-sawing between the realistic and the romantic view of women's abilities is of course characteristic not only of the detective story but of other branches of light fiction.

V

SIX WONDERFUL OLD WOMEN

And Other Lady Detectives in England: the 1920s, 1930s and 1940s

And frequent hearses shall besiege your gates.
Alexander Pope,
'Elegy to the Memory of an Unfortunate Lady'

THE FIRST WORLD War had shown that it was possible for women to tackle strenuous and demanding work, and there were areas where the lesson had an immediate and permanent effect. In November 1918 twenty-five women were appointed to the Metropolitan Police Force in London, principally for the purpose of patrolling streets to keep an eye open for untoward incidents; among their duties was the task of wheeling drunkards to the nearest police station on a stretcher-like conveyance known as a barrow. The women were fitted out with an unbecoming uniform which invited ribald comment from the public, and their male colleagues treated them with hostility and ridicule for many years. To begin with they were denied the power of arrest; their small force was disbanded in 1922 and almost passed out of existence, but a reprieve was granted for the original number of twenty-five, who were left to form a nucleus from which a new detachment could be built. In the same year the CID employed one woman whose function had more to do with social welfare than criminal investigation: she dealt with women and children involved in cases of sexual assault, taking statements and doing her best to soothe the afflicted.

The duties of policewomen in fiction were less circumscribed. Protecting the crown jewels, uncovering the identity of master criminals and astounding their associates, were the usual occupations of these privileged ladies, whose work never brought them in contact with anything squalid or tedious. Fictional lady detectives had been in existence for some twenty years before the London Metropolitan Police Force actually extended its ranks, in 1883, to include two women who were employed to supervise female prisoners: Mrs Paschal's exertions on behalf of the Detective Department at Scotland Yard were chronicled as early as 1861. Another imaginary division, the Female Department (1911), had Baroness Orczy's Lady Molly as its star (see Chapter I). These characters were very glamorous and flamboyant, in contrast to the image of gloom and rigidity that quickly attached itself to the real-life female wardress or vigilante, in boots laced to the knee and a two-inch leather belt. However, it wasn't long before the tougher qualities of the policewoman acquired a special glamour in books which inflated the standard battleaxe figure into a fast-moving, loud-mouthed adventuress.

The celebrated detective who is frumpish in appearance and abrupt in manner is probably best exemplified in Nigel Morland's Mrs Pym, but this character had a forerunner in Mrs Emily Ollorby who appeared briefly in Edgar Wallaces' *Traitor's Gate* (1926). Mrs Ollorby, we're told, is 'one of the cleverest women detectives on the books of Scotland Yard' and follows her profession by addressing inconsequential remarks to possible wrongdoers in the street. 'We fat women have our romantic moments,' she declares, adding: 'I'm not sensitive. If I were, I should be dead.' She's ugly, and cheerful about it, as she barges her way into the homes of plotters and makes oblique allusions to their past and future misdeeds. This is her method of detecting, and we know it pays off because the author tells us so. Mrs Ollorby is a stout and strong woman, and her mind works by a process which is never revealed to the reader. Edgar Wallace, of course, is writing not detective fiction, but a far more loosely structured type of thriller in which the villains never pretend to be otherwise, the heroine suffers because of a mystery about her parentage, and the hero remains stolidly upstanding until he's put out of action by a thump on the head. It is not exactly high-class entertainment, with its dullness, its uninspired implausibilities, its conventional wastrels and gentlemen and master crooks. Mrs Ollorby fits into the basic pattern as a figure of fun just sufficiently distinctive to form a kind of linking device for the rather diffuse elements of the plot.

It is possible that Nigel Morland had Mrs Ollorby in mind when he dedicated *The Moon Murders* (1935) to Edgar Wallace '. . . who originally outlined the character of Mrs Pym for me'.

But his own creation goes much further. Mrs Pym in action is a figure straight out of the *Beano* or the *Dandy*, tearing about London in a preposterous hat, indulging in dangerous driving, snarling at her subordinates, coming up slap against gangsters with WHAMS and THUDS. She's a hooligan lady, who prospers at Scotland Yard in spite of masculine opposition to become 'the only female detective with high executive rank'. At the time of her first appearance her age is given as thirty-nine (some time later her date of birth was moved back four years, to 1892), though in the text she's referred to as 'an old woman', perhaps because of her 'stringy grey hair and drab clothes'. 'The name's Pym,' she says. 'Plain Palmyra Pym.' It's her first statement, delivered with contempt and defiance to get her blow in first. Ultimately, she is taken at her own valuation because she gets results. Her method of working is somewhat lacking in finesse:

'. . . I am going to clear up this case!' She banged her fist on the commissioner's desk, the gooseberries dancing madly round her hat.

Sir Michael gulped, and the veins began to stand out on his forehead.

'Oh, I see; and you think you will do it?'

'I know I shall do it!' Mrs Pym barked back at him. 'A woman is more capable of getting inside a mystery than any man living. I've had a hard life, Mr Commissioner, and I've dealt with criminals, in one way and another, for years. I shall completely ignore red tape in its every manifestation, and I shall bring the criminal to you—yet!'

Her odd idea about women's powers is amplified later: '. . . There's one way a woman knows her way around, my lad, and that's in knowing men. It's got nothing to do with cleverness or anything else; every woman from a daily help to the Queen of England can gauge a man quicker than a flea can hop' (*A Rope for the Hanging*, 1938). She may hold firm to this generalization but it does nothing to affect the feeling she keeps for her own sex: 'complete contempt'. At one point, however, she declares: 'I am not a feminist, but I believe that women should stick together.'

The inconsistency is in part a result of the popular author's inability to deal with the implications of the situation he has devised. A high-ranking official at Scotland Yard, who is also a woman, is going to find herself at the centre of controversies which have nothing to do with her capacity for the job. If she doesn't take the view that she's a woman of exceptional talent and disposition ('There's nothing sloppy and feminine about me,' snorts Mrs Pym), then she will be forced to uphold the proposition that there is nothing in a person's gender that renders her ineligible for a post. Mrs Pym is an exceptional lady in everyone's view, but the narrative presentation of her character changes. At the beginning of the series she is 'masculine to the core'; Nigel Morland has cut across the difficulties inherent in the theme by keeping his heroine firmly at the level of caricature. She resembles the conservative person's nightmare idea of the type of woman who demanded the vote; sheer awfulness makes her succeed. It would have been going too far to make her a Feminist, since the term had very unfashionable connotations in 1935, but the trappings remain. She is lumbered, among other defects, with an extreme antipathy to her own sex, since this is an aspect of the ludicrous impatience attributed to aggressive women.

Mrs Pym did not remain masculine for long, however, though her behaviour was hardly modified. Once she'd been accepted as a popular detective it was necessary to refurbish her image, so 'for all her gift of being at home in a man's world, she was not that most depressing of creatures, a masculine woman.' By 1951 (*The Lady had a Gun*) she is more seemly in appearance, her hair is arranged neatly and her tweed suit comes from Bond Street. Twenty-five years later (*Mrs Pym and Other Stories*, 1976) the reader is still being assured that the detective 'is not that major horror, a masculine woman', though in other ways she has now reverted to the knockabout manner of the early stories. She's not a masculine woman, though her speech has taken on a gruff, sub-Cheyney flavour: 'Son, I've had trouble all my life. This is my case and I'll damn well handle it Pym fashion.' 'I found the body and I'm in charge,' she declares, for all the world like a domineering eight-year-old. We know she's feminine because she can tell the sex of a criminal by instinct: 'It was a man and you're blind if you can't see that.' However, she has long passed the stage when 'feminine nausea' overcomes her at the sight of a corpse. A woman lying stabbed to death in a boat evokes the remark, 'Lug her to the bank and we'll have a look-see.'

The detective's blustering and barging keep the action going; her method of working is never subjected to scrutiny in the light of reason ('I've got a good memory and I play hunches because women work that way—it's the same as logic, but it's quicker'); speedy driving and fast reactions get her out of many a nasty fix. If a street brawl erupts in a disreputable spot, Mrs Pym is likely to be found wielding a lethal handbag in the thick of it. It is not only her personality that 'seemed to hit you with a whack, like a wooden stake'.

Apart from instant dramatic effect, there is a very good reason why the author chose to make his central character female: it enabled him to circumvent restrictions placed on a Scotland Yard detective without excessive loss of credibility. A woman may be thought to hold scant respect for 'masculine' conventions and institutions; she is without an inhibiting sense of tradition in professional matters, and can be impatient of formalities as well, if she is a person of forthright opinions like Mrs Pym. 'I came here to look at the matter from a new angle, and I am not interested in precedents or departmental politics,' the detective shouts. The author is going all out to exploit the glamour of unorthodoxy and originality of spirit—the same objective is at the centre of 'Mark Cross's' Daphne Wrayne adventures, described later in this chapter, though it's handled in a different manner.

Actually, Mrs Pym's unorthodoxy consists principally in her refusal to abide by police rules governing the treatment of suspects. She's for ever threatening to harm her prisoners ('With infinite slowness she brought the buzzing spindle towards the man's bare flesh . . .'); the reader knows it's largely bluff, because Assistant Commissioners, however eccentric, don't do that sort of thing, but it achieves results: 'I'll talk—ease off, ease off!' 'Listen, you poor fish, I got this job because I have no kind feelings,' says the delinquent sleuth. 'I go after your sort and get 'em. Because the police play fair, they can't handle gangs. I don't give a damn for your feelings and I can handle you . . .' She's bolstered up by professional authority without having to relinquish amateur privilege; she is too tough to bother about fair play but her motives are good and her end justifies the meanness. People may lose their ears when Mrs Pym is around, but only if they're suitable candidates for mutilation. Proposing to light a little fire on a person's chest is the nearest 'the ruddy woman busy' gets to playfulness. Torture, or the prospect of it, is just an efficient means for extracting information. Mrs Pym is really 'a nice-minded woman' who finds it difficult to utter the word 'brothel'. 'Fastidious' is not an adjective one would readily apply to this character, but the author doesn't hesitate to do so.

The stories are not detective stories in the strict sense. Mrs Pym's natural opponents are gangs and gangsters, marked from the start by their distinctive names: Saccorovia, Fioka, Cyprion, Tcherpachen. These are 'dirty brutes' to be got off the streets, and Mrs Pym tackles the cleaning-up job with all the gusto of a manic charwoman. Even when the problem has a domestic location she doesn't modify her aggressive manner: 'What's all this I hear about a disturbed broom-cupboard?' she barks.

There isn't much room in the books for social comment, and when it occurs it is usually in the form of an unexpected fact relating to the colourful lives of the poor. A woman whose husband has been murdered wonders when she can ' 'ave 'im', since the cakes she has laid in for the mourners are going stale (*A Rope for the Hanging*). Shott (a police officer) takes charge, because Mrs Pym can hardly be expected to know about the rituals governing life in the slums. Indeed, thoughtless official behaviour sometimes did aggravate hardship: one real-life policewoman, Lilian Wyles, described in *A Woman at Scotland Yard* (1950) her surprise at finding that young victims of sexual assault were reluctant to allow their knickers to be taken away for examination, since most of them possessed only one pair. The pioneer policewoman handling 'delicate' tasks, apprehending shoplifters, interviewing suspected women and children or visiting ex-prisoners really had very little to do with her fantasy counterpart. In fiction it is the pursuit that matters, the triumph for the individual detective, the routing of an adversary evil enough to place the whole exercise on a plane of high significance. In unsophisticated detective fiction the climax is often reached at the moment of confrontation between the two characters representing social good and social damnation. The 'better' the novel, in literary terms, of course, the more these qualities are blurred to accommodate complexity in feeling and motive.

The cult of unorthodoxy in the service of order and justice

97

determined the behaviour of many fictional detectives, since it involves a built-in interest and glamour which is lacking in conventional lives. It's an economical way to achieve results, to get the romance of the illicit into a narrative whose primary objective is to uphold the concept of law and its workings. One way of accounting for originality of approach is to make the protagonist a woman, new to authority in the public sphere and therefore untrammelled by preconceptions:

> ... If the big brains at Scotland Yard were not held in by the red tape that is so unfortunately necessary in the public interest, and were allowed to break the technicalities of the law a hundred times a month as do I and my colleagues, I am afraid there would never have been any need for myself and my irregular force.

'The big brains held in by red tape' has an unavoidable association with damaged heads, which the author, who is not primarily concerned with the felicity of his images, probably did not intend. The speaker is Daphne Wrayne, heroine of many semi-detective novels by 'Mark Cross' (Archibald Thomas Pechey). Daphne Wrayne has placed herself at the head of a philanthropic enterprise devoted to stamping out crime. She and her four male colleagues, whose identity is not disclosed to the public, undertake their investigations free of charge, out of sympathy with the victims of criminal acts and in order to protect property and uphold social justice. Daphne Wrayne, an ex-barrister, and her four 'Adjusters' are all rich individuals who have no need to charge for their services, and the non-commercial nature of the organization is continuously stressed as an indication of its *bona fides*. Grateful clients are advised to get off a cheque to their favourite charity.

To begin with, the Adjusters have their own way of dealing with wrongdoers. In *The Shadow of the Four* (1922) a pack of would-be murderers are soundly whipped, drugged, and placed in coffins to be discovered by the police on Wimbledon Common. But picturesque treatment of this kind is soon discontinued. The Adjusters bend the law to suit themselves (though it is never the law that is broken, only its technicalities), and once Scotland Yard has learned to trust them, they hand over their bowled-out criminals for conventional punishment.

Daphne Wrayne is one of those idealized characters whom everyone finds irresistible. She is endowed with every virtue and advantage to ensure as wide a basis as possible for her appeal.

'. . . I've been badly at war with myself all these last few months [she says]. One half of me has been crying out for you, marriage, a home, children. They mean such lots to a girl like me.'

'They're waiting for you, my dear,' he said quietly.

She smiled, but almost bitterly.

'Don't I know it? But there's the other side of me—the side that has made me want to do things all my life. The side that wouldn't let me lie soft at home and spend money like other girls; that sent me to Newnham to study law and make a name for myself at the Bar.'

The girl is wistful and sincere, resolute, fun-loving and intellectually brilliant, and these qualities are lumped together without the least concern for plausibility. The author has it both ways: Daphne can do no wrong. She's a dear headstrong little person. She's sweet and stern at the same time. Cleverness doesn't keep her from going on about feminine intuition, which plays an unduly large part in her successes. One might put up with the noun if it weren't always accompanied by the adjective: '. . . It was just that intuition on which we women always rely'; 'being a woman myself I'm interested in your wife's intuition'; 'we rely on instincts we women'; 'women's instinct'—these are among the touches devised to keep the narrative light and fanciful.

At this level, indeed, the woman detective is always either conforming to, or deviating from the rules laid down for her sex; there is never any question that sexually determined qualities might be wrongly labelled. Nausea induced by the sight of a corpse is 'feminine nausea'; a liking 'for things which did not hang together and which challenged her imagination' is 'a purely feminine liking'; the barrister's view is contradicted by the 'woman's view', and it is the latter that's sound, because it is based on instinct. This is a very simple method of applauding the odd, the quirky, the unexplainable with its charm for the reader. 'Being a girl, I work backwards,' says delightful Daphne Wrayne. 'My sex, as you know, is primarily governed by intuition—instinct—impulse—call it what you will.' Womanliness, of course, is inconsistent with professional detachment ('I've always kidded myself up to now that I was getting decently hard-boiled—same as a doctor or a nurse—not because I want to be, but because I've got to be. And now for the first time I'm finding I'm not a pukka crime investigator, I'm just a woman') and this is often turned to an advantage. It is sympathy for the wronged that gets Daphne Wrayne going, generosity that determines her efforts on behalf of others, winsome obstinacy that causes her to rely on instinctive feelings, and a pretty weakness for showing off that makes her delay calling in the Yard until the last minute.

The stories are constructed in accordance with a rudimentary detective pattern: a crime has been committed, some blameless person is in trouble, and the Adjusters are called in. There's often a crucial inconsistency in the case which mystifies everyone except Daphne Wrayne and the reader. When a person's character changes after his brother's death, it really isn't difficult, given the context, to deduce that one brother has assumed the identity of the other (*The Secret of the Grange*, 1946). If an unforgiving businessman makes friends with his oldest enemy, we may conclude that it's part of a devious scheme for revenge (*Murder As Arranged*, 1943). Occasionally a plot is enlivened by a fairly ingenious twist (*The Mystery of Joan Marryat*, 1945, for example); but generally the author relies on a few standard devices which he repeats with trifling variations. The clandestine organization, the play-acting and the colourful altruism are what absorbs his interest. Daphne Wrayne is available to interview clients in the Conduit Street office, but the four Adjusters keep out of the public view, even getting themselves up in monks' robes to preserve their anonymity. ' "Hoods!" he commanded. "This chap mustn't see us." ' It's the secret society of the girls' papers (see Chapter VI) transposed into a superficially adult setting.

Daphne Wrayne is a paragon, but Jane Carberry is a fool—not an apparent fool, gleefully disarming suspects and all the time observing and scheming in the interests of detection, but an actual fool. This heroine of five novels by Beryl Symons, beginning with *Jane Carberry—Detective* in 1940, is an attractive fifty-year-old of the upper classes who draws a crowd in the street when she has occasion to sweep her own doorstep. Her mental processes are not impressive ('What was it Dick said I had to be? Lucid. A pleasant-sounding word'); however 'She arrives at knowledge which others miss. How? I cannot tell.' In fact it comes in the form of visions and intuitions. 'Are you going into one of your goofy states?' asks one of her friends, for once using the right word. Pressed to explain her reasons for stating a fact, Jane has only tautology to offer: 'I know because I know.' Her actions are not determined by reasoning: 'Something is dragging me somewhere. All so vague. Where does it want me to go?' It wants her to go to the scene of a crime, of course, and once she gets there she finds herself curiously receptive to disembodied emotions: '. . . I understand now why that fright seized me as I sat here. I was sitting over the grave of Mrs Moffat's curse on her daughter . . .' She naturally attaches great importance to her dreams:

'Why do you suspect this man so strongly?'
'Because of that dream I had, just before the storm.'
'Forget dreams, madame. The police demand facts, not fancies.'
'But I dreamed the jewels and the thief or thieves were in the plane, and they were.'

'Scotland Yard chokes in the dust of hard and fast facts,' declares the enlightened lady, who is in no danger of doing so herself. It's the old conflict between the practical and the inspired. It is amusing and entertaining to bypass the labours of the dogged, the plodding and the sober, to alight brilliantly on a solution without preliminary groundwork. This truism is at the centre of novels more substantial than Beryl Symons's.

Intuition is extended to constitute a tangible faculty in F. Tennyson Jesse's detective heroine, Solange Fontaine (*The Solange Stories*, 1931); she is 'gifted by nature with an extra spiritual sense that warned her of evil'. Armed with this useful attribute, she sets out to rectify a few breaches of justice. The author is quite frank about her reason for making the character female: 'Although I intensely dislike the modern newspaper mode of thought which considers a woman "news", I pandered to it so as to be able to sell my stories more easily,' she tells us in the introduction.

The stories, indeed, are somewhat scrappy and melodramatic; the initial departure from reality—the 'extra sense'—is grossly backed up by instances of telepathy and spiritualism. Justice effected by supernatural measures is alien to the prosaic, logical spirit of deduction. It can only make an unproductive deviation. In *The Solange Stories*, the poor heroine is often made to feel chilly and uncomfortable as 'evil' is transformed into an pprehendable force. F. Tennyson Jesse was a competent, painstaking novelist whose reconstruction of the Thompson/Bywaters murder case (*A Pin to See the Peepshow*, 1934) confounds one of the fundamental assumptions of detective fiction, that the innocent have nothing to fear. In one Solange story, 'The Canary', the author adumbrates the point which she developed later to such good effect:

'. . . Unless something very unforeseen happens to save her [Solange says], Mrs Brownlie will be tried for the murder of her husband, and there is no doubt she will be found guilty. And then . . .'

Miss Leman's ruddy countenance deepened in hue. 'They wouldn't . . . they wouldn't hang that poor little thing? No, no, they wouldn't do that?'

'They would, indeed. A jury is made up largely of husbands and a judge is generally a married man,' said Solange dryly.

But the stories are not up to that standard of that novel in their transcription of reality, the interplay between character and conditions that tends to social disaster. Something very unforeseen *does* happen: a faked séance turns into a real one, and the innocent wife is saved from arrest. Without a supernatural agency to work on her behalf, let alone a female detective, Edith Thompson (named Julia Starling in Tennyson Jesse's novel) hangs. As much as anything else, the moral climate of the era is against her. It seemed at times that the distinction between adultery and murder was not very clearly marked, one act of wrongdoing indicating a disposition towards the other. The members of the jury are no freer from bias than anyone else. If Solange Fontaine had been an ordinary detective with no more than normal faculties, operating at a more mundane level, she might have been engaged with credible social issues. But as the author freely admits, her talents didn't run in the direction of formal complications of plot: '. . . I have never been able to imagine what on earth happens next,' she wrote. 'With me the host's body may remain on the floor (or at the desk) of the library to all eternity . . .' She did what she could with her detective, and turned out 'thrilling' tales.

Another disappointing character is Mrs Elizabeth Warrender, who on the face of it would seem to have many advantages— the Fabians and scholars G. D. H. and Margaret Cole as authors, orthodox puzzles to engage her attention, and a personality well within the tradition of the female sleuth. She is 'The Mother of the Detective'* who is able to see the wood as well as the trees. She begins by solving the mystery of the stolen silver when her pompous son is stumped. She knows 'Gladys [the maid], you see', and so she's not puzzled by Gladys's strange behaviour. Her deductions are generally based on a truism or convention: '. . . Men always sleep heavily in their own homes, and wake up all in a muddle.' It's the Miss Marple brand of 'specialized knowledge', but without the stylization that puts Miss Marple in a class of her own. Mrs Warrender too is a modest, recessive, meek old lady who discounts her successes; but in her case the reader can't really give her too much credit either. She's not only an unlikely detective, she's an impossible one. The Coles have simply gone too far in their efforts to exploit the 'least-likely' convention. The next stage—and it's not much further—is to make the detective feeble-minded.

'Mrs Warrender did wish that she had more adequate brains,' and so does the reader. Thinking distresses and muddles her: 'She hadn't a theory; as far as she had anything it was a confusion between two mutually inconsistent and equally silly ideas.' What she does possess in abundance is luck, the kind of luck that directs her to the spot where she's going to see and recognize the one person with a motive for the crime which has been committed. In *Fatal Beauty* (1939) it is a vengeful ex-housemaid, now the proprietor of a beauty salon, who has been sending her old employer skin preparations doctored with arsenic. She does this after a lapse of fifteen years, you see, because she was once dismissed without a character. Before the

---

* The title of a story in *A Lesson in Crime* (1933). Most of Mrs Warrender's adventures are recounted in the form of longish stories, some of which were reissued separately as novellas.

denouncement, she has been a little rough with her employees, but there are no indications of lunacy in her behaviour. However, we have to suppose that she's been waiting all this time for Mrs Mortimer to fall into her clutches, keeping a good supply of poisoned lotions for the occasion. When Mrs Warrender glimpses the diabolical beautician, whom she recognizes as the maid Hicks, she knows at once what has happened.

Hicks, or Madame Rose as she calls herself, is not the only one of the Coles' characters whose actions are out of proportion to the provocation. Gordon Lake, in the full-length novel *Knife in the Dark* (1942) gives in to a murderous impulse because he's taken exception to his wife's treatment of refugees. He is a humane person who resents the infliction of further cruelties on those who have suffered in occupied Europe. Kitty Lake is rude to the Polish Jewess Marta Zyboski, so Gordon waits in the dark with a little Maori dagger, and that is the end of Kitty. It's impossible not to think of the ruthless rhyme:

> Late last night I slew my wife,
> Laid her on the parquet flooring.
> I was loath to take her life,
> But I had to stop her snoring.

The result of the imbroglio is that the unfortunate refugee is placed in danger of being hanged for murder. 'Oh, the stupid man!' cries Mrs Warrender, referring to the police inspector. 'Can't he see she didn't do it?' A telegram is despatched to the real culprit who rushes to give himself up in a further access of chivalry. That is the end of Gordon Lake. 'A terrible tragedy,' says Mrs Warrender.

Mrs Warrender's Profession is the obvious title for the collection of stories published in 1939; it's a joke, of course, and it is also ironic, since the heroine is never anything but an old-fashioned amateur. 'Lots of people can be very unpleasant and not be murderers,' she says, sounding just as childish as rough Mrs Pym, but solemn-eyed with righteousness. If we take the statement out of its context, we can hear the pertness in her voice. She is, however, the type of sleuth in whom silly young girls confide: ' "My dear," said Mrs Warrender . . . "of course I'll do anything I can to help. But what *can* an old lady like me do?" ' The old lady's sharp eyes immediately fasten on the one clue in the case. She dashes about in the heat and makes herself ill and shaky, for which she is scolded by her son. When she meets with a setback, she feels 'inclined to cry'. A tearful detective is just about the most paradoxical image connected with the business.

Mrs Warrender keeps house for her son James, the professional investigator, whom she treats with the usual mixture of deference and faint ridicule. Men are creatures apart, to be humoured and used. She doesn't mind if James takes credit for her deductions: this is just endearing male vanity which must be pandered to. She knits socks, and wears her hair in plaits wound round her head. She's alarmed by men who roar at her. She has a strong moral sense, of course: 'She had been indignant with him [a person who is about to be murdered] for playing fast and loose with Vivienne Murray; whatever people might say, she thought there was no excuse for that sort of thing in a grown man.' She stands for the values of decorum and concern. The vulnerable and mistreated (usually female and young) attach themselves to her and expect her to work wonders, which she does, though not entirely by her own efforts. As we have indicated, luck is on her side; this amounts to a failure of construction in the stories.

The plots are exceptionally trite in any case: it seems that the heroine's weakness and lack of wits have brought the detective story to a fairly low level. There are no complications to provide intellectual satisfaction. What we find is a sweet old lady, a stereotype of lowbrow detection, solving tiny puzzles in her own sphere, not at all embarrassed to state the obvious: 'You see . . . if he was really killed, it must have been—he must have been killed by somebody. And the question is—who?' The Coles succeeded, to a remarkable extent, in keeping all their serious interests out of their fiction.

The more conventionally feminine the type, the more hesitantly and apologetically its exemplars speak. The masculine lady detective grunts and grumbles. She is not subject to the usual social pressure that inhibits rudeness. 'Don't leave your sentences unfinished in that stupid way,' barks Matilda Perks, a creation of Ralph C. Woodthorpe, addressing one of her neighbours. This type of lady is not meant to seem ill-mannered of course; she is merely frank and forthright and this is commendable. The narrative attitude makes the distinction plain.

Miss Perks is an honest person and she is to be admired for this reason. She is a natural opponent of the shifty and the whimsical. She informs her acquaintances that they're fools and ninnies. The schoolmistress's power of discernment cuts through any amount of subterfuge, and as a former teacher of small boys, Miss Perks is no more baffled by murder than she is by lesser naughty deeds.

She appeared in 1935 in *Death in a Little Town*, and she can pass for a detective only to the extent of being ahead of the police in deducing the facts from the evidence. Even this is not greatly to her credit, however, since it turns out that she has actually witnessed the crime. A scoundrel and blackmailer has been done to death in a Sussex lane. Someone has hit him on the head with a spade. 'If somebody had to be murdered, there could not have been a better choice,' states Miss Perks, coming straight out with the truth as usual. The fact that it is man-slaughter, not murder, doesn't lessen the culprit's guilt, as far as the author is concerned. Retribution is demanded, and so he dies on a train in Serbia with a bullet in his heart.

The device of the picturesque exit is the usual way to deal with the killer who must expiate his wrongdoing but doesn't really deserve to hang. Miss Perks has known all along that Frank Thornhill is guilty, but she never intends to pass on her knowledge to the police. To this extent, she acts in accordance with her own judgement. Sergeant Whalebone has taken away the murder weapon, but Miss Perks for once is reticent about putting a name to *that* particular spade. The book has a curious, somewhat bleak atmosphere, compounded by the eccentric tendencies of many of its characters, all unprepossessing in various ways. One very weak-kneed suspect is rude to his wife, not at all in the manner of Miss Perks: 'What are you standing there for, like a fat, stuffed pig?' he shouts. 'I thought I told you to tidy the place up.'

Miss Perks's brother Robert, 'a charming old gentleman' with whom she lives, suffers from an uncommon mental quirk or disability which causes him to undress in public. 'Robert took off his trousers and the garment beneath them, and stood up.' 'Robert in some ways is a child,' says Miss Perks defensively. It's an odd note to bring into a detective story, and it doesn't stop here. Nudism is the subject for discussion at a disastrous tea party. 'What do these people do?' one of the guests in-

quires. 'Do they merely sit or stand about in their skins? . . .
It must become rather dull, I should imagine, after the sensations of the first few minutes.' Then there is the young tramp,
quite unconnected with the story, who breaks into a lady's
bedroom in her absence and dresses up in her silk lingerie. The
incident has amused Sergeant Whalebone (the association with
corsets must have been irresistible) and he recalls it as he goes
in search of the lethal spade. The blurring of sexual distinctions
takes the form of perversion or deformity, though of course
these words are never used. Miss Perks herself has a black
moustache, and this perhaps accounts for her failure to marry.
She holds decided views on the subject.

'You have no husband in view at present?' she demanded.
Kate raised her eyebrows.
'Not at present,' she said stiffly.
'You ought to get married,' said Miss Perks. 'Every woman
ought to get married. That's what women were meant for. I
ought to have had a husband myself. I was a fool. I've
regretted it since. It can't be helped now; but you mustn't
make the same mistake . . .'

This is the advice she hands out to a young woman on their
second meeting. There is a suggestion that they won't meet again.
Josephine Tey's Miss Lucy Pym is more successful in her
relations with girls. They positively overwhelm her with admiration and attention when she comes to lecture at a physical
training college run by her old schoolfriend Henrietta Hodge,
and this is a little strange because Miss Pym is middle-aged,
pert and plump, not at all a suitable object of adoration. However, 'Oh, Miss Pym, you are a *poppet!*' they cry. The book is
Miss Pym Disposes (1946) and the heroine is one of those mild,
unassuming characters who have had celebrity thrust upon
them. Miss Pym has written a book on psychology, no less,
based on nothing more abstruse than common sense, and 'in-
tellectuals' fed up with Freud and Jung have made it into a
bestseller.
Miss Pym is charmed with the good manners and high
spirits of the girls at Leys College, with the exception of
Barbara Rouse, a swot and a cheat, whom Miss Hodge in-
explicably favours. The headmistress is an obstinate lady who
has marked down to Miss Rouse the prime post among those

traditionally offered to college leavers. By all the rules of fairness and suitability it should have gone to brilliant Mary Innes; but opposition only gets Miss Hodge's back up. 'What you think or do not think of my decisions is immaterial,' she tells her staff, who are nonplussed. But what Miss Hodge has done is to make disagreeable Rouse a fit subject for retaliation. A pin is removed from a piece of equipment in the gymnasium where she practises early in the morning; it crashes on top of her and kills her. The culprit is not Innes, as Miss Pym supposes, but her beautiful, wilful friend 'Beau' Nash—though Innes is ready to take the blame on herself. Miss Pym's detecting really consists in the discovery of a rosette off a dancing shoe, dislodged in a crucial spot—and all her psychological insight doesn't keep her from assigning it to the wrong owner. Nash, without thought or remorse, lets drop that it belongs to her. But this is not a detective story which ends with the culprit taken away in handcuffs. 'I am entirely in your hands,' Miss Pym tells Innes, when she still believes her guilty, 'because I am quite incapable of sending anyone to the gallows. I know what my plain duty is and I can't do it.'

It's an interesting moral point, which is not part of the usual scheme of detection fiction (*Miss Pym Disposes* is subtitled 'a crime story'), where a person's guilt is rarely complicated by mitigating factors. In fact the girl who has caused the accident gets off apparently unscathed, while Innes pays for being implicated in the act, though only to the extent of renouncing the post which caused all the trouble. As a detective novel, *Miss Pym Disposes* is not up to the standard of other works by Josephine Tey; there is something a little offhand in the treatment of the central tragedy, and this creates an imbalance, since it is clearly the personalities involved and not, for once, the puzzle aspect of the crime that interests the author. What is called for is either a more serious or a more idiosyncratic approach.

But Josephine Tey made excellent use of the college setting, always an especially appropriate background in stories of murder. The school or college adapts remarkably well to accommodate the detective theme. Sayers's *Gaudy Night*, Nicholas Blake's *A Question of Proof* and Gladys Mitchell's *Laurels are Poison* are prime examples of what might be said to constitute a sub-genre. The enforced closeness of the staff, pupils going in for self-assertion in various ways, are bound to generate tensions which may easily (taking into account the suspension of social restraints) erupt in violence. There is no more plausible or efficient way to get the suspects into an interesting relation with one another. Fads, obsessions and eccentricities flourish in the overcharged atmosphere. Rivalries may get out of hand, with dramatic results.

The traditional girls' school story has character development as its basic and enduring theme; in detective fiction, of course, the emphasis is shifted to the warped personality masked by an amiable front. The hidden depths will turn out murky, to say the least. It's a pleasant, not too serious way to subvert the process of moral improvement. The culprit, however, is less often a deranged schoolchild than someone more tenuously connected with the establishment. The fourteen-year-old murderer is a figure that really needs to be offset by a situation of out-and-out farce. This was a speciality of Nancy Spain, who created a girls' school bearing the very suggestive name of Radcliff Hall. ('In passing,' the author assured her readers, 'perhaps it is only right to say that the school was named more for the red cliffs of clay upon which it was built than for any other reason.')

To Radcliff Hall are summoned Nancy Spain's delectable detectives, Miriam Birdseye and Natasha Nevkorina, looking respectively like a witch and a tart, in accordance with two extreme modes of feminine ascendancy. *Poison for Teacher* (1949) is really a detecting romp with high camp overtones: ' "*Who turned on the urns?*" cried Miss Lipscoomb in a terrible voice.' 'Dears' and 'darlings' abound, along with horrid children and tearful young men. Miriam Birdseye ('a genius') is a revue artist turned sleuth, and darling Natasha is an ex-ballet dancer who is perhaps not so Russian as her name implies. On a whim of the author's, the naughty ladies have set out to travesty the procedure of detecting. 'Are they *men* whom you catch?' asks an interested party who is quickly put in his place: 'Oh dear no,' says Miriam. 'My partner quite often catches women . . . Or so she says. You must ask her about hers. I cannot remember them.' (*Not Wanted on Voyage*, 1951.) The detective's method is not exactly systematic: '*One* I caught by luck. Another went raving mad and tore up a draper's shop. Another was drunk. They were all more or less mad.'

The theatrical Miss Birdseye can assume a part at will, without the aid of crude disguise. Nancy Spain has a great deal of fun with the conventions of stage and school life: Miss Lipscoomb cannot open her mouth without sounding 'exactly like Arthur Marshall'. The Miriam Birdseye novels (there were seven altogether) are exceedingly frivolous and extravagant, not at all in the spirit of painstaking, classic elucidation. They are very bright and clever, but they lack the intricacies of construction, the economy and ferocity of wit that mark the difference between spoof (which is ephemeral) and satire (which endures). The lady detective, in Nancy Spain's double incarnation, is all ribald innuendo and pleasing artifice, and she operates in an atmosphere of protracted Christmas party spirits. The criminal is the performer who *fails* to bring off a trick, with gruesome results. ' "Now, with your permission," [says the murdering conjuror] "I shall saw my wife in half." And then, unfortunately, he did so.'

The author positively embraces the erratic, the personal and the whimsical, instead of eschewing these qualities in the interest of a plain, authoritative effect. The result is decorative but insubstantial, like icing detached from its cake. 'I never read detective stories,' remarks a character in *Poison for Teacher*. 'They appear to me to combine all the worst faults of the crossword puzzle and the Grand Guignol, with none of the compensations.' One way to avoid this judgement is to make a mockery, in the most lighteated way, of both conventions. Certainly no one reads these stories to pick up clues, consumed with curiosity about the identity of the murderer. *Everyone* in the narratives is playing a part, when character is established exclusively in terms of affectations. The real and the fake are not to be distinguished. Our deepest interest is not engaged, though we may applaud the effervescence, the sweet ruthlessness, the fancy dressing.

Birdseye et Cie is the name of Miriam's detective agency which has few employees and no objective but to banish tedium from its precincts. Catching murderers is no more serious than catching butterflies, and requires an equal amount of lurking, pouncing and flapping about. Dottiness and flamboyance are the ingredients that count, in Nancy Spain's view of detecting. The inconsequential takes precedence over the pompous and the sententious.

The lady detective is gaudy, eccentric, gruff, tough or modest; she is odd or ordinary, altruistic or personally motivated. She may exploit the characteristics attributed to women or discount them altogether to assume a mannish guise. She is least satisfactory, perhaps, when she is made into a high-powered, romantic figure like E. Phillips Oppenheim's Baroness Clara Linz ('he watched with obvious admiration the approach of a very beautiful woman . . .'), whom prime ministers, dukes and generals consult (*Advice, Ltd*, 1932). Baroness Linz may expect to command a fee of a thousand guineas for recovering stolen property; her detecting, such as it is, is carried out in lush circumstances. The tales themselves are dreadfully insipid, like party drinks a long time flat. It's equally impossible to summon up enthusiasm for the exploits of Oppenheim's other investigating heroine, Lucy Mott (*Ask Miss Mott*, 1936), with her reckless admirer Violet Joe.

When the woman detective is imported into a different genre (the thriller, in the case of Oppenheim and his contemporary Edgar Wallace) she is bound to suffer a certain diminution: this is not the place to display remarkable techniques of elucidation. The most that can be hoped for is resourcefulness, and this is certainly a characteristic of Selwyn Jepson's protagonist Eve Gill (*Man Running*, 1948), an impetuous girl who befriends a fugitive and determines to protect him from the consequences of his own chivalrous folly. He is the dupe of a heartless adulteress, who in turn is enthralled by a suave seducer. The pseudo-sophisticated touches don't procure a great distinction between this and the children's adventure story which it resembles. Eve Gill, setting off in wire-rimmed spectacles to take up a post as lady's maid, is behaving exactly like the typical *Girls' Crystal* heroine who is also adept at pretending in a good cause. The motive is the same: to get someone out of a scrape. In *Man Running*, the brave girl carries her playacting right into the murderer's den at midnight.

Like many story-book heroines she is able to make infallible judgements of character: 'He was no more a criminal than I was; I told myself so, and did not ask myself how I knew.' It's a simplifying device which avoids unnecessary speculation in the narrative. She *knows*, that is enough. There is no need for the heroine to be characterized as a detective; she is just indulging a sense of adventure and an impulse to see right done. Any quick-witted girl who acts to promote a state of justice is a detective to this extent.

Lying is difficult, as Eve Gill's fugitive realizes when he tries to concoct a story to delude the police:

'Where did you exchange clothes?'
    'A pub in Chelmsford.'
    'In the public bar? Didn't it cause some comment?'
    'We walked out of the town a bit, changed behind some bushes.'
    'Which bushes?'
    'Dammit!'

It requires a great deal of skill to make a false set of actions plausible; and this, of course, is what detective writers do all the time. The truth is overlaid with a number of possibilities which have to be stripped away like shoddy wallpaper. The classic, Chinese-puzzle type of story depends for its impact upon the virtuosity with which the deception is handled. This particular mode, of course, had become unfashionable by the mid-1950s when the crime novel was beginning to supplant the detective story as a popular art form. The events which make up the story were expected to reflect more clearly the circumstances of real life, and this meant treating the detective, male or female, as a more humdrum creation. There were survivals from the past, of course, and a few of these were adapted successfully to meet the requirements of a new generation of readers. There is still a place for omnipotence and idiosyncracy. But somewhere between the opposing figures contrived by the humorist and the moralist, the woman detective is beginning to emerge as a credible, complex character.

VI

FROM SYLVIA SILENCE TO THE SILENT THREE

Sleuths and Secret Societies in the Schoolgirl Papers

Adventures improbable as Hans Andersen ...
Kenneth Allott, 'The Children'

DETECTION AS A theme, and sleuths as super-heroes, became vital ingredients of British boys' papers well before the turn of the century. Sherlock Holmes's popularity in the *Strand*, which was of course a magazine for adults, found echoes in that of Sexton Blake, Ferrers Locke, Dixon Hawke, Nelson Lee and countless others. The Amalgamated Press followed up its boys' paper successes with a new range of periodicals for girls: the *School Friend* ('the Bessie Bunter paper') in 1919, *Schoolgirls' Own* in 1921, and then *Schoolgirls' Weekly*, which ran from 1922 until 1939, when it was incorporated with the *Girls' Crystal*. In the last two papers there was greater emphasis on careers, adventure and suspense than on schooldays.

Most of the early stories were sentimental or melodramatic, but later on they became lively and addictive, with inventive—even mind-boggling—twists of plot and counter-plot. Mystery-solving was a strong feature of the genre, pursued with relish by diverse adolescent girls ranging from exploited Cinderellas and orphans to heroines with specific functions and talents like girl aviators and racing drivers, whose jobs were ostensibly far removed from detection. Even Bessie Bunter, the plump and comically obtuse fourteen-year-old schoolgirl, unravelled obscure puzzles and outwitted international schemers from time to time. Tessa the Trapezist of Tarranto's Circus, Film-Struck Fay, Greta the Girl all Animals Loved, Susie the Pride of the Factory, etc. were all adept at bringing criminals or miserable meanies to justice. But these amateurs were overshadowed by the specialist girl detectives who had more than their fair share of surface glamour and in the 1920s and '30s stood out in girls' fiction as symbols of emancipation and adventurousness. In the interests of circulation, these magazine heroines were designed to appeal to a very broad audience; daring rather than depth was the keynote, and they were nothing if not colourful.

Theirs was a world of happy hunches and hooded helpers. As well as the string of adolescent sleuths whose investigations succeeded more by pluck than judgement, there was a proliferation of schoolgirl Secret Societies, whose detecting exploits were conducted against a background of candlelight confabs in ancient crypts or clock towers. Their masks, hoods and floor-length robes not only kept out draughts and mouldering damp but ensured anonymity. This was essential, because as well as uncovering criminal gangs the secret societies took on conniving prefects, corrupt headmistresses and even, when occasion demanded, some of those fiendish Nazi administrators who managed to hold down the whole of occupied Europe, but proved no match for the English schoolgirl with her sleuthing hackles up.

Atmosphere was as important as pace in the stories, and the Amalgamated Press authors were more skilful in creating a build-up of mystery and suspense than the writers who manipulated American girl detectives like Nancy Drew and the Dana Girls (see Chapter VIII). The Nancy Drew saga is loaded with the trappings of mystery fiction but somehow lacks atmosphere, while in the Amalgamated Press adventures a vivid sense of scene frequently compensates for certain inadequacies of plot structure. The brooding aura of abandoned buildings, of rambling country houses with something fearful clomping around their ancient corridors, and of course the cloistered intensity of English boarding-school life are established with conviction. The writers (almost all of them men using feminine pseudonyms) churned out hundreds of thousands of words of detective fiction week after week. It is not surprising that they fell back on several stock devices of the mystery story. Romantic and highly charged objects like Eastern 'idols', bizarre jewellery and half-obliterated old documents were often central to the action, and when these began to seem repetitive a dash of supernatural suspense would be thrown in to stir things up. However, even when menaced by exotic perils and surrounded with ghostly paraphernalia, the teenage detective heroines generally remained brisk and determinedly down-to-earth.

The earliest regular full-time girl sleuth in the Amalgamated

Press story-papers was Sylvia Silence, whose exploits began in the opening issue of the *Schoolgirls' Weekly* (October 1922). Utterly English and slightly stilted Sylvia antedated the more glossy Nancy Drew by several years. Both girls started their careers by helping their investigator fathers, who were quickly relegated to off-stage roles. Almost all the young female investigators were followers in their fathers' footsteps rather than police-trained professionals. Mothers were either non-existent or merely psychological wallpaper. In this respect girl-detective stories resembled the boarding-school fiction that had been popular since the first decade of the twentieth century, when Angela Brazil neatly swept away domestic restrictions by transporting her heroines from hearth to hockey pitch and throwing in plenty of communal high-jinks. Sylvia Silence was originated by John W. Bobin (writing as Katherine Greenhalgh) who was responsible for several thrillers in the Sexton Blake series. At fifteen Sylvia was heralded as 'The Girl Sherlock Holmes', but it is her father who has more obvious affinities with Conan Doyle's celebrated character; Mr Silence, like Holmes, spends a lot of time in an ancient dressing gown, playing a violin. He does not, however, in the context of these children's periodicals, inject himself with cocaine, and he also differs from Holmes in his attitude towards his assistant. Sylvia bears little resemblance to the pedestrian Dr Watson and soon proves to be her father's equal in solving mysteries. Mr Silence encourages her efforts to go solo. Sylvia is not only intelligent and intrepid, but 'slender and winsome' and the possessor of 'a wealth of bronze-brown hair'. (Curiously, red hair seems to be a statutory requirement of the teenage sleuth; in England they sport most shades of auburn from dull rust to frightful flame; across the Atlantic Nancy Drew abandoned blondeness for Titian tones somewhere in the course of the saga, while Judy Bolton was a redhead from the start.)

Good looks were not exclusive to Sylvia but occur in all her successors, and in another way she set the pattern too: her two inseparable companions when working on a case are Jacko, a large grey monkey, and Wolf, 'an Alsatian ... with an intelligence little short of human'. Long after Sylvia had bowed out of the papers, Amalgamated Press authors continued to equip their teenage detectives with superb specimens of this breed. (It is interesting to note that in this area the English girls differed

SYLVIA'S PLUCKY LEAP.

One of the sails of the windmill had come to rest parallel with the platform's edge, and, with an agile leap, Sylvia Silence sprang on to the sail and clung to it with her hands.

Sylvia Silence; a *Schoolgirls' Weekly* illustration, 1922

from their American equivalents who seemed to prefer boy-friend assistants to dogs.) By the middle of the 1930s the doggy-detective reached its zenith with Valerie Drew's Alsatian side-kick being promoted to solving several mysteries on his own, as 'Detective Flash'. Sylvia's style of investigation is simple rather than subtle and the action of 'The Case of the Missing Pendant' (the first of her adventures) is characteristic. Trapped in an abandoned windmill 40 feet above ground, but determined to get free in order to prove her friend's innocence, Sylvia fear-lessly fiings her body into space, and manages (just) to grasp one of the windmill's sails. Her weight draws it down until it is low enough for her to drop off. She lands in the millstream, and the first story ends appropriately with supersleuth Sylvia 'dripping but triumphant'.

Bobin created another teenage detective for the *Schoolgirls' Weekly*'s companion paper, *Schoolgirls' Own*, in 1930. He updated his own image by dropping 'Katherine Greenhalgh' and adopting the prettier pen-name of 'Adelie Ascott'. His Lila Lisle appears in seven complete series, and is always known as 'the Girl Problem Investigator', which somehow makes her sound like the sympathetic editor of a women's magazine letter page rather than a detective. Much more stylish than her predecessor, Lila wears artificial silk stockings and smart court shoes, cloche hats and well-cut fur-collared coats. In the first story ('At the Haunted Grange') she is introduced as 'a slim figure streaking over the grass'. Modernity and robustness are emphasized by her 'shingled red-gold hair' and the fact that she cares 'nothing for the wintry nip in the air' and is only 'thinly attired in a sweater and running shorts'. Unlike most A.P. girl detectives, Lila does not work with an Alsatian but, like Sylvia, she has a monkey companion. Less staid than her predecessor, Lila is, however, no more discerning in her sleuthing, which is conducted largely through the process of linking up conveniently placed clues by mad chases or semi-psychic guesswork.

With Sylvia and Lila, Bobin seems to have been taking trial runs at the girl detective character. In 1933 he turned out a more attractive and better defined investigator for the *Schoolgirls' Weekly*. Valerie Drew might well have owed something to Nancy Drew, as her name suggests, and indeed her first mystery, like Nancy's, was concerned with clocks. However, her personality soon became distinctive. Valerie has many natural advantages including 'red-gold hair' (of course) and violet eyes; she is as sporty and as fashion-conscious as Lila Lisle, epitomizing both her role and her decade by striding around in crisp tailor-mades, divided skirts or slacks, and sometimes carrying a businesslike walking stick. Valerie's popularity survived changes in authorship: Bobin died two years after he had produced the character but the stories continued, at first anonymously and then in 1937 under the name of 'Isobel Norton', which might have been a blanket pseudonym for a group of writers. Valerie appeared regularly in *Schoolgirls' Weekly* until it folded in 1939, and she was then transferred to *Schoolgirl* until that ended with the wartime paper shortages of 1940. In the early stories she is eighteen, and endowed with less than adult competence; she progresses, however, during the course of the saga from a sort of superior sixth former to an extremely sophisticated young woman. In 1938 she owns a 'delightful Park Lane Flat' and is able to pilot her own aeroplane. (Girl aviators were about equal in status with girl reporters and detectives as symbols of feminine independence and grit.) Valerie possesses an enviable range of skills: she understands deaf and dumb language, accurately reads the messages of signal flags hoisted on ships or coastguards' cottages, 'speeds along country roads' in her 'trim sports car', and can successfully navigate yachts, motor boats and sail-planes. There is occasionally an over-glossy touch about her; however, this is mitigated by her very practical and engaging relationship with Flash—he is the gratifying type of dog who never fails to come up to scratch. If Valerie is holed up in a crumbling disused coalmine she can order Flash through a crack in the seam, 'Find X—you know his scent! Find him *now* and bring him here!' and he will immediately do so. Canine co-operation of this nature was of course satisfying for schoolgirl readers whose own dogs, however endearing, were likely to be less obedient and far less skilled.

A 1938 serial shows the kind of problem Valerie is often up against. The almost demented Headmistress of Edenview School asks her to solve the mystery of strange happenings at her establishment: water becomes polluted, and phantom figures appear, as well as a green monster in the sea. Valerie eventually puts things right, of course, but initially her assignment seems difficult, to say the least. As the aeroplane she is piloting touches down on Haunted Island, the school's old clock tower (a favourite prop of 'Adelie Ascott' and 'Isobel Norton') splits from top to bottom 'with a cracking sound like the bark of a powerful gun . . . Two tall chimneys of stone swayed and trembled dizzily. And then—then it all began to totter . . . and the whole tower collapsed like a pack of cards.'

'The School on Haunted Island' was in fact a reworking of 'Valerie Drew Schoolgirl Detective', a 1933/34 serial. Valerie's development from schoolgirl to smart young thing is clearly shown by her different status in the two versions. In each case she moves into the school to investigate a mystery; in

Tenderly Valerie removed the message from the injured pigeon. Then she stared at it in amazement. It was in code!

Valerie Drew and her Alsatian assistant Flash; drawn by C. Percival for the *Schoolgirls' Weekly*, 1934

the earlier story she poses as a sixth-former but in 1938 her cover is that of games mistress. In 'Valerie Drew Schoolgirl Detective' the sleuth quickly gets to grips with a malevolent secret society known as the Veiled Judges. This was not Bobin's first attempt at a clandestine group. As 'Gertrude Nelson' he had already written for *Schoolgirls' Weekly* in 1932 a highly successful serial, 'The Quest of the Silent Six'. Two years later his follow-up to this, 'The Silent Six Under Canvas', proved equally popular. Valerie Drew did not appear in these J. W. Bobin stories; girl detective and secret society themes were occasionally intertwined, but they generally developed as separate branches of story-paper fiction. The Silent Six was not a disruptive secret society like the Veiled Judges but 'a swift, silent band of schoolgirls' who were 'pledged to right a great wrong'.

Valerie's adventures came to an end in the early 1940s, but another detective in the Amalgamated Press girls' periodicals continued to flourish. Noel Raymond, a male investigator, was regularly 'starred' in *Girl's Crystal* from its first issue (as *The Crystal*) in 1935 until 1951. His creator was Ronald Fleming who—unusually in the A.P. girl's papers—did not use a feminine alias for these stories but wrote as Peter Langley. (He was usually known as 'Rhoda Fleming' or 'Renee Frazer'.) Noel differed from his predecessors in ways other than his gender; he was not in his teens but his mid-twenties, and being masculine and tough he had no need for an Alsatian assistant. However, in 1937 he acquired a different kind of helper in the person of his niece, June Gaynor, with whom readers were obviously expected to identify. Noel also bears little resemblance to the sleuths of boys' papers, who were usually either derived from Sherlock Holmes or were supermen-adventurers equipped with pseudo-scientific apparatus to pep up the slog of sleuthing. Known as the 'debonair detective' Noel Raymond is closer to Lord Peter Wimsey, whose nonchalant manner and style of speech he sometimes adopts:

> 'I wonder,' murmured Noel, as he slipped a Russian cigarette from his gold case and lit it thoughtfully, 'what's the correct procedure when a chappie's goin' to meet a girl he's never seen who signs herself, "Yours distractedly", and looks on him as her only friend? A bit awkward, what?'

Noel tackles all his assignments with panache, from putting spunk into spineless teachers to thwarting master criminals or spies. His mental capacities are equalled by his muscular prowess and agility; the latter is frequently illustrated by his unorthodox methods of effecting rapid entrances and exits: 'His gaze scrutinized the ivy-covered wall and fastened on a rain-pipe. Noel's eyes lit up. Rain-pipes were child's play to him!'

There are lots of females in Noel's saga. Numberless teenage girls appeal to him for help because 'his eyes, steel blue and a little amused, invited confidence' (to say nothing of those 'whip-cord muscles') but the detective never shows any signs of sexual awareness or exploitation. He was an awesome example of the clean-limbed and clean-minded young Britisher who seemed to delight the Amalgamated Press writers and readers, managing always to combine manly strength with boyish frankness, un-attainability with chumminess. Noel Raymond became more predictable and conventional with the passage of time—' "Great Scott!" exclaimed Noel, under his breath, "The mystery deepens!" ' Nevertheless he was exciting and romantically appealing to girl readers until the middle of the 1940s; after the war June Gaynor, his teenage assistant, played a more prominent part in the stories—like Valerie Drew's canine helper she was promoted to solving mysteries on her own. It was, perhaps, June's increasingly casual attitude towards 'the world's most fascinating detective', whom she addressed as 'nunky', that finally transformed his image from debonair to domestic, and took away his last vestiges of glamour.

As a sleuth June Gaynor is not particularly original or inspiring; she is less distinguished than Lila Lisle and Valerie Drew, and even her eyes are of an ordinary colour. In the Noel Raymond adventures violet eyes are instead bestowed upon the detective's main sparring partner—Rosina Fontaine—who needed them to send out 'mocking gleams' whenever she encountered the sleuth. Noel always manages to triumph over his female adversary in the end, but he never quite knows where he is with 'Rosina the Baffling', and is frequently surprised to find her natty little pearl-handled revolver suddenly nuzzling his neck. Rosina is as ruthless as she is beautiful; she is an expert not only in disguise but in housebreaking and escapology. Unlike the upright Noel, she is equipped with what the Amalgamated Press authors considered exclusively feminine duplicity. She has the added qualification for deviousness of being non-British—she is French, and therefore has all the destructive fascination with which women of her country are lumbered in the tradition of English romantic fiction. A typical instance of Rosina's failure to play fair occurs when Noel prevents one of her attempted jewellery thefts. She concedes defeat, but the violet eyes are still glittering with guile as she murmurs:

'It was fun whilst it lasted. Do you mind?'
She produced her dainty gold case, extracting a cigarette. Noel retained his grasp on the girl's wrist as he produced a lighter, snapping it open. The girl leaned forward, a faint smile on her lips as she approached the cigarette. The next instant there came a faint explosion: a startled shout escaped Noel's lips as he staggered back, his eyes smarting and blinded by some treacherous tear-gas.

And of course no trace of Rosina—or the jewels—is left on the scene except the echo of her mocking laugh, and possibly a whiff of her heady French perfume. Valerie Drew also came up against a Gallic villainess called Marcelle Dauphine, but this lady eventually reformed and became the girl detective's ally.

Once Valerie and Noel had been phased out of the girls' papers, a new detective appeared in *Girls' Crystal* who seems to be a diluted amalgam of them both. Vicky Dare and her Alsatian assistant Rex were featured for a year and a half from 1951 to 1953 in tales by 'Judy Lewis' (Reg Thomas); the final events of Vicky Dare's career, however, were presented in pictures and not in stories. When the Amalgamated Press produced the new *School Friend* in 1950 it concentrated on picture strips, and became the first girls' paper to achieve a circulation of a million. Soon the format of *Girls' Crystal* was changed to correspond with that of the tremendously successful *School Friend*, and not surprisingly other publishers quickly launched picture papers for young female readers. Hulton, inspired as well by the popularity of their 1950 illustrated boys' paper *Eagle*, brought out *Girl* in 1951. This was to feature several girl sleuths in the course of its thirteen-year run. The first cover-girls of this glossy weekly were Kitty Hawke and her All Girl Air Crew, drawn by Ray Bailey, who were, of course, devised as female counterparts of Dan Dare and his team of space explorers. Girl aviators had been extremely popular in magazine stories of the 1930s and 1940s, but they did not survive long after the war when the prevailing mood in the girls' papers was one of back to normality, i.e. domesticity. This movement away from careers for women is depressingly highlighted by the change in character of *Girl*'s vividly drawn and well-defined early heroines. The girl aviators faded away, to be replaced eventually by less enterprising stereotypes like Angela, Air Hostess (1958). Despite their superficial glamour, airline stewardesses were in a sense only glorified waitresses. It seemed that the leading characters in the girls' periodicals nad reverted to their pre-1930s role as backers-up of men. After the collapse of Kitty Hawke & Co. the cover of *Girl* was given over to Wendy and Jinx, Schoolgirl Detectives. This engaging pair held sway for a number of years, and their crisp attitude and up-to-date appearance obscured the stories' basic lack of inventiveness: their problem-solving was conducted against a background of stock situations and devices like sports or school rivalries, debating society feuds, and so on.

Another attempt at a sleuthing heroine in *Girl* was Penny Wise, Private Detective, who was drawn by Norman Pett (the originator of 'Jane' in the *Daily Mirror*). Penny, though she always looks fetching and fashionable, unfortunately lacks Jane's gusto. She is one of those invincible females whose hunches always pay off, and she gets a great deal of help from her former boyfriend, Bill. The picture-strip format imposes severe limitations upon the creators of detective exploits, but the writers and artists of the *School Friend* were better than *Girl*'s contributors at working within these restrictions—even though *Girl* had the advantages of bigger pages, full colour and general glossiness. It was in the 1950 *School Friend* that the secret society finally eclipsed the girl sleuth as an effective symbol of intrigue and adventure. The Silent Three, the most celebrated and addictive of these underground groups, was the first to appear in picture strip, but in essence it was a refurbished version of clandestine organizations that had been featured since the early 1930s in story form in the Amalgamated Press papers. It occupied the front and back cover pages of the first issue of the *School Friend* (20 May 1950) and continued to crop up regularly until the late 1960s; it is parodied today in Posy Simmonds's strip cartoon in the *Guardian*, her 'Silent Three' having their roots in this earnest trio of schoolgirls. In the austerity of the postwar years, the *School Friend*'s readers were captivated by the romance of mysterious meetings by flickering candlelight, and the thrill of dressing up in long hooded robes—particularly while clothes rationing continued! Stories of the Silent Three were based on the impeccable formula of solving a mystery and righting an injustice. It is easy to see the affinities of this 1950 secret society with J. W. Bobin's Silent Six, which he originated for the 1932 *Schoolgirls' Weekly* and revived in another long-running serial for that paper two years later.

The Six were juniors who had banded together under the leadership of Shirley Carew 'to fight for fair play and the suppression of sneaking at Highcroft School'. They are always on the scent of some mystery or other, or of some act of 'cruel persecution of a scholarship girl' to put down. They are in fact quite at a loss if there is no immediate problem for them to unravel: 'Wednesday again, girls! What are we going to do

The Silent Three; an illustration by Evelyn Flinders for the *School Friend*, 1950

with ourselves this afternoon? There isn't anybody for the Six to ladle out a little justice to, is there?' In the illustrations to these early stories the Silent Six appear to be not so much hooded and robed as totally enveloped in their picturesque garb. Rather surprisingly, however, each member of the society manages to conceal her robe under her gymslip when necessary by winding 'the long length of black material around her slender waist'. (Bulging bellies beneath the box pleats would, one imagines, have militated against the anonymity that was essential for schoolgirl secret society members.)

As well as having the right garments the Silent Six were properly equipped with the other important trappings of the genre: passwords, the replacement of the names of the society's members by numbers, and access to movable flagstones or secret passages that could be entered through panels in the school hall. Shirley, as well as carting her robes around with her, usually conceals a small screwdriver about her person in case of emergencies. This comes in handy not only for prising up those flagstones, but for unscrewing doors or windows when the Silent Six are trapped by their enemies in an outbuilding or windmill.

During the 1940s the *Girls' Crystal* took up the secret society theme with relish. C. Eaton Fearn, the paper's editor, as 'Gail Western' produced 'Secret Leader of the Hooded Four' as early as 1940. By the mid-'40s he was writing frequent secret society adventures including 'Hilary and the Phantom Three' (a vendetta with an unscrupulous senior prefect) and 'Her Feud with the Secret Three', which featured an unpopular prefect and a daredevil trio consisting of Linda Hale, Mary Walton and Patsy O'Dare (whose 'shures', 'darlints', 'bedads' and 'spalpeens' would quickly have announced her identity to the world at large, despite her concealing dark dressing gown, white hood and mask).

A feature common to most of the stories is a Headmistress's ban on the secret society, whose members are then under the threat of expulsion on discovery. They have, of course, been maligned by the villainess of the piece, whose beastly schemes they are out to frustrate. The horrid prefect or mistress gets the society blamed for wrecking studies, planting booby traps or carrying out petty thefts. Another convention of the stories is that the secret society is usually formed by three or four girls who share a study. The perceptive reader might sometimes have felt that the group would have functioned more efficiently through quiet, uninterrupted study confabs, which would have spared them the problems of getting trapped at midnight in draughty crypts from which escape is hampered by their floor-length robes. Of course the hidden though awkward meeting-place is justified when a member of the society who has suffered unjust expulsion during the previous term returns secretly to prove her innocence. She lurks on the school premises, but can only meet her confederates in a concealed place; fortunately the Amalgamated Press fictional schools were well set up with underground passages, ancient towers with secret escape routes, and fountains in whose ornamental gargoyles important and confidential messages could be hidden.

Stewart Pride, who was to become the first editor of the 1950 *School Friend*, made a significant contribution to the secret society genre. As 'Dorothy Page' he wrote 'The Fourth Grey Ghost', a serial which started in the *Girls' Crystal* in 1948. This had a new angle—the girl helper to a boys' secret society. Penelope Cartwright is the daughter of the Headmaster of Harcourt Abbey Boys' School. A meek demeanour seems to be indicated by the knitting bag which she constantly carries, but actually this is just a repository for her robe. She is really resourceful and intrepid, and saves the day for the boy members of the society whose adversary is a crooked Senior Master. This story is memorable on several counts, and one of them is the lively style of the illustrations provided by Evelyn Flinders. (When the Silent Three's adventures began in the *School Friend*, Evelyn Flinders and Stewart Pride were once more to co-operate in the creation of a secret society thriller.) The Grey Ghosts were resurrected in the 1949 *Girls' Crystal* ('The Elusive Grey Ghost'), and as 'Joy Nesbit' Stewart Pride produced several other variations on the underground organization theme. More than one of his heroines became adept at whisking off her long black hooded robe and stuffing it into her knitting bag. The elasticity of the material was surprising!

Another author in the hooded-helper genre was Reg Thomas, who used the pen-name of 'Jane Preston'. In his 'Girl Helper of the Hooded Four', Rita Marsden becomes the only female member of a secret society: she comes up against a lot of anti-feminism before the other three fully accept her, and is subjected to some nerve-racking initiation tests, which she passes with flying colours. There are unusual features in this particular mystery—when things begin to flag the leading characters participate in desperate horseback chases and escapes across the moors. Rita has the best of two sub-literary worlds, for when she is not enveloped in her green monk-like garb she helps at her father's riding stables, where she makes 'a trim, workman-like figure in sweater and jodhpurs'. She does some actual detecting, but mainly gets along with the use of that old standby, feminine intuition; for example, the first time she sees the expelled boy whom the Hooded Four are trying to vindicate she knows instantly that 'It was utterly impossible that a boy who possessed such steady eyes could ever do anything under-hand.'

One other Amalgamated Press writer was regularly attracted to the secret society theme: Horace Boyten (writing as 'Enid Boyten', but not to be confused with the creator of Noddy, although he set some stories in a school called St Claire's, just as she did) occasionally placed his 'daring schoolgirls' against a dramatic background in Nazi-occupied Europe. In a *School Friend Annual* the 'Hooded Owls' (teenage girls, of course) are, under the noses of the slow-witted Nazis, able to smuggle a young French boy resistance worker to the beach, where a British torpedo-boat is waiting. This story was published in 1949; soon afterwards the Silent Three came into being, and Boyten was the third member of the group that was responsible for this extremely successful series. He and Stewart Pride worked out the storylines, and Evelyn Flinders produced the drawings. The illustrations succeed in conveying not only pace, but a sense of character not often achieved in picture stories. The saga was dashingly told in balloon captions and pictures, occasionally amplified by small blocks of narrative text.

In 'The Silent Three at St Kit's', Betty Roland is another of those unfortunate characters who have been unjustly expelled, and she decides to hide at the school and form a secret society to prove her innocence. The other two members of the society are her erstwhile study-mates, Joan Derwent and Peggy West. They all look very attractive, with their chic curly hair, and their red-and-white-striped blazers: they also wear their green robes, hoods and black masks with a touch of elegance. During the course of the first story the society is outlawed as a result of

Cynthia Drew's scheming. This tyrannical Head Prefect is mixed up in the illegal salvaging of bullion from the wreck of a ship sunk during the war. The Headmistress bans the secret society, but at last Betty, Joan and Peggy triumph, and at the school assembly the Head calls for 'Three Cheers for the Silent Three'. As they put their robes away Peggy says, 'Perhaps one day we may need them again, who knows?' They do, of course—frequently—at St Kit's and at other schools. Wherever they operate, they find an abundance of crypts, caves and ivy-covered towers; and positive labyrinths of underground passages. They manage as well to keep a remarkably plentiful supply of candles. Like the members of all those earlier secret societies in the *Girls' Crystal*, they are not only adept at sorting out the problems of the underdog and bringing rogues to justice, but at getting their robes quickly out of sight; the Silent Three stuff their disguises under their blazers, without even a minimal lump to make their involvement in secret society activities obvious to anyone. One story informs readers that they *always* carry their robes about their persons, on the offchance that the secret society may suddenly need to spring into action. The sheer competence of the Silent Three is of course breathtaking. When threatened with discovery, for instance, they blow out their candles in concerted movement, as their leader raps out, 'Escape plan "B" in operation! Make for the secret door!'—and like lightning they hop out of the crypt and vertically ascend 'through the walls' to the roof of the old clock tower and safety. It is easy to see that the Silent Three, though rooted in the earlier Amalgamated Press juvenile detective and mystery stories, also owed something to the supermen and women of films and television. Long serials featuring this trio continued to appear in the *School Friend* and its successors until the late 1960s, and most of their picture stories were reissued in the monthly 'libraries' associated with the weekly papers. Their eventual phasing out was not entirely due to the retirement of Evelyn Flinders, because in some of the reissues other artists were used to draw Betty, Joan and Peggy. School stories began to lose their popularity in the 1960s, and the editors of girls' periodicals decided that stereotypes like pony riders, ballet stars and pop singers were more attractive objects of reader identification than plucky schoolgirls like the Silent Three. However, there is still in today's girls' papers a strong thread of psychic mystery-solving which is a rather bizarre offshoot from the brisk and basic sleuthing of girl detectives like Valerie Drew, and the strange rituals of underground schoolgirl societies.

VII

CAREER GIRLS AGAINST CRIME

'She-dicks' in America from the 1920s to the 1960s

Often on a work of grave purpose and high promise is
tacked a purple patch or two to give an effect of colour.

Horace, *Ars Poetica*

AFTER THE FIRST World War, female detective fiction in
America began to move away from the high-flown towards
gutsy crime-fighting stories in which action and independence
were the keynote. The mood seemed to reflect the growing
emancipation of women. Authors strove for a new sense of
naturalism and gave their feminine sleuths a more professional
and 'hard-boiled' approach. The slightly staid lady detective
was largely superseded by the she-dick, the female ferret and
the crime-busting babe. However, these were not always so
progressive as they seemed on the surface; the slick operators
and the refined Victorian investigators were still sisters under
the skin. Professionalism in the heroines and in the style of
the stories was not consistent. A female private eye might
kick off as a crisply aggressive crime-fighter, yet suddenly
lapse into the stilted speech of the decorous early detectives.
She was, in a sense, what we now know as the statutory
woman in her particular genre.

The postwar stories are characterized by vivid images and
jargon; their settings are equally colourful, from glamorous
foreign parts to sleazy Chicago slums; from grand opera and
ballet to vaudeville, amateur dramatics or honky-tonks. The
she-dicks come from similarly diverse backgrounds. Some are
gracious, couturier-gowned ladies; others are 'ordinary'
working women—strippers, film continuity girls, teachers,
nurses, nuns and journalists. (Liveliest examples of the last
group are often found in Hollywood films of the '30s and '40s,
in which actresses like Joan Blondell and Rosalind Russell
were successfully cast as competent, wisecracking reporter-
sleuths.)

Like their predecessors, the American women detectives of
the 1920s frequently supplemented the process of logical

deduction by acting out their hunches. Mocked-up events to catch a crook, in which the (disguised) sleuth played an integral part, became set-pieces. The new independence of women was to some extent reflected in the genre. Several female detectives were paid professionals who worked alone, exercising ingenuity and initiative; others had male partners, but were resolutely cast in the auxiliary role. In most of the stories there are entanglements with romance as well as crime.

Frederick Arnold Kummer's Elinor Vance (*Diamond Cut Diamond*, 1924), though capable of solving cases on her own, is not a career detective. She is a woman of independent means, and as much a Lady Bountiful as a lady investigator. She happily lays out thousands of dollars on elaborately structured schemes to prove the innocence of a client or to catch the real criminal. She has, however, more powerful strings to her sleuthing bow than mere money. Men, whether they are her friends or her opponents, are overwhelmed by Elinor's physical charms: 'He could combat the girl's intelligence, her gay insolence, but her beauty always left him helpless.' Elinor is also loyal to her own sex and understands it in a way that is unusual in the traditions of popular fiction. 'I know women,' she explains 'quietly' to a lawyer associate who protests against her 'digging up these unfortunate women [and] sympathizing with them'. She has apparently decided that it is more fun for a rich lady to cast herself in the role of 'a female Robin Hood' than to spend her surplus cash on travel or art: 'I've been everywhere from Tokyo to Kalamazoo. . . . As for art, it's too often merely an excuse for rotten studio parties . . .'

Elinor's involvement with crime is in fact spurious. She is really a throwback to those elegant ladies who, in so many Edwardian romances, engagingly dispensed largesse and manipulated events so that the reputation of a hard-done-by but virtuous heroine could be redeemed, thus enabling her to fall into the arms of a proper suitor. Hulbert Footner's Rosika Storey, who also came on the scene in the early 1920s, is another superior, ladylike character who unravels the mysteries and problems that afflict lesser mortals; she conducts her criminal cases, however, with more punch and panache than Elinor. Rosika has chosen to be known as 'Madame' Storey, ostensibly because 'no-one [sic] would believe that a woman as beautiful as I could still be unmarried—and respectable', but one suspects that she has also insisted on this form of address because it suggests a socially elevated position and a romantic foreign background. She is a self-styled 'practical psychologist— specializing in the feminine', but honest enough to admit that she embarked on a career in detection because she needs money to buy the Fortuny gowns she favours, to say nothing of maintaining her Gramercy Park establishment. On her pay-roll is Bella Brickley, the secretary who records Rosika's triumphs in an uncritical and adoring manner which recalls Mary Granard's view of Lady Molly of Scotland Yard. The Gramercy Park ménage also includes a pampered pet monkey, which perhaps is meant to indicate Madame's occasionally bizarre tastes and her contempt for certain prevailing conventions. (Although unrecorded, it is a sure bet that besotted Bella rather than rarified Rosika has to tackle the unsavoury mopping-up that living with a monkey demands.) Rosika, though she's extremely attractive to men, maintains aloof indifference towards would-be seducers or suitors—except of course when it is necessary in the interest of criminal investigation to give one of them a little temporary encouragement. Even then she remains very much in control of the situation and apparently stays chaste throughout the half dozen or so books that comprise her adventures.

Most of these are collections of short stories, though *The Underdogs* (1925) is a full-length novel. In Bella's first-person narratives there is a great deal of contrivance and inflation, but in spite of this, and in spite of some stilted dialogue, a sense of life and immediacy comes across. 'Young, tall, exotic [and] always right', Rosika Storey is 'giant-souled', a cross between goddess and giggly girl: 'She seemed to exist in an atmosphere miles above ordinary people [but] when we were alone together, she threw off her public manner with relief, and emerged, keen, human, lovable and full of laughter.' Rosika and Bella propound a rather woolly brand of feminism:

Mme Storey's wonderful mind was wholly feminine; her success was due to the fact that she refused to force it into masculine channels of thought. She worked by intuition, that swifter and surer process of reasoning. Unfortunately in a man-ruled world, intuition is at a discount, and Mme Storey was obliged to spend a good three-fourths of her time proving to judges, juries and other men, that her unerring intuitions were true according to their cumbrous rules of logic and reason.

Rosika can afford to be contemptuous of pedestrian methods of crime investigation; even when blindfolded (as in *The Underdogs*), a psychic route to the solution becomes open to her. Later in the same story, when posing as a housebreaker, she is enraged at the anti-feminist attitudes of some of her fellow-thieves. She possesses not only commanding beauty but a voice to match: 'If you had heard that voice in the dark you would have known that it belonged to a notability' ('The Murder at Fernhurst'). She also has the gift (very useful in a detective) of bringing about instant reform in hardened criminals and con men. A holiday trip with Bella in Monte Carlo, described in 'The King of the Gigolos', not surprisingly becomes another case. Madame's teasing of Raoul d'Aymara quickly converts the impressionable youth from gorgeous but conniving gigolo into a likeable and honest lad: she 'made him look like one of our nice American boys'. In the same short story Rosika demonstrates her nonchalant pluck when she needs to examine 'a dark stain' which has spread across rocks hundreds of feet below the cliff top. She dismisses hysterical 'remonstrances from the Frenchmen' and persuades them to improvise a sling in which they hoist her over the edge. Bella of course is appalled: '. . . I saw her swinging between rock and sky . . . clinging to the rope above her head with one hand and holding a cigarette in the other. . . . The village people were staring, as at a marvel.'

Men from various walks of life including police inspectors, janitors and criminals try to win Rosika's favours. Her lack of response must have been very deflating for them. Readers might have felt that, in contrast, the warmth which Madame reserved for her underling contained a hint of lesbianism, and Bella's unrestrained admiration for the woman whom she describes as 'my mistress' seems to endorse this. The innocence of their relationship, however, is spelled out in *The Underdogs*: '. . . Alone together we're just like pals. We laugh and joke together. She treats me like a sister . . .' In this novel Rosika pretends to be a crook in order to break into the underworld. To outwit a gang of housebreakers who 'spring' potential recruits from prison, she gets herself arrested and jailed. The narrative at this point makes a serious comment about prison conditions and their effects on the women who are incarcerated, especially if they are first offenders. It is characteristic of Rosika, who of course succeeds where the entire New York police force has failed, that she delivers the gang's master criminal but not his underlings to the authorities: as she points out to Bella, she is concerned with punishment for the slave-driver but is prepared to give the slaves a chance. The 'slaves', though thieves of long standing, respond to Madame Storey's inspiring influence, as a result of which 'they might be said to lean over backwards in their determination to be straight'.

Rosika had one foot in the postwar world and the other in the socially rigid society that preceded it. Her confidence and strength of personality were echoed by Bertha Cool, who was, however, decidedly more modern. 'Beefy' Bertha was dreamed up in 1939 by A. A. Fair, who as Erle Stanley Gardner was already the successful author of the Perry Mason stories, and new chronicles of her exploits continued to appear until the early 1970s. The title of the first book, *The Bigger They Come*, is appropriate: everything about Bertha is larger than life. She is the senior partner of a private detection agency, known originally as Bertha Cool—Confidential Investigations, and later as the Cool-Lam Agency. Her associate is a shrewd and efficient young man, Donald Lam. Bertha appreciates his sleuthing skill but very much enjoys being the boss-woman and sometimes makes a point of putting him down:

> Bertha was built like an old-fashioned freight locomotive. She had short legs, a big torso, diamond-hard glittering eyes, and as she came barging into the office it was quite evident that she wasn't in her most amiable mood. She always liked to rely on the prerogative of her sixty-odd years and be the senior partner. (*Cut Thin to Win*, 1966.)

Those 'diamond-hard eyes' are referred to several times in each book. Bertha is adept at flashing them around and taking in the likely financial status of a prospective client. Her primary job at the beginning of a case is to collect as large a retainer as possible. Bertha's voice is 'rasping' and, like her 'diamond-hard' or 'little-pig' eyes, only softened by the prospect of plenty of cash:

'Money,' Dawson said, snapping his fingers, 'is nothing.'
Bertha's face softened. 'I see,' she cooed.

The sound of cooing is not, however, often heard from Bertha, who is more usually 'a hundred and sixty-four pounds of greedy-eyed, money-hungry anger'. She is a widow who seems to have forgotten whatever marital joys might once have lightened her life. Her attitude towards most men is contemptuous: ' "He's a fragile little pipsqueak," Bertha said, "and when you shake hands with him just give him a token shake. If you squeeze the least bit you'll hurt his arthritis . . ." '

Nevertheless Bertha has to depend on Donald to do most of the fieldwork. The two sometimes work in collaboration, but Bertha, one imagines, would be too conspicuous to snoop silently in the wings of a crime. Donald uses his sharp wits and his sex appeal when he is probing a mystery, but Bertha applies to sleuthing problems what is described in *Some Women Won't Wait* (1958) as her 'steam-roller skills'. Crackling dialogue and colourful images bring about strong reader-involvement; quips and wisecracks deflect grandiose sentiments and debunk pompous personalities. There is always an inventive following-up of clues, as Donald 'stages' events whenever such action is likely to push his investigations further.

Bertha's aggressive toughness of course makes her topple over from realism to caricature, and the author indulges in a lot of conscious hamming-up. In *Some Women Won't Wait* we find a memorable vignette of Bertha—pursuing a case with Donald in Hawaii, she abandons her girdle and adopts native garb, then a brief bathing suit. Donald gleefully blesses the Hawaiian air and the local drinks which have 'a wallop that can jar a babe as hard-boiled as Bertha Cool', making this formidable character 'who put sex in mothballs years ago' consider taking up the hula.

Although the tone of the Cool-Lam stories is often flippant, Bertha, like Rosika Storey, is a full-time, professional and paid detective. Possibly because they could command proper fees for their services, these two women seem to be the most over-confident of the female investigators of this period. There were other professional women who took up detection as a sideline to their main careers. Nurses, with their caring and competent air, seemed to inspire confidence in members of the Police Department (who used them as incognito assistants) as well as in the patients they nursed and their families. If, somewhere in the middle or even on the edge of a murder case, the right kind of woman could be planted by the police on a nursing assignment, she would be sure to ferret out information vital to its solution in the intervals between giving her patient alcohol rubs and hot milky drinks. Mignon Eberhart's Nurse Sarah Keate is an ideal police auxiliary. Sarah is more than ready to work on her own initiative as well, occasionally bending both the truth and the law, and even resorting to petty crime to cover the tracks of a fellow-nurse on whom suspicion of murder would otherwise fall. The police might be her superiors in the business of crime-solving but neither they, nor the male doctors whom she could also cut down to size, ever intimidated her.

The stories are Sarah Keate's first-person narrations. The style of the first book (*The Patient in Room 18*, 1929) is stilted and laboured in comparison with some of the later adventures. Sarah is on the surface the archetypal dedicated nursing sister. She describes herself as an 'old maid' but is resolved not to follow the accepted pattern of ageing spinsterhood—a combination of fat, sentimentality and ineffectiveness. She prides herself on being 'a keen and clear-minded woman' with 'more than the usual amount of determination'. She is certainly a nurse of the nitty-gritty type rather than a hand-holding ministering angel. In her own words, she is 'middle-aged . . . inclined to embonpoint and neuralgia . . . and about as fanciful as an oyster.' Sarah is a bit of a martinet with her juniors, for whom she cultivates a deliberately brusque or sarcastic attitude. In some of the books, however, there is one younger colleague—usually pretty and very feminine—for whom she has a strong affection; there are shades here of the bracing but slightly suggestive chumminess that was found in the English girls' boarding school stories of the same period. In *The Patient in Room 18* Maida is the favoured one, and their relationship is one of mutual admiration and reassurance. Sarah writes confidingly, in a moment of vanity: 'Maida professes to a great admiration for my hair.' She goes on to state 'It is not my intention to rhapsodize over Maida', but she does—frequently.

I had grown accustomed to Maida in her stern white uniform. Now her black hair and the sword-blue of her eyes and the vivid pink that flared into her cheeks and lips at the least touch of excitement—all this, above a wispy, clinging dinner-gown of midnight-blue that was somehow barely frosted in crystal beads, affected me as much as it did the boy . . .

Soon after this Sarah finds herself studying Maida's 'slim shoulders and gracefully alert carriage', her 'victorious' yet not arrogant manner, and so on. In *From This Dark Stairway* (1931) the pretty and romanticized young nurse who sparks off Sarah's admiration is Nancy Page, a golden-haired, soft-eyed and engagingly dimpled girl whom Sarah considers 'the essence of femininity'. She also admits to 'a sort of partiality for that young man'—Larry O'Leary, who is a private detective at the beginning of this long series of books, and later becomes a police lieutenant in the Homicide Bureau.

The stories follow a pattern; Sarah stands on the sidelines and criticizes the ineptitude of the official investigation before she is roped in (always displaying some reluctance) to assist. In the course of her adventures it becomes evident that any hospital which employs Sarah Keate is inviting disaster. Her presence in a medical institution is a sure indication that several murders will shortly take place. Sarah, on the whole, remains unruffled by the discovery of corpses in the elevator, the mysterious disappearance of a patient from the charity ward or the sense that she is being watched constantly by a menacing unseen presence. She stolidly continues to act the part of an autocratic 'auntie' to the patients, adroitly popping thermometers under tongues and making reassuring noises, even when other nurses get jittery and whisper together in frightened clusters. (Her colleagues are surprisingly lacking in moral strength and stamina under this kind of stress, despite Sarah's insistence that even in situations of danger nurses should be carried along by the habit of discipline—by 'baths and diet trays and clean linens and dusting and bed-making and charts and doctors' calls'.)

In all her crime stories, Mignon Eberhart makes good use of physical atmosphere to create a build-up of suspense. There is usually a psychic sybil on the staff who foretells impending doom for the nurses who are about to report to the wards for night duty. The heavy mood that exists between three and five o'clock in the morning, and the shut-in feeling of the dark night ward with only its 'green shaded light about the chart desk' are well conveyed. The sense of menace and claustrophobia is heightened in *The Patient in Room 18* by days of incessant rain, and in *From This Dark Stairway* by a hot and humid spell that adds to the general murkiness; the summer darkness comes oppressively, 'like a black, secretive mist, creeping along . . . into corners'. Sometimes atmospherics are overdone, and there are rather too many shadowy corridors where 'a sort of subdued terror' lurks 'in the very walls'. Of course the sick-rooms would be darkened at night, but when murder has already been committed on the premises it seems short-sighted of the hospital administrators to keep the stairways, the hall and even the nurses' home so dimly lighted. There are other contradictions: for example, all the hospital lights go off suddenly when Sarah is the only person on duty in a ward at night, and it then becomes apparent that this generally efficient and resourceful nurse has not even equipped herself with a torch, although 'down that black emptiness, only five nights ago, two men had been violently done to death . . .' The usual ingredients of the hospital drama are, however, on the whole convincingly used, from patients hovering between life and death to the mysterious purloining of hypodermic syringes: 'Morphine is not something that one carries about in a pocket or vanity bag . . .'

The crime-solving adventures of Sarah Keate continued into the 1950s. She was not the first of the sleuthing nurses, though certainly one of the most popular. Her predecessor was Mary Roberts Rinehart's Hilda Adams (known also as 'Miss Pinkerton'*). The author, who advised young writers to stick to areas of life known at first-hand—'If you are a housewife living in the South, why try to tell a story of French Colonials in North Africa?'—drew to some extent on her own nursing experiences. *The Buckled Bag* (1925) begins with a longish justification of a nurse's involvement in crime, particularly of her double-dealing in obtaining a patient's confidence—'A trained nurse sees under the skin of the soul'—and then

---

* After Allan Pinkerton, a writer and private investigator whose name became synonymous with detection.

possibly denouncing him, or one of his relatives, to the police. Hilda seems to think that it is only legality and not scruples which prevents the clergyman or the doctor from using information obtained in confidence in the same way. In her opinion, nurses, not being legally barred, need have no doubts about passing on anything they have learned from their patients.

Hilda is initially drawn into sleuthing by George Patton, who starts as a small-time country detective and eventually becomes a police inspector. Her career in crime-solving gets off to a bad start; while she is out shopping in a department store and preoccupied by thoughts of the challenges that her new work will bring, someone cuts her handbag off her arm, so that she returns home 'depressed and ill-humoured'. However, by the time she embarks upon her last adventure (*Haunted Lady*, 1942) Hilda Adams is not only efficiently solving complicated cases but is confident enough to enjoy an autumnal romance with Inspector Patton. (Early in the series her age is given as twenty-nine; in *Haunted Lady* she is 'rather a rosy thirty-eight-year-old cherub'.) There are occasional hints of love interest between the nurse and the police inspector throughout the saga, but these are kept in a low-key mood with Patton making the overtures—'Outside of the temper she's rather a dear person, and I'm fond of her . . .'—and Hilda brushing off his 'nonsense'.

Sometimes there are duels between the two on account of Patton's masculine over-protectiveness and Hilda's feminism: 'If there is anything that takes the very soul out of a woman, it is to be kept from doing a thing she has set her heart on, because some man thinks it dangerous. If she has any spirit, that rouses it.' Patton also annoys Hilda when he accuses her of allowing her emotions to affect her judgement: she prides herself on a factual approach. She is high-minded in certain ways, and even in the interests of unravelling a murder mystery does not, for example, resort to eavesdropping (Nurse Sarah Keate does so unashamedly, like Susan Dare, another of Mignon Eberhart's women detectives; see pages 142–3). Without deliberately listening, however, Hilda often picks up threads of enlightening conversation as she moves quietly in her rubber-soled shoes around the houses of the private patients whom she takes on at Patton's instigation. The process of justifying her double role continues over the years; both she and Patton are quick to resent suggestions that she is the police's 'stool pigeon'. Hilda uses the argument that, since the criminal acts against society, society must use every means against the criminal. She hoists this belief 'as a flag of truce to my nurse's ethical training' and is at pains to point out that

> Although I played a double game, no patient of mine had suffered. I was a nurse first and a police agent second. If it was a question between turpentine compresses . . . and seeing what letters came in or went out of the house, the compress went on first, and cracking hot, too. I am not boasting. That is my method . . .

Despite the charm that Hilda Adams held for George Patton, she strikes the reader as a dedicated but pedantic and not especially appealing woman. Joan Blondell, who played Hilda in a film version of the stories, made her more sympathetic.

Also dedicated to her work—or rather her vocation—and enjoying some detection on the side is Sister Ursula, about whose cases 'H. H. Holmes' produced two full-length books and several short stories in the 1940s. Sister Mary Ursula of the convent of Martha of Bethany solves crimes not only in the context of the law but of the Church: 'One doesn't joke about murder in the confessional.' She may talk in quiet meaningful tones but she is a character to be reckoned with. Her father was a Chief of Police in Iowa, and Ursula, before illness prevented her, had intended to join the Force; instead she takes the veil. Her health recovers and, though she has abandoned her early ambitions, when she suddenly finds herself a witness in a difficult murder case she ponders deeply on the facts and soon comes up with the solution. After this, from her convent seclusion she becomes 'an unofficial adviser to one police lieutenant in several other cases'. In the short story 'Coffin Corner' (1943) Sister Ursula elucidates a long-ago murder mystery through her understanding of the game of cribbage. She also demonstrates her very worldly knowledge of football in this episode. Nuns of course are bizarre figures in the brash and sometimes brutal world of detection but, like nurses, they crop up from time to time, adding a touch of originality to the genre (see Chapter XII).

Police officers welcomed assistance from Nurses Keate and

Adams, and from Sister Ursula, but this was not always the case with Hildegarde Withers, the 'spinster schoolma'am' created by Stuart Palmer, whose investigative efforts were described by Inspector Oscar Piper as 'hurling a monkeywrench into the machines'. Hildegarde is an American variant of the eccentric, unmarried female sleuth who has proved such a popular archetype in English detective fiction. She is firmly middle-aged and must have retired early from teaching, for she seems to have plenty of time on her hands for solving 'puzzles'. There are about eighteen books in the series, beginning with *The Penguin Pool Murder* in 1931 and ending with *Hildegarde Withers Makes the Scene* (1959) which was co-authored by Palmer and Fletcher Flora. Hildegarde is the type of woman who seems never to have been young, but always stolidly mature. She is prompted by vanity to reminisce about her 'heyday' though she admits to having had little personal experience of romance. In fact the acerbic Inspector Oscar Piper, with whom she is on first-name terms, is in Hildegarde's estimation 'the only man in her life even though she detested him one day and mothered him the next'. She *does*, however, have an orange-hued poodle called Talleyrand, which she alternately bullies and indulges. In her apartment Hildegarde provides snacks and reassurance for both dog and police inspector.

The stories always get off to a good start with immediate and dramatic action. A 1941 episode, 'Green Ice', for instance, begins with a smash-and-grab raid on a Manhattan jeweller's shop, while in the opening pages of a 1959 novel (*The Green Ace*), 'a great big dead beautiful naked dame' is found by two traffic cops crammed against the back seat of a speeding Buick. Stuart Palmer manages to maintain pace and gusto throughout the books, so that even the predictability of the set-piece psychological battles between Hildegarde and Oscar becomes acceptable. Hildegarde Withers is 'a private investigator without portfolio' who cherishes lost causes. Convinced that she can teach the police a thing or two, she busybodies around headquarters, ostensibly selling tickets for charity bazaars and barging into whatever problem is currently preoccupying Inspector Piper. She listens in on her radio to police calls so that—embarrassingly for Oscar—she can arrive early on the scene of certain crimes. She is frequently ruffled by the police inspector's contempt for her 'fancy-sleuthing' and when he insultingly calls her 'an amateur snoop' she informs him tartly that 'There's such a thing as being *over*trained.'

Hildegarde brings her 'famed intuition' into play by sleeping on a problem and expecting to come up with the correct answers in the morning; but she is not quite so reliant on psychic short cuts as some other women detectives, and does a lot of painstaking following-up of clues and tracking of possible culprits. At times she seems the typical 'old sketch' of popular fiction—dowdy, with a taste for extravagant and hideous hats, and emanating an 'odour of soap, violet sec and chalk dust'. The last is surprising for, as mentioned earlier, she rarely seems to get near the inside of a classroom; to use Oscar's succinct phrase, she's for ever 'up to her bustle' in crime. Throughout the stories, the robust quality of the inspector's vocabulary makes an amusing contrast with Hildegarde's prissiness. Hildegarde Withers has been featured in films as well as in books; she was portrayed successively by Edna May Oliver, Helen Broderick and Zasu Pitts, all actresses well equipped to put across the 'spinster schoolma'am's' wry and resolute personality.

During the 1930s and early 1940s there was a proliferation of she-dicks who were pretty enough to bowl men over wholesale. Most of these girls, though putting themselves in situations of risk to do their detecting work, were not paid for it. Crime investigation was a secondary job and on the whole their main careers were glamorous. Rose Graham, for example, in Karl Deitzer's 1937 story 'Murder at the Movies' is a Hollywood continuity girl. She spots the killer of a star actor simply by bringing her professionally trained eye and ear for detail to bear on the murder case. William Irish's 'Angel-Face' (in a short story of the same name in 1937) is another once-off crime-solver with an entertainment-world background; she is a stripper who becomes an amateur detective in order to prove that her brother is innocent of a murder charge. Gipsy Rose Lee's 1941 novel, *The G-String Murders*, also featured a stripper-sleuth, and the combination of these two diverse talents has a certain bizarre attraction.

Susan Dare is probably the best-known of this group of young and attractive detectives. Mignon Eberhart recorded her adventures in *The Cases of Susan Dare* (1934), a collection of separate episodes. Susan differs markedly from Nurse Sarah Keate, the author's earlier female investigator, in being nubile and having a regular boyfriend, Jim Byrne. Susan is livelier than Sarah, not so verbose and less inclined to moralize. She works alone more often than her predecessor although Jim, who is a reporter on the Chicago *Record*, collaborates with her on several cases. Initially, as a writer of crime novels, Susan has no desire for active involvement, but after stumbling into a murder mystery her interest is aroused and she begins to spend more time on detection than writing. 'Playing God' by manipulating fictional characters is, of course, an author's prerogative, but Susan, as an investigator rather than a crime-writer, has to be able 'to confirm with hard facts that queer divining rod of her own consciousness'. For this kind of confirmation Jim, more objective than Susan, is helpful when she can 'only push out blind tentacles of something that was perilously like intuition'. The stories include, as well as Eberhart's usual sense of atmosphere and frisson, trails of carefully defined clues for the reader to get to grips with (though there are one or two irritating moments when it becomes obvious that Susan has solved a case by being aware of a fact that has not been passed on to the reader). Susan effectively supplements her 'woman's' intuition with more down-to-earth feminine know-how, as she explains to Jim when he asks, 'It's her lipstick?' 'Yes. It was in her coat pocket; that's why she sent for her coat . . . You can see a smear of it on her lips now. It's called claret—a rather soft crimson. Any woman would note the exact shade.'

Susan is a lively example of the appealing young girl sleuth of the 1930s; it is surprising that her exploits were featured in only one book, whereas Sarah Keate, Mignon Eberhart's less engaging earlier heroine, sprawled her way across many volumes. Perhaps Susan was a little *too* normal, too much like the girl next door, to excite readers. At this time there were plenty of 'ordinary' girl characters who, when thrust into situations of danger and suspense, proved to be competent sleuths. (Most of these are not really so 'ordinary' however; they are beautiful, intelligent and making their marks in their chosen professions apart from detection.) In Paul Gallico's 'Solo Job' (1937) Sally 'Sherlock' Holmes Lane is a reporter for the New York *Standard*, and she is led by her 'nose for news' into the thick of a fearsome baby-killing racket. She's engaged to Ira Clarke, 'the big ugly night editor', but resents his efforts to keep her out of danger:

> 'You're just a girl, Sally, after all, and—' He stopped there, because Sally suddenly drew her hand from his and straightened up. Then he said, 'Well, aren't you?'
> Sally shook her head. 'No. No, Ira, I'm not. I'm a reporter . . . Ira, look! I love you, my dearest, and shall until I die. But I won't let it—let you make me weak. I've always worked alone. I can stand on my own feet, Ira.'

Sally sometimes carries her desire for independence too far. For instance, when she voluntarily puts herself into a particularly nasty and perilous trap she doesn't take the obvious precaution of mentioning her plans to anyone beforehand. She is rescued only because Ira has ignored her demand to let her do things alone, and has kept a watch on her all the time. Feminist independence in the end flies out of the window as Sally, from the confines of Ira's arms, says 'Always watch over me. Oh, my darling, my darling! . . . It *is* what you're here for!' At this point—if not before—it must also have been obvious to readers that romance, and not sleuthing, was what Sally was there for. However, she is gifted with certain capacities which give her a headstart in detection; she is sensitive not only to 'the appearance but the aura of evil'; also she has 'no patience with detective-story disguises' but simply alters her pretty, platinum blonde good looks when necessary by fasting and going without sleep. Not surprisingly, in view of Sally's lightweight personality, there is no sequel to this story.

Another Sally is made of sterner stuff: Sally Cardiff appeared in Vincent Starrett's story 'The Bloody Crescendo' (1934), later republished as 'Murder at the Opera'. (Starrett had written *The Private Life of Sherlock Holmes* in 1933 and created several fictional male detectives before introducing Sally.) 'The Bloody Crescendo' has touches of perception and realism. Sally, for example, though bright and beautiful in the young she-dick tradition, displays at times a confidence in her own abilities which seems, to others, rather unpalatable. She makes it clear throughout to Arnold Castle—the young man who wants to marry her but resents her 'detective activities'—that she has no intention of abandoning her sleuthing for the kitchen sink.

At the end of the story they reach a happy compromise, with Arnold accepting the auxiliary role:

'Do you know, Sally, I think I'm a little afraid of you! It's rather alarming to contemplate—er—having a detective in the family . . .'

Miss Cardiff blushed a little.

'Don't be silly,' she said. 'There'll be times when I'll be grateful for a good old Watson!'

Sally approaches crime-solving with a rather macabre non-chalance (she hums softly to herself while weighing up the facts of a murder case and 'laughs delightedly' when discussing the details with others). Unlike most of the fictional women detectives she is suspicious of 'intuition' and suggests that it might in fact be related to personal conditioning: 'Intuition was a funny thing. It whispered to Dallas—a man—that a woman had done this deed. To Sally Cardiff—a woman—it whispered that a man had done it. Perhaps she, also, was prejudiced.'

'Leslie Ford's' Grace Latham, who came on the sleuthing scene in 1934 in *The Strangled Witness*, also makes no claims to psychic capacities: 'My batting average in the crystal ball league is zero point zero.' She is a widowed socialite with two grown-up sons, and the important man in her life is Colonel John Primrose, a handsome but bossy character who is attached to Grace but underrates her intelligence and sometimes insults her: 'Do as you're told, Mrs Latham. And stay in the car. Don't get out of it, and don't go anywhere until somebody goes with you. You're not in Washington DC, and you're in everybody's way. Don't you be a—.' Grace Latham, the heroine of several books, is a likeable lady who is rather more genteel than the usual run of women investigators of this period. She is an amateur, but can go a long way on her own initiative in un-ravelling a crime; however, it is usually the cocky Colonel who pulls the final plums out of the pie, and Grace seems spine-lessly ready to accept his dismissive assessment of herself: 'The diamond bracelet, I supposed, was what he was talking about . . . It didn't seem to make any kind of sense. But as Colonel Primrose had said, I had no right to set myself up as a technical expert on a commodity I had so little of.' It is interesting that these stories with their irritating thread of anti-feminism should have been the work of a woman: 'Leslie Ford' was the pseudonym of Mrs Zenith Jones Brown.

Theodolinda ('Dol') Bonner in Rex Stout's 1937 novel *The Hand in the Glove* (published two years later in England as *Crime on Her Hands*) refuses to allow any man to patronize her. Even when she's questioned by a member of the State Police who suspects her of murder, Dol is not at a loss for words: he leads in with 'Never believe a woman when she's in a hole'; her response, delivered 'in her coolest tone' is:

> 'You're being silly, Colonel. I dislike all men anyway, and I particularly dislike men in uniforms with military titles because I detest war . . . I dislike you very much. You are the north wind type, there is nothing to you but velocity; in anything requiring insight or subtlety you are merely a nuisance . . .'

Many women of course have come up at one time or another against bullying misogynists like this soldier-turned-policeman, but have shrugged off the experience. Dol's counterattack, and the general aggressiveness of her feminism, spring from an old wound. After her father's 'ruin and suicide' she became 'a poor girl instead of a rich girl' and was jilted by her fiancé at the time when she most needed his support. Dol determined then to achieve economic and emotional independence: 'I'm quite young, and it may turn out that I'm merely conceited and my pride has been hurt, but I *think* I'm clever. I'm going to try to be.' Sleuthing for Dol is a serious business, and never a matter of unpaid dilettantism. (It is rather surprising that she flipped a coin to decide between landscape design and detection—the only two careers available in which she felt she could be her own boss.) Dol didn't always work solo; at the beginning of *The Hand in the Glove* she has a female partner (Sylvia Raffray) in her investigation agency, but this girl drops out in the first chapter. Dol also appeared in one or two Nero Wolfe novels; her activities, and those of Sally Colt, another girl detective, triggered off some resentful remarks on 'she-dicks' from Archie Goodwin.

The toughness of Dol's personality is not echoed in her physical appearance. Her skin is cream-tinted and transparent, her eyes are a 'remarkable combination of caramel irises and jet lashes', and she has 'the grace and bearing of a dancer'. All this of course suggests affinities with the typical heroines of light romantic fiction, but Rex Stout resists the impulse to dilute Dol's anti-masculinism, and there is no conventional clinch on the final page. She parries all advances and insists that she hates being touched. The only male for whom she has affection is her young brother Dick, and she is working hard to put him through a good school.

The Hand in the Glove, apart from overdoing Dol's feminism, is convincing in its characterization, and has more depth of content and intricacy of structure than the average female sleuth story of the period. Murder is not used merely as a prop for mystery and detection; something of its nauseating reality comes across when Dol suddenly finds herself confronting a corpse for the first time. There are other grisly episodes (animals are trapped and slaughtered in a particularly brutal way) and the mood of the book sometimes contrasts starkly with the simple 'goodies-versus-baddies' atmosphere of other contemporary stories of detection. The reader is made aware of some of the real-life problems that might be especially difficult for women detectives to cope with. There is a sense of realism too in Dol's frequent reassessing of her achievements and failures. She prides herself on her professionalism, yet succumbs to 'quixotic impulsiveness in wiping the fingerprints' when she thinks these will incriminate the wrong person. She often doubts her own efficiency: 'Detective? Piffle. She was nothing but a darned female quidnunc.'

Dol Bonner was probably the last of the young and likeable girl sleuths of her decade. During the 1940s most of the new American female detectives were older women—Miss Julia Tyler, a retired classics teacher; hefty Amy Brewster, who is a lawyer and financial expert as well as something of a sleuth; Hannah Van Doren, the bloodthirsty crime-writer known as 'Homicide Hannah, the Gorgeous Ghoul', and so on. Gale Gallagher, however, whose exploits were first recorded in 1947 in *I Found Him Dead* seems the natural successor to nice girls like Susan Dare and Rose Graham, and realists like Dol Bonner. There are two Gale Gallagher books; the second is *Chord in Crimson*, 1949. They are not only narrated by Gale, but her name appears on the title-page, presumably to give a sense of authenticity: in fact, the writer was Will Oursler. Gale has her own agency, the Acme Investigation Bureau, and she is a 'skiptracer'—a specialist in finding persons who have gone missing, leaving unpaid bills. She also gets drawn into murder mysteries. 'In the tag end of the twenties' she is attractive but case-hardened and extremely professional, stalking the streets with a Colt .32 concealed under her 'stunning' clothes. She warns off predatory males by advising them 'to stay out of the arms of the law', and is not afraid of operating on her own in sleazy locales.

Gale as a detective is following in the footsteps of her police-man father, who died in the course of his duties. She has a sense of dedication but a wry awareness that many of her efforts may be fruitless: 'I work for the law but any cop knows power isn't always on the side of justice.' Like Dol Bonner, Gale frequently examines and analyses her own working methods: 'I was getting mad in spite of myself. I always get too emotion-ally involved with my cases.' She admits that 'there are times when I don't like my work. I feel too sorry for people.' The books are full of action, atmosphere and brisk dialogue that lifts itself off the page. Gale appeared on the scene at the end of the 1940s and, with her wit and low-key toughness, she provides a link between the crisp career girls of the 1930s and the future heroines of the genre. She is a forerunner, not of the superwoman-adventuresses of films, television and popular fiction during the 1950s and 1960s, but of the serious and in-telligent women detectives who then emerged in books on both sides of the Atlantic.

VIII

A SWEET GIRL SLEUTH

The Teenage Detective in America

'. . . What queer enterprises they sometimes engaged in.'
                                        Mark Twain

THE GIRL DETECTIVE was a natural development of the girl
who solved trivial mysteries as a sideline, but she wasn't classified as a standard figure in juvenile fiction until the first Nancy
Drew books began to appear in 1929 and 1930.

From the early years of the century, American girls had been
on the move. The Camp Fire Movement (founded in 1911 as
an alternative to Girl Scouts) got them out of the drawing-room
and into the woods, where they proceeded to shed restrictive
layers of clothing: 'Bless your heart, little Kitty, you won't
know yourself in green bloomers . . .' Technical advances in
locomotion were quickly celebrated in girls' books: there were
Motor Girls in 1910, Flying Girls in 1911, girls dashing about
on motor cycles even before the First World War had made
this mode of transport a commonplace of modern life. By 1917
girls and women were 'doing everything in the world, even
running elevators', although the heartfelt complaint of many
English heroines was reiterated in American books: 'too young
to do anything but keep the home fires burning!' Finding a
suitable outlet for one's energies is always cause for jubilation:
'I always wanted to be an agriculturette, and now I'm going
to!' Immediately after the war we find stories of conservation
and reconstruction, and then the old staples of orphans and mis-
placed fortunes were dragged up again. The Camp Fire Movement still flourished, but it had acquired somewhat lush and
pretentious overtones: 'Goodness! How-ow I love the woods!
. . . It—it seems to me as if the woods were the lesson-book of
the light . . .'

Work, with its connotations of independence, self-esteem and
usefulness, still held its own glamour. Postwar fiction demanded
a new type of heroine, a cleaned-up embodiment of Flaming

149

Youth, with all the energy and purposefulness of the working girl and none of her restrictions. The amateur sleuth, a figure that satisfied a number of apparently conflicting requirements, was the obvious answer. She took some time to evolve: it was not until 1929, when American women had had the vote for ten years, that adolescent girls were presented with their own irresistible heroine: Nancy Drew.

Nancy has genuine heroic quality unconnected with the literary value of the series. A product of commercial expediency, planned to exert the maximum appeal for the greatest number of readers, she was tailored to correspond with the child's wish for excitement and entertainment. Didacticism and sentimentality were not part of the package. Social and moral observation is contained in the stories only in the form of the preconceived idea: certain values are taken for granted, including a view of femininity which actually conflicts with Nancy's behaviour. ('Good' girls in the stories are often sweet, meek, self-effacing and prim.) The author tackled this problem simply by ignoring it, which provides an economical but not very satisfactory solution. Nancy has never had to waste time wishing she were a boy; for all practical purposes she *is*. She's a winner, a high-flyer, a fast thinker, a champion. She drives a blue roadster, knows how to handle a speed-boat and an aeroplane, round up steers, keep control of an unruly mount and stun a would-be kidnapper with a single blow. The stories certainly pander to the spirited girl's reluctance to accept the notion of her own physical inadequacy.

The author, 'Carolyn Keene', achieved a neat blend of conservatism and innovation. There is no indication in the books that Nancy's activities are out of the ordinary—indeed, the narrative tone occasionally attains a primness suggestive of magazine fiction for the suburban miss: 'Nancy turned to see a strange sight. A woman, wearing a tight-fitting black dress and large peaked hat, with a stole half covering her face, was tiptoeing across the carpeted room, heading for the desk.' As far as the format is concerned, the 'problem-solving' element in children's fiction is simply re-located at the centre of the theme. Sleuthing was not exactly an unprecedented activity, with precocious tots like Honey Bunch (heroine of a series for very young children) solving their first little mysteries at the age of four. At the simplest level, the typical children's story is one in which something is wrong, or puzzling, or mildly unjust at the beginning so that it can gradually be put right. In detective fiction the troublesome occurrence is serious, involving criminal activity that threatens the whole community, though there's always a distressed individual for the detective to take under her wing. As a consequence of her ability to uncover crimes, the eighteen-year-old sleuth is largely unrestricted, allowed to board planes at will, take off in pursuit of absolute strangers and even stay out all night. She is subject to none of the minor, irritating pressures of home life and this makes her an object of strong vicarious satisfaction for the juvenile reader.

The original 'Carolyn Keene' was Edward Stratemeyer, founder of the syndicate which still produces the Bobbsey Twins and Hardy Boys adventures. Stratemeyer drafted the first three stories shortly before his death in 1930, when the pseudonym and the idea passed to his daughter, Harriet S. Adams, who has been responsible for the series ever since. *The Secret of the Old Clock* (1929), Nancy Drew's first mystery, is a straightforward tale of an unjust inheritance ('It makes my blood fairly boil every time I think of Ada and Isabel Topham getting all of the Crowley fortune'). A queer old gentleman named Josiah Crowley has seen fit to place instructions relating to his last will and testament inside a clock, apparently in order to cause the maximum inconvenience to his heirs. Nancy tracks down the clock and its secret, earning gratitude from the real beneficiaries and praise from her father: 'You're a regular detective, Nancy!' Soon he's referring to her as his assistant, and this gives her a semi-official standing since he is the celebrated criminal lawyer Carson Drew.

Nancy's adventures quickly become more exciting: in the second book of the series she's uncovering a hidden staircase and exposing the trickery behind an apparent haunting. This, in fact, is the most persistent theme in the Nancy Drew saga; the girl sleuth's world is populated to a remarkable extent by crooks who specialize in faking ghostly phenomena for the purpose of furthering a wicked objective. Nancy has only to approach a river for a phantom canoe to appear gliding along it. A vanishing horse (*The Invisible Intruder*, 1939) almost fools her friends, but the young detective isn't short of an explanation: 'It was probably a tremendous balloon stretched over a mechanical horse which the rider guided by remote control.'

She's right, of course; she knows the lengths that criminals will go to to achieve their ends.

On another occasion (*The Clue of the Broken Locket*, 1945) a haunting is simulated by means of 'an ingenious arrangement of wires, sound projector, and a film clip'. Sensible, grown men are scared away from the place but not courageous Nancy: 'I ... want to inspect that phantom ship at close range.' None of the apparitions in the stories has a numinous quality, though some are more farcical than others ('It was that skeleton, I tell you ... He just reached out and bit my finger'). Ghostly voices are for ever warning Nancy to mind her own business ('I have a message for you from the spirit world. Direct from your grandfather Drew') but the girl's well-founded scepticism is never shaken. Like every heroine of the era gifted with common sense, she knows that anything mysterious must have a rational cause. (In children's fiction in general, up to the 1960s, magic and time-travelling were acceptable forms of the supernatural; ghosts were not.) There is nothing subtle or understated about the ghosts which Nancy and her friends encounter. Luminous figures are seen at the keyboards of organs, wraith-like shapes emerge from walls, and, as a last resort, comic-strip phantoms are constructed from odourless gas. There is no attempt to engage the reader's imagination; the author provides the ghostly paraphernalia without the atmosphere of a haunting. The thick-witted individuals whom Nancy is up against are dreadfully prone to overdo their visual effects.

The girl detective is intrepid to the point of foolhardiness: in every story there's a thrilling moment when she is dragged off by a person of evil appearance, soon to be threatened with the prospect of never seeing daylight again. Her constant disappearances are bad for the peace of mind of her friends: ' "Oh!" Bess cried out. "Nancy is in danger again! What can we do?" ' Often a last-minute rescue is staged by Nancy's father, Carson Drew, by her friend Ned Nickerson or by her female subordinates Bess and George. The young sleuth thrives on danger, which she pursues with gusto; she's never deterred by the prospect of ill-treatment. She is gifted with a head that can withstand incessant knocks. She may lose consciousness, but never her nerve or her self-possession. As soon as she comes round she's off on the trail again.

Blows intended for Nancy are sometimes diverted, and the

NANCY WAS A PRISONER IN THE TOWER!

The Clue in the Crumbling Wall

One of R. H. Tandy's illustrations for the original
'Nancy Drew' series, 1939.

detective is forced to minister to her unconscious friends, who lie strewn around her in unhappy profusion (' "They might have fallen right into the fire!" Nancy thought, shuddering'). No one is ever seriously hurt, however, though Nancy's side-kick George has a nasty experience when she impersonates the detective in order to throw a villain off the scent. Poor George is abducted, drugged, and reduced to a state of nervous prostration: the erstwhile tomboy lies abjectly on a couch in her mother's living room and feebly begs Nancy to give up the case (*The Clue of the Velvet Mask*, 1953). George doesn't recover until she's forced to pull herself together in order to save Nancy and Bess who have got themselves into a tight spot: 'In their prison room Nancy and Bess were suffering intense discomfort.' It's a characteristic plight.

George Fayne and Bess Marvin are cousins, antithetical in appearance and behaviour. George is normally boisterous and adventuresome; Bess is flirtatious and rather timid. They're happy to follow Nancy's lead; and, in a sense, they represent opposing tendencies that are fused together splendidly in the young sleuth. Nancy is hyperactive but never hoydenish; she's always on the side of dignity and order. Threats, bashings, drenchings and hauntings can never undermine her serenity. Bess's blonde prettiness is of the type associated with silliness, whereas Nancy's denotes intelligence and *savoir faire*. (Nancy acquires 'titian' hair later in the series, but she is blonde to begin with.)

Nancy has no mother to inhibit her independence of spirit: a housekeeper named Hannah Gruen acts as a surrogate parent, but remains very much a background figure. Well-bred Nancy treats Mrs Gruen with affection and respect; but the glorified servant knows her function and never exceeds it. When the girl attempts to discuss her current case (*The Clue in the Crumbling Wall*, 1939), Mrs Gruen has nothing more constructive to offer than futile pleas for caution. In fact caution, or the instinct for self-preservation, is altogether outside the scope of the stories; Nancy can take outrageous risks because she's indestructible. Many nasty characters mean to do her harm, and come pre-pared with a variety of weapons to achieve this purpose. The detective cannot set foot in a boat without ending in deep water. Her car is frequently sabotaged, dangerous objects come hurt-ling towards her, drawbridges start to rise when she's half-way across them. If she goes to a party, the chances are that someone will attempt to smother her in a pile of coats.

Every one of the rules laid down for adult detective fiction during the period known as the Golden Age is infringed in the Nancy Drew stories. There is no mystery about the identity of the criminals; plots and sub-plots are welded together by a series of preposterous coincidences; the triumphant conclusions are not presented as a result of logic or even of plausible chance. If Nancy sits down on a park bench to think about a case she's interested in, she will soon be joined by a talkative stranger who knows something relevant to it. If a robbery takes place, the thief is liable to turn up unknowingly on Nancy's doorstep to apply for a job. The girl can spot a wrongdoer at first sight. Her unreasonable assumptions are invariably correct. She sees connections where none could possibly exist. She's helped, too, by clues in the form of strange messages which drop out of the air, as if propelled into space by a whimsical deity ('Floating towards her, seemingly out of nowhere, was a small white paper'). These may be attached to the leg of a carrier pigeon, or simply become dislodged from the bole of a tree when Nancy is walking under it.

In the interest of simplification, all the quasi-mysterious and perplexing forces in the stories are centred on a romantic object —a 'clue'—which needs only to be interpreted correctly for everything to fall into place. (It's a more facile version of the traditional riddle or magic formula in a fairy tale.) This involves a radical displacement which gives the stories their trite and artificial quality, but it also provides a necessary focus for the juvenile imagination. In adult stories of detection, 'clues' are simply pointers to the actions or the identity of a criminal, but in children's fiction the object itself must encompass the whole attraction of the plot. The old albums, stage-coaches, dancing puppets, scarlet slippers and so on, are sufficiently quaint and intriguing to produce an instantaneous effect. They're all, of course, objects with a traditional appeal for girls—stagey or sentimental—unlike the twisted claws, sinister signposts and broken blades of the corresponding boys' series, which belong to an order of symbols distinctly masculine. The Hardy Boys would be embarrassed by a case which started with a ballet dancer's shoe. In the Nancy Drew saga at least, there is very little attempt to extend the atmosphere generated by each picturesque device. In fact Carolyn Keene hardly bothers to differentiate, in any real sense, between the various settings provided for Nancy's mysteries. Ordinary or bizarre, they're all evoked in the same flat manner by an author apparently deficient in the sense of place.

Of course the formula, which imposes incessant movement upon the characters and a snappy, monosyllabic style upon the narrator, is largely to blame. The prose is consistently workmanlike and graceless. Things are kept continually on the boil by a series of fake climaxes. Potential disasters are averted almost before they have had time to register. Lives are endangered and saved at the drop of a cudgel. Occasionally the matter-of-fact quality of the characters is carried far enough to produce unintentional wit: in *The Bungalow Mystery* (1930), for instance, a man imprisoned in a cellar complains to Nancy that he hasn't been able to get in touch with his wife 'since I've been tied up here'.

Absolute freedom of action, an absence of mundane disabilities and a surface gloss contribute to Nancy's appeal. She is not the type of heroine who succeeds in triumphing over a social handicap (usually of age or gender), solving the mystery in order to prove everyone mistaken. Her function is even more straightforward than this—she is invincible to begin with. Whatever she does is right. If she is rebuked for unseemly behaviour it is by a person abysmally crotchety and old-fashioned ('When I was a girl, girls stayed home and learned to cook and sew and mind their own business'), or someone whose religious views make him see the world in a very static way, as when an exceptionally bigoted person of the Amish persuasion (in *The Witch Tree Symbol*, 1963) informs her that she ought to be at home 'cooking and cleaning'. In *Nancy's Mysterious Letter* (1932) the detective is taken severely to task by a rude old postmaster: 'Now, when I was young, girls didn't go round inviting men below their station in life to come into their homes. That's the reason we have so much lawlessness these days . . .' But these are only token gestures, included to indicate that Nancy is subject to disapproval like any ordinary teenager. The reader knows that the critic is not speaking from a reasonable viewpoint.

In every sphere that she enters, Nancy competes on equal terms with professionals, with adults and with boys of her own age, and always comes out on top. At the same time, she has managed to hold on to every quality traditionally associated with femininity—good looks, an affectionate disposition, kindness to strangers, perfect taste in dress, self-deprecation, graciousness, even the ability to respond correctly to displays of masculine prowess. 'Oh, Ned . . . you'll break a bone,' she is heard to murmur on an occasion when her boyfriend hurls himself against a secret door in the dungeon where they're imprisoned.

Nancy's relationship with Ned Nickerson is kept as bland and unobtrusive as possible. Ned is handsome and obliging, and this is all the characterization that is necessary. The first quality is essential to emphasize Nancy's status, the second because the detective needs someone who will act on her instructions. 'Are you willing to help me solve a mystery?' she asks; Ned really has no option. In the context, it's the only relation that is possible. Only minor characters may become engaged or married. When they do, incidentally, they develop emotional problems which are presented in terms peculiar to the genre: 'It's the iron bird that's coming between us!' a disgruntled fiancé cries in *The Clue of the Broken Locket*.

Ned protects and rescues Nancy on the few occasions when he's called upon to do so, but Nancy has the larger social function of protecting the property and inheritances of the rich. The people about to be done out of their rights are always well-bred, cultured and genteel, whereas the typical crook can be identified at once by his absurd name—Bushy Trott, Adolf Tooker—and low behaviour. He's the natural product of a slum, a place of no morals and no culture: '. . . Windows were broken out, roofs sagged, and the yards were choked with weeds. Nancy knew that only the most poverty-stricken lived along the docks. There were few persons to be seen in the vicinity, and those she did pass stared at her so hard and were so disreputable in appearance that she hesitated to question them.' A clean, modest and deserving person of the lower classes will always inhabit a country cottage or a seaside shack. Nancy, of course, is invariably charitable to the underprivileged but the kind of order she upholds has its origins in a middle-class ideal of stability and judicious authority. She's a vigilante, never a reformer, and there is no need for her to question her own motives since the evildoers in the stories always represent a principle of pure badness. There is no room for ambiguity at any level.

Everything about Nancy and her circumstances is perfect to begin with; there are no personal complicating factors to interfere with the stylized mechanics of the chase.

The other distinctive American girl detective is Judy Bolton, heroine of a series which ran from 1932 to 1967. The author, Margaret Sutton, is more concerned with superficial realism, at least to the extent of devising a recognizable personality for her central character. Judy is a small-town Pennsylvanian girl, a doctor's daughter who is fifteen when the stories begin: 'All her life Judy had pined for a mystery to solve but thus far none had come her way.' *The Vanishing Shadow* opens the sequence of thirty-eight cases which the girl tackles in a far more unassuming and less spectacular manner than Nancy Drew. Judy has quirks of temperament, she is capable of injustice and mismanagement, she is restless and obstinate. Of course she is essentially good-hearted, courageous, intelligent and astute, and it is these qualities that find an obvious outlet in the business of amateur detecting. Judy has to manufacture her own mysteries, in a sense: the wrongdoing in the books is really no more than a projection of the girl's craving for adventure. The important factor is Judy's nature, and this interacts with the external facts of the plot to produce a special emotional atmosphere which is a long way in feeling from the antics of the supersleuth. The girl is just sufficiently self-aware to acknowledge the psychological benefits of the exercise in deduction:

'. . . Sometimes I wish I were a boy.'
'And you would be—'
'A detective,' she broke in quickly. 'A great one who goes into all kinds of dangers. I wouldn't mind that—afterwards. There would be that thrill of finding out things. You can't imagine what a satisfaction there is in hitting on a real live clue.' (*The Vanishing Shadow*)

One of the author's objectives is to express a sense of wonder in concrete, romantic and accessible terms. Judy comes closest to stating her philosophy in *The Trail of the Green Doll* (1956) when she remarks: 'Every day *is* a mystery, Peter, because you never know one minute what wonderful, beautiful, or even terrible thing will happen the next. That's what makes life so exciting and—and wonderful.' Margaret Sutton could hardly have been more explicit about the fact that Judy's talent lies in making the most of everyday experience; the green dolls, musical trees and so on are merely symbolic. The author has made a creditable effort to invest these emblems with depth and significance—they stand for more than the equivalent objects in the Nancy Drew stories—but the narrative method is plainly at odds with the constant implications of sensitivity in the heroine. When she's not actually in thoughtful pursuit of a clue, Judy's perceptions are almost as banal as those of the typical Camp Fire enthusiast going into ecstasies in the woods.

The discrepancy arises because the author has not succeeded in avoiding sentimentality; the stories suffer from a pervasive maudlin undertone which comes to the surface at intervals. (It's not unusual to find bathos passing for sensitivity in juvenile fiction; it's perhaps a legacy from J. M. Barrie who caused Peter Pan to remark that death 'is an awfully big adventure'.) When Judy, in an early exploit, gets into difficulties at her new school, a sympathetic friend comments that the only thing *she* learned there was 'how to choke back tears'. 'I'm learning that too,' Judy confesses, exhibiting—in the author's terms—a kind of moral courage which complements her physical bravery ('Judy, aren't you afraid of anything?' her timid brother asks, before she succeeds in making a town hero of him).

The stories have their own peculiar mood—a kind of tawdry romanticism which saturates the narrative. Like Nancy, Judy is adept at exposing trickery, clearing up misunderstanding ('she's dehaunted more houses than you could shake a stick at, including her own house at Farringdon'), and restoring lost relations to their families. But the plots are always subordinate to the evocation of atmosphere. It is perhaps significant that many of the starting points for Judy's strange experiences are represented by something fleeting and intangible—vanishing shadows, disembodied voices, invisible chimes. A mysterious note is sounded, and then there is the chase, the trail of cardboard villains far less convincing than the most extravagant phantom. And at the centre of it all is the nice, unpretentious, average high school girl with her cat Blackberry, her friendships and enthusiasms, and her passion for straightening things out.

Judy advances to the age of twenty-two and marries reliable Peter Dobbs, an FBI agent who detects in the public sphere while she continues to do the same in private. She's a sleuth who lacks official recognition even at the lowest level ("A detective!" Pauline gasped. "Why, Judy, only men are detectives. Can you imagine anyone taking a mere girl on the police force?"); since she's not consulted, she has to go around taking special note of odd or off-key occurrences and tracing each to its source, for her own satisfaction as much as anything. She has no career in her own right, although she does take a short course at a business school 'in order to be able to help Peter with his work'. She acts as his secretary, of course: it is one of those convenient domestic relationships of executive and assistant which prevailed in romantic fiction of the 1940s and 1950s. However, Judy retains a certain amount of gumption since she is the heroine of an action-filled children's series:

'. . . Perhaps the Woman's Page should be the back page so that hubby can enjoy the headlines while wifey ponders the recipes' [her brother jokes].
    'Speaking from wifey's point of view,' Judy retorted, 'she is just as interested in the headlines as he is. She might even want to know the story behind them . . .' (*The Trail of the Green Doll*)

Perhaps the fact that she contrives to lose her wedding dress in a haunted house might be seen as a comic gesture of dissent, or at least reluctance to assume the usual self-effacing role. Marriage is certainly not the end of adventure as far as Judy is concerned. Even on her honeymoon she's hot on the trail of a gang of smugglers.

Energy and spirit are the qualities that count in the girl detective's world. Curiosity, too, becomes a valuable attribute when it's attached to a proper objective; it sheds the connotations of poking and prying which otherwise inform it. The dark secrets ferreted out by the young investigators can always bear exposure—indeed they are invariably the better for it. There is nothing really nasty in the wood-shed or anywhere else; if a skeleton is found hanging in the closet it will turn out to be the property of a medical student, which somehow makes it an object of considerable ordinariness. Houses are never haunted by anything more sinister than a white sheet. All a girl detective really needs is sufficient courage and common sense to keep her imagination from running away with her. The properties borrowed from the Gothic novel—the ruined castles, moss-covered mansions and twisting passageways—are drawn in lightly and prettified, so that they may fascinate without alarming the reader.

Nancy and Judy were followed by many girl sleuths who lacked the style of one and the stamina of the other. Carolyn Keene's detecting schoolgirl sisters, Jean and Louise Dana, for example, decipher strange messages and rescue prisoners exactly in the manner of Nancy Drew, with no refinements of character or behaviour to give them credibility. Like the original detective they acquire deep problems to ponder ('Had the porcelain cow been hurled deliberately by someone who wanted to harm Louise?'); they are frequently overtaken by mishaps upon the road ('Louise quickly twisted the steering-wheel to the left, endeavouring to avoid the tremendous mass of cheese'); and people whom they annoy are as likely as not to shove them down a well ('It's so damp and slimy in here'). They attend a boarding school whose accommodating head-mistress positively encourages them to get off on the trail of crooks. The school setting, in fact, furnishes nothing more distinctive than an unpleasant classmate whose function is to generate a little apparent friction, expose herself to constant humiliation by her profitless bragging and thereby enhance the Danas' triumphs. Lettie Briggs is the stock sneak of the school, mean-spirited and spiteful.

Kay Tracey is another American schoolgirl detective with a misguided adversary in the classroom: 'Kay and the Worth twins . . . were accustomed to Ethel Eaton's lack of good sportsmanship.' The dreadful girl is always trying to get even with her enemies, just to add a slight complication to the very mundane plots. (The stories are written by Frances K. Judd.) Kay is a conventional sleuth who acts with no thought for her own safety, searches carefully for clues and sometimes gets into a desperate plight. When it's all over she is told that she deserves the biggest part of the credit. This is formula-writing at its most flaccid, and there is little ingenuity in plot to compensate for the inert prose.

As a general rule the girl-detective pattern is more effective and coherent when detecting is the heroine's sole activity, whether she's a schoolgirl or a wealthy amateur; the overlap of

"LET'S FOLLOW HIM!" CRIED JEAN.
The Portrait in the Sand   *Frontispiece (Page 127)*

The Dana Girls on the trail of a crook; drawing by
F. Warren, 1943.

career and mystery themes in children's fiction often had a disastrous effect on both. An adventurous nurse, air hostess, journalist or copywriter is usually a hybrid figure, unsatisfactory in respect of both pursuits. A rather vapid glamour attaches to stories of this type, with the heroine's 'career' representing the gateway to romance, in every direction. The 'mystery' element is included simply because the authors are not capable of sustaining interest at a level of verisimilitude. Stories featuring career-girl sleuths contrived to distort the original impulse behind the creation of the girl detective. The priority is no longer intelligent application (however fancifully it's dressed up) but conventional femininity of the most puerile kind: 'She tried to look especially appealing and demure because she wanted to get her information in a hurry.' None of the 'glamour' detectives (Cherry Ames, Vicki Barr, Connie Blair, Beverley Gray and so on) is acceptable even as a fantasy figure, because their silliness and lack of form force us to take them at their surface value: no ulterior force could survive in the bland air of these stories. All the plots are based on a central assumption which invalidates the detecting role: if a girl is sufficiently well-behaved and glossy she may travel to a foreign country at the expense of her employers, prevent a robbery or a kidnapping, acquire a certain amount of credit and marry her immediate superior in the profession. The unadulterated detective, on the other hand, with her searchlight and her magnifying glass, stands for productive eccentricity and independence; she's a valid archetype at least partly because she has no counterpart in the real world to get in the way of her symbolic implications. She evolved, as we have seen, at a moment in time when optimistic ideas about women's capabilities prevailed (ten million American women were actually in full-time employment, although the imminent Depression would reduce this figure by one-fifth). And, whatever the limitations of the stories themselves, the girl detective, in her proper historic context, remains a classic feminist symbol —a unique figment of popular culture.

IX

GRANDMOTHERLY DISGUISE

Miss Marple, Miss Silver and Mrs Bradley

... All goes to plan:
The feud between the local common sense
And intuition, that exasperating amateur
Who's always on the spot by chance before us;
All goes to plan, both lying and confession,
Down to the thrilling final chase, the kill.
W. H. Auden, 'Detective Story'

BY 1930 THE pretty English village was considered the most effective setting for a crime story, and Agatha Christie took the convention a step further when she based her new detective in a cottage in St Mary Mead, providing her at the same time with a deceptive appearance and a deferential manner calculated to delude the most astute murderer. Miss Jane Marple is the dear old lady of English popular fiction, in a direct line that runs from *Cranford* to 'Miss Read'. Her curls are snowy, her cheeks pink and her manner inconsequential. A couple of generations earlier she would have worn a mob-cap and sewn patchwork quilts. She exudes benign gentility. But beneath the fluttery and fragile exterior is a powerful capacity for deductive logic which leaves Miss Marple in no doubt about the wrong-doer's motive and procedure. Everything about this lady is surprising, even her inversions of popular judgements, which quickly became a stock-in-trade. 'There is a great deal of wickedness in village life,' she reiterates, to the delight of readers who probably felt it was time to divest the country cottage, hollyhocks and all, of its more facile associations. It has to be done gently, of course: there is no attempt to subvert the reader's basic assumptions about moral order. Agatha Christie is simply concurring with Conan Doyle's observation that horrid passions may rise as easily on the village green as in the heart of Soho. Of course she is out to make the most of the contrast between cosiness and cupidity.

The story of the *Murder at the Vicarage* (1932) is told by a vicar who doesn't underrate Miss Marple's potential. 'There is no detective in England equal to a spinster lady of uncertain age with plenty of time on her hands,' he states. There is a note of wryness in his tone; he is referring to nosiness, not disinterested elucidation. But one of the author's objectives is to transmute the unappealing habit of gossip into a socially useful activity. Detective fiction provides the only context in which excessive interest in the doings of one's neighbours may have a beneficial outcome, even if the process of gathering information remains distasteful: ' "Quiet men, like Colonel Hillingdon," said Miss Marple, "are often attracted to flamboyant types." And she added, after a significant pause, "Lucky—such a curious name. Do you think Mr Dyson has any idea of—of what might be going on?" ' (*A Caribbean Mystery*, 1964.) Miss Marple's insinuations offend a Canon who recommends Christian charity, but the reader is quite well aware that the dear old lady possesses that quality in abundance. Her speculations are by no means gratuitous. She is simply fortunate in having found a way to exploit and dignify a slightly unsavoury preoccupation. Before she has completed her first case the vicar's young wife refers to Miss Marple as an old cat, but the epithet is later softened to old pussy, once it has been established that she is neither motivated by malice nor subject to misconceptions. The term is apt, of course: we know Miss Marple is fluffy in appearance and possesses claws which are kept out of sight until she is about to pounce on a murderer.

Agatha Christie has taken a common term of criticism applied to women novelists in the Victorian era—narrowness of experience—and shown how the deficiency can be turned to good account. Miss Marple's own experience of life is neither wide nor deep, but she has a very productive familiarity with other people's. She has spent a lifetime observing the untoward in St Mary Mead. Her method of detecting works by extension —applying the principles that got to the bottom of a small contretemps like the disappearance of a quantity of shrimps from the fishmonger's—and analogy: ' "I always find one thing very like another in this world," said Miss Marple.' This is presented as an endearing mannerism:

'And perhaps he reminded you of someone?' prompted Sir Henry, mischief in his eye.

Miss Marple smiled and shook her head at him. 'You are very naughty, Sir Henry. As a matter of fact he *did*. Fred Taylor, at the fish shop. Always slipped in an extra 1 in the shillings column. . .', *A Murder is Announced* (1950)

Miss Marple attributes her successes to specialized knowledge, by which she means knowledge of the characters involved; she has just sufficient gumption to repudiate the term 'feminine intuition' which is bandied about on several occasions. It is not intuition but accuracy of thought which leads her, time and again, to a pertinent conclusion. Otherwise she behaves with impeccable femininity, according to the popular and pejorative definition of the term: she simpers, flutters, flatters, dithers, and is subject to apparently meaningless digressions in conversation. Invariably she exasperates the bluffer and more stolid type of policeman: 'For about ten seconds Inspector Neale stared at Miss Marple with the utmost bewilderment. His first idea was that the old lady had gone off her head. "Blackbirds?" he repeated.' But the old lady's confusion is on the surface only, to amuse the reader who knows what is coming. Miss Marple's thoughts are always in order and the significance of her remarks will soon strike the Inspector with appropriate force: 'Craddock caught his breath. She'd got it! She was sharp, after all.'

In fact Jane Marple is both sharp and fluffy, intelligent and muddle-headed, timid and resolute, inquisitive and fastidious, self-effacing and persistent, unworldly and cynical. Her character is composed of contradictory elements for maximum effect. If she had a counterpart in real life it was the author's Victorian grandmother who was continually surprised by human gullibility. But the requirements of detective fiction supervened before a note of realism could be transcribed. It is well-known that Agatha Christie was not so much a novelist as the inventor of a novelty, a peculiarly intricate and entertaining type of puzzle. All the complexity and originality she could muster went into the construction of the story; her characters, apart from a handful of principals, are rarely more than cyphers. The principals—Poirot, Jane Marple, Mrs Oliver, Tommy and Tuppence Beresford—have a greater number of personal characteristics and mannerisms and this causes them to stand out although they lack substance. They have, however, exactly the right degree of presence to fulfil the function enjoined to them.

For her subsidiary figures Agatha Christie had a whole range of stereotypes to draw from, whom she adapted to her own purposes. Everyone in England in 1930 was familiar with the mild vicar, the brisk nurse, the adenoidal kitchenmaid, the effusive spinster, the gruff colonel, the pampered actress and the reliable doctor. These form part of the cast in innumerable works of farce, romance and melodrama. They are instantly recognizable; their appearance seems to rule out moral or psychological ambiguity. Their lines are predetermined and, in the detective story, this merely adds to the reader's enjoyment when one of them is decisively unmasked, a process which involves a complete reversal of character. But it really isn't difficult to keep up a façade when the façade is all there is. The pretence of integrity in the face of impending exposure would lack conviction in a serious context—but it conforms to the rules of the detecting game.

Until about 1957, Agatha Christie's plots were ingeniously composed of interlocking segments. This was the area in which she excelled; her tone and style have always been less satisfactory. The former is often whimsical or sententious, the latter unremittingly bland. She was involved in the delineation of a world of safety and complacence where the precise moment of a misdeed could be established by reference to an unfailing custom:

'... She must have been murdered around five o'clock, because otherwise ...'
Miss Marple cut in. 'Because otherwise she would certainly have taken the second tray into the drawing-room?'

This observation is taken from a fairly late story, *A Pocket Full of Rye* (1953); in the 1930s and 1940s the details of social behaviour held an even greater significance. In *The Body in the Library* (1942) Miss Marple's suspicions are alerted because the eponymous corpse is got up in an unlikely outfit. A common young lady on her way to an assignation, even one in a field in the middle of the night, would be sure to display an excess of finery. Miss Marple is accustomed to housemaids on outings who scramble over rocks in unsuitable shoes, whereas 'a well-bred girl . . . is always very particular to wear the right clothes for the right occasion. I mean, however hot the day was, a well-bred girl would never turn up at a point-to-point in a silk flowered frock.' On the strength of these remarks the reader is forced to the conclusion that persons who swelter in the heat have an advantage in upbringing over those who merely suffer from twisted ankles. But the rules about dress were laid down as strictly for one class as for the other. The shopgirl at the seaside in a sensible skirt and plimsolls would have been the laughing-stock of her companions.

It is clear that the author was happy with the social arrangements of the pre-war era and these lent a certain clarity and simplicity to the detecting process. It isn't until the early 1950s that a note of disenchantment occurs, and it is sounded with the facetiousness that usually implies intolerance of new ideas: '. . . Juvenile Delinquency is—that's what is the rage nowadays. All these young criminals and potential criminals. Everyone's mad about them . . .' The underlying theme of *They Do It With Mirrors* (1952) is misguided philanthropy, and the story is set in a kind of new-fangled rehabilitation centre administered by a crank: '. . . Nothing's thought of or considered here except a lot of whining boys and young men who want to live easily and dishonestly and don't care about the idea of doing a little hard work. What about the decent boys from decent homes? Why isn't something done for them? . . .' The voice of unimaginative common sense is heard more than once in the novel: '. . . Makes me a bit sick, sometimes. Daresay I'm wrong and old-fashioned. But there are plenty of good, decent lads about, lads who could do with a start in life. But there, honesty has to be its own reward—millionaires don't leave trusts to help the worth-while . . .' Even Miss Marple is impelled to speak out in defence of the neglected qualities of decency and respect for law, though her tone remains characteristically tentative: 'The young people with a good heredity, and brought up wisely in a good home—and with grit and pluck and the ability to get on in life —well, they are really, when one comes down to it—the sort of people a country *needs*.'

Miss Marple stands for intelligent, moderate conservatism although, in the tradition of the deferential female, she is always hesitant about proffering an opinion. She has been brought up to accept masculine authority. In one sense, of course, her principle activity is subversive of this concept, although basically it is designed to support the theory that a woman's talents will find a suitable outlet in her own sphere. Miss Marple is simply an older version of the sweet but shrewd little woman of magazine fiction, to whom the adjective 'fluffy' was also applied. She works in an undercover way to gain her own ends—or to prove her point. There is no authentic feminist voice in the stories, though occasionally a character may give vent to an outburst of simple-minded feminism:

'Women have a much worse time of it in the world than men do. They're more vulnerable. They have children, and they mind—terribly—about their children. As soon as they lose their looks, the men they love don't love them any more. They're betrayed and deserted and pushed aside. I don't blame men. I'd be the same myself. I don't like people who are old or ugly or ill or who whine about their troubles . . .'

The speaker, naturally, is an attractive and self-assertive young woman who intends to make the most of her gifts, and it is interesting to note that in 1952 she incurs less narrative disapproval than she would have done twenty years earlier. In 1962, however, a character in an Agatha Christie novel—not a stupid man—can proclaim unthinking endorsement of the old cliché about women being a separate, irrational species:

'. . . It may be considered, I suppose, that Marina has occasionally treated some man badly. But there is nothing to cause any lasting ill-will. I'm sure of it.'
'What about women? Any woman who has had a lasting grudge against Miss Gregg?'
'Well,' said Jason Rudd, 'you can never tell with women. I can't think of any particular one offhand.' (*The Mirror Crack'd from Side to Side*)

Miss Marple is interested in order, not progressiveness. She is perfectly satisfied with society as she has known it, and her own unchanging position there. Even the supermarkets and housing developments which finally reached St Mary Mead in the early 1960s do not encroach on the little nest of Queen Anne and Georgian houses which make up the essential village. The manor house may have changed hands but it still contains a study, library and drawing-room where an unnatural death can take place with full dramatic effect.

Priorities and preoccupations in Miss Marple's world remain basically the same: it is the stories themselves that undergo a radical change. Narrative control began to slacken at about the same time as the mode became plainly inappropriate to the spirit of the age. *The 4.50 from Paddington* (1957) is the last Miss Marple novel that can rank with the best of Christie. It starts off in splendid style: a superfluous woman is throttled on a train, the body is flung down an embankment and later conveyed surreptitiously to a convenient sarcophagus; it remains here until it is discovered by the young woman who is acting on Miss Marple's behalf. ('I haven't got the physical strength nowadays to get about and do things,' laments the poor old lady who has become the next thing to an armchair sleuth.) Lucy Eyelsesbarrow, Miss Marple's stand-in, is an Oxford graduate who earns a great deal of money by taking temporary housekeeping posts. 'To the amazement of her friends and fellow-scholars [she] entered the field of domestic labour.' In a serious novel this strange choice would require a great deal more justification than it gets here, where it is made to seem merely expedient and sensible. The clever girl has studied the market, noted an area of serious shortage and exploited it. Perhaps the author is making an oblique point about the high value placed upon efficiency in domestic matters and the comparative disregard for scholarship, but she certainly doesn't consider her deputy heroine's action wasteful or perverse. A First in Mathematics ensures accuracy in household budgeting, after all.

Miss Marple arrives in the neighbourhood posing as Lucy's aunt, and sweeps up to the great house in a taxi to denounce the murderer, who reacts by calling her 'a devilish old hag'. Refined old ladies who dabble in detection must expect this kind of abuse in the penultimate scene, but there is always a strong man on the spot to see that it stops short here. 'He lunged forward at Miss Marple but this time it was Cedric who caught him by the shoulder.' The novel has several interesting complications which are deftly worked out—in the 1962 film version of the story these are removed, along with a number of important characters, and the result bears out the proposition that an Agatha Christie plot should not be tampered with, even in the interest of straightforwardness. The remaining structure is very bare indeed: it is nothing but a vehicle for Margaret Rutherford's characterization of Miss Marple, which of course bears little resemblance to the lavender-and-old-lace sleuth envisaged by Agatha Christie. She is no longer a dear old auntie but the stock, unacknowledged lesbian figure of popular fiction, the stout golfing lady of forthright views. (Incidentally, this figure was resurrected in the 1970s in Joyce Porter's lady detective, the Hon. Constance Morrison-Burke: see Chapter XII.)

Like many authors whose output was prolific, Agatha Christie succumbed in the end to self-parody, weariness, and slapdash technique. She did Miss Marple no service by packing her off to the Caribbean, where the gaudy vegetation provided an unsightly backdrop for her pink knitting wool. The experience so disconcerts the old lady that she bursts into the bedroom of a wealthy invalid in the middle of the night, 'playing Nemesis'. 'Mr Rafiel, will you trust me,' she says. 'We have got to stop a murder being committed.' 'It's a damned good joke,' Mr Rafiel thinks later; but really the comparison of Miss Marple with an Avenging Fury is unsuitable to the point of bathos. It is one result of pushing the contrast between role and appearance too far. The misleading expression is actually perpetuated in the title of a later novel: *Nemesis* (1971), in which Miss Marple is sent off on a bus tour for the purpose of ferreting out information about a crime which took place in the past. A similar reconstruction is effected in *Sleeping Murder* (published in 1976 as Miss Marple's last case, though it was written, surprisingly, in the 1940s). For the sake of the author's reputation, it would have been better to let both corpses lie; though for weakness of plot neither of these comes anywhere near the unspeakable last novels, *Elephants Can Remember* (1972) and *Postern of Fate* (1973).

A Caribbean Mystery is the novel in which we learn that Miss Marple was never as ignorant of sexual matters as she seemed. Perversion and illicit desire were among the human foibles that could be studied closely in a village. Miss Marple, a canon's niece, is actually brought to reflect that the whole business was more enjoyable when it was labelled Sin—but this is a social, not a moral, comment, slipped in by the author in a moment of exasperation with modern life. On the whole, there is something dreadfully sugary and smug about Miss Marple which the very mild narrative irony does little to alleviate:

> 'My outlook, I am afraid, is a very petty one,' said Miss Marple humbly. 'I hardly ever go out of St Mary Mead.'
> 'And yet you have solved what may be called an international mystery,' said Sir Henry. (*Miss Marple and the Thirteen Problems*, 1932)

Naturally she claims no public credit for her perspicacity and she certainly isn't paid for her services to the police force: she is that exasperating amateur who is always on the spot as a chance visitor or nosy-parker. No one comes officially to consult her: in this respect she is unlike Miss Maud Silver, heroine of thirty-two detective novels by Patricia Wentworth, whose London flat at 15 Montague Mansions is constantly invaded by distraught young women who fear for their own lives or someone else's. Miss Silver is equally self-effacing—'When she comes into a case the police come out of it in a blaze of glory'—but she is a professional enquiry agent, one of those high-class specialists whose fame is passed around by word of mouth.

Patricia Wentworth (Mrs G. O. Turnbull) also wrote historical romances and thrillers in the Sidney Horler tradition; the first reference to Miss Silver occurs in one of the latter, *Grey Mask* (1928), when the lady detective is described as 'a sleuthess—a perfect wonder [who] has old Sherlock boiled'. The 'strange turn of events' which caused the transformation of a dowdy middle-aged governess into an efficient 'sleuthess' is never recounted; throughout the series there are tantalizing references to 'the rather horrible case of the poisoned caterpillars', which may have marked the start of Miss Silver's celebrity, but unfortunately it was never written up.

Grey Mask is a routine period thriller with a chivalrous and impetuous hero who returns to England after an absence, revisits his old home (now empty) for reasons of sentiment and immediately stumbles upon 'a cheery sort of criminal conspiracy carrying on like a house on fire in my mother's sitting-room'. The plotters, suitably disguised in grey rubber masks, are about to embark upon the usual course of murder and misappropriation. Thrills for the reader and dangers for the characters abound: 'A bullet hole, by gum!' The *sang-froid* of the hero, the exuberance of tone and the melodrama, so characteristic of the 1920s, had all been modified by 1937, when the second Miss Silver novel appeared; but it wasn't until *Lonesome Road* (1939) that the structure of the classic detective story was adopted. In this case, unusually, Miss Silver is called in before the event and manages to avert it. No one dies by foul means, though one of a group of apparently civilized people is guilty of the intention to murder. Cosmic justice is effected when the miscreant perishes suitably in a trap that he has himself prepared: 'The verse which Rachel had not been able to finish finished itself: "They have digged a pit and fallen into it themselves." '

In fact, the Miss Silver novels come into two categories, with the emphasis either on straight detection or romantic danger. In the latter, the identity of the criminal is never in doubt, and in one instance at least—*Danger Point* (1942)—the presence of Miss Silver is quite unnecessary. The heroine, left to die in a rock pool, is rescued by a young man acting on his own initiative without prompting from the lady detective. Miss Silver's usual triumph is sacrificed to a romantic climax. However, in the sphere of detection this novel marks the introduction of a standard device to complicate the issue: the criminally careless murderer who confuses the identities of two women simply because one has borrowed a distinctive garment belonging to the other. In *The Silent Pool* (1956) the first victim goes to her death 'in Adriana's coat'—a suitable fate for an elderly, ineffectual woman who takes an uncontrollable fancy to material patterned in huge black and white squares with an emerald stripe. The device is used with slightly more subtlety in *The Chinese Shawl* (1943), when a girl wearing a black dress is accidentally slaughtered. In this case Miss Silver is put on the right track because of something apparently very trivial, 'the difference between a bit of silk and a bit of lace':

'. . . Only a very short-sighted person to whom all black materials look alike at a little distance could have mistaken that heavy silk for so different a material as lace.'

March smiled quizzically.

'How acute—and how feminine! That is where you will always have the advantage of me. I am only a man.'

Miss Silver smiled in return.

'Gentlemen always say that when they are feeling superior,' she said. 'It is still a handicap to be a woman, and they know it. You must not grudge us any of the slight advantages it confers.'

There is another occasion (in *The Brading Collection*, 1952) when Miss Silver is obliged to rebuke Randal March for coming out with a similar platitude about the workings of what he terms the feminine mind. 'You cannot divide minds into sexes,' Miss Silver replies. 'Each human being presents an individual problem. . . .' It is by no means a deep observation, and its implications are not followed up, but it is the closest Miss Silver gets to intelligent comment in the entire series. Just for a moment she ceases to appear lovably eccentric and begins to sound thoughtful. But the narrative view of the astounding old lady is made to coincide with the views of two facetious though genuinely respectful young policemen. 'Maudie's moralities' is the term applied by Frank Abbott to Miss Silver's pronouncements on justice and human wickedness.

Of course, many of the defects and deficiencies popularly attributed to women may acquire a positive value in the context of detective fiction. The popular feminine virtues, too, can find new forms of expression. As well as nosiness—the most basic requirement of the lot—persistence, obstinacy, conservatism, respect for propriety, concern for others, and attention to detail are all qualities which may play a vital part in establishing the truth of an occurrence. A typical generalization about women —they 'see what is immediately before them better than men can, because they never look at anything else' (Schopenhauer) —takes on a new meaning when the objects under scrutiny are clues in a murder case. Certainly Miss Silver's natural powers of observation enable her to see what is directly beneath her nose without the aid of a magnifying glass. However, it is in detecting emotions, states of mind and secret desires that she is especially adept. In this sphere too she has a natural advantage: the opportunity to take part in kitchen gossip.

Frank Abbott lay back in his chair and looked at her, a spark of malice in his light blue eyes.

'May I ask where you received these interesting confidences?'

He got a smile which he had done nothing to deserve.
'When I was helping with the washing-up after lunch at
Mrs. Underwood's.'
He smiled back at her.
'That's where you take the bread out of the poor police-
man's mouth. I can't very well drop in and help with the
washing-up . . .'

Randal March and Frank Abbott are the two young policemen with whom Miss Silver is most closely associated, though
the former virtually drops out of the series after he has married
the chief suspect in a murder case (*Miss Silver Comes to Stay*,
1951).* Aristocratic policemen *will* keep turning up in this
type of fiction, and it's impossible not to feel exasperated by the
time of Miss Silver's twenty-third case, when Frank Abbott's
blue eyes, sleek fair hair and aloofness of temperament are cited
yet again. Miss Silver's social antecedents are more obscure: she
possesses no inherited wealth or influence or physical distinction.
Her favourite relative is a niece with the unmistakably common
name of Ethel Burkett. She has no assets but a natural refine-
ment, a capacity for delivering the unspoken reproof, and a
high order of intelligence.

In fact, Miss Silver's social circumstances would appear more
plausible if the stories had actually been set in the Victorian
era, when governessing was one of the few resources of the
genteel girl who needed to earn a living. 'There had been years
when she had hoped for nothing more than a life in other
people's houses, and in the end a bare existence on such sparse
savings as could be wrung from her salary'—this miserable
fate was not so inevitable a destiny in the 1950s when the
comment was written. But Patricia Wentworth was not at all
concerned with registering changes in modern life: all the
novels are set in a kind of hiatus in time, an unreal era that
contains many features of the period between the wars. Information about ephemeral attitudes and fashions is put across
in a covert way. One of Miss Silver's strongest characteristics
is dowdiness, and dowdiness, before the 1960s and the fashion
for antique clothing, was often associated with the age of

* The interesting relation between a detective and a possible murderer
has been explored in greater depth by, among others, E. C. Bentley and
Dorothy L. Sayers.

Victoria—hence the black cloth coats, the black laced shoes and hats decorated with bunches of cherries which make the detective look exactly like a person of no consequence. This of course is disarming for the criminal and therefore a source of vicarious gratification for the reader. By a kind of natural extension Miss Silver's outlook and position are given a Victorian flavour too.

'Terrifyingly intelligent, conscientious, sincere, religious, dowdy, and prim,' in the view of Randal March, Miss Silver is also 'a perfectly kind and just human being' whose approach to detecting is based on the one humanitarian principle connected with the procedure: the need to protect the innocent. This overrides considerations of propriety, so that the middle-aged sleuth can gossip or eavesdrop if the opportunity occurs. She is never guilty of babbling, misjudgement or indecorum. She is a modern heroine only in the sense that she has achieved success in her chosen profession, and financial security 'by her own intelligent exertions'. She is by no means typical. 'There was only one Maudie—let her remain unique', Frank Abbott concludes after envisaging, with some dismay, a proliferation of Miss Silvers at the Admiralty, the War Office, the Air Ministry. An unusual access of nostalgia has caused him to place a high value on the old-fashioned virtues which he sees embodied in Miss Silver. 'Security—that is what the Victorians had, and what perhaps they paid too high a price for. They had slums and child labour, and culture was only for the few, but at least their children were not dragged from their beds to take refuge in underground shelters, and their slums were not blasted into rubble.'

A note of social criticism is sometimes sounded, but it is always kept at a superficial level. 'I feel sorry for the children,' [Miss Silver remarks]. 'Fancy going out into the world under the impression that you can always have your own way!' The experiment in child-rearing that prompts this observation is part of a fanciful approach to living that affronts Miss Silver's conservative views. At a place named Deep End (in the 1953 novel *Anna, Where Are You?*) a number of characters far gone in silliness have banded together to form an artistic community. Of course they are nurturing a crook in crank's clothing. 'It was Augustus Remington's violet smock that gave him away.' When he is not murdering bank clerks, Augustus acts the part of a gentle soul who does exquisite needlework and worries about his vibrations. Patricia Wentworth has a great deal of fun at the expense of people who flit around in pea-green garments and go in for herbal preparations. Miss Silver's common sense does not extend to a recognition of the sound basis of much country lore; but it does enable her to exact obedience from the freely-developing children who soon respond to benevolent discipline. This is inevitable: her ability to impose order in the schoolroom is not to be gainsaid. It is a quality that stands her in good stead, in case after case, when she comes to deal with unruly adults who murder one another without restraint.

Miss Silver is unique in more ways than one: she is excused the basic feminine role because she has a part to play in confounding the disruptive elements in society: 'Spinster Miss Silver certainly was and had never desired to be otherwise.' With her knitting, her faith in divine providence and her admiration for the works of Tennyson, she is just sufficiently eccentric to appear quaint when she is not being authoritative; in another type of fiction the qualities would have denoted hopeless conservatism or blandness. Miss Silver's age and disposition exempt her from the need to seek, on her own behalf, a sentimental solution. Patricia Wentworth is careful, however, to place a young romantic couple at the centre of each of her plots; charming girls and upright young men form honourable alliances in story after story. They are all interchangeable. Sometimes the girls are allowed temporary employment: modelling, painting miniatures and working as a wartime secretary are suitable occupations. Occasionally they are hard-pressed at work so that protective feelings may be aroused in the breasts of their suitors. When the blows fall, the girls pass into a kind of dazed stupor; distress hides their natural sweetness of disposition. Someone is murdered and the girls themselves or the young men fall under suspicion. The scene is set for the appearance of Miss Silver: '. . . How I heard about Miss Silver was from a girl who was in a perfectly dreadful murder case, and Miss Silver put it all right and found out who had really done it . . .'

This artless tribute (in *The Key*, 1946) sums up the plots of all the novels. Like Agatha Christie, the author found a formula that suited her, but it was one which allowed considerably less scope for repetition. She gains her effects, not by taking risks which sometimes pay off brilliantly, like the creator of Miss Marple, but simply by arranging each group of players and events to form a standard dramatic pattern. She opts for conformity all along the line. At best, the narrative style is smooth and competent; the stories contain no ingenious twists or flourishes. No invigorating shocks are administered to the reader. To begin with, the nice young couples are above suspicion, which narrows the field of enquiry; then, in many cases the author adopts an attitude to one of her characters which isolates him or her at an early stage. (No attentive reader of *The Watersplash*, *Poison in the Pen*, and *Out of the Past*, for example, will fail to spot the murderer straight away.) *Spotlight* (1948), for instance, is a fairly satisfactory detective novel right up to the last chapter when it becomes plain that the most likely person *is* the murderer. He is the least attractive character in the author's terms.

Very facile psychological explanations are sometimes provided to account for criminal behaviour. A number of Miss Silver's murderers are unoccupied old ladies who were weak in the head to begin with. ('She wore Mr Tattlecombe's raincoat and used the kitchen poker . . .')Others are predatory, black-hearted, humourless women in their thirties with a lust for power. The rage of the underprivileged is another corrosive emotion which may easily get out of hand: 'I always hated you —always—always—*always*! Why? Are you really such a fool as not to know? You had everything and I had nothing— except your damned charity! . . .' When the murderer is a man the motive is just as obvious, and subject to rather less variation: it is simply 'the lust of gain in the heart of Cain', as Miss Silver expresses it.

Corruption and goodness are absolute qualities so that the detective is never placed in an ethical dilemma. At the end of each story, 'virtue [has] been vindicated, crime exposed, and justice done in the manner of the Victorian tract'. In fact, nothing distinguishes Patricia Wentworth's novels but the character of Miss Silver and even this is not presented in three-dimensional terms. The detective, who is not at all a frivolous person, produces a frivolous effect.

The traditionally feminine activity of knitting is given a fairly obvious symbolic slant in the stories of Miss Marple and Miss

Silver. Each detective is an expert knitter, whose woolly garments progress at roughly the same rate as the movement towards a solution in a problem of murder. The process is inexorable: stitch by stitch or step by step. Knitting, although it has sinister connotations which go back to Madame Defarge and the knitters round the guillotine, chiefly represents feminine industry and apparent harmlessness; the latter quality is underlined by the fleecy white shawls and leggings which 'depend' from Miss Silver's needles. Another detective who knits for relaxation is Mrs Beatrice Adela Lestrange Bradley (later Dame Beatrice); but there is nothing homely or endearing about Mrs Bradley's finished woollen articles: 'She took out a nondescript piece of sorry-looking knitting, and keeping her eyes on the iron gates by the lodge, commenced to knit, quickly and badly.'

This image is a long way in feeling from the soft white wool of Miss Silver, or Miss Marple's 'embryo bootee'. In fact the author, Gladys Mitchell, is satirizing one of the minor conventions of detective fiction, just as she subjected others to a process of bouleversement. In the first book of the series the detective herself gets away with murder, thereby establishing a motif that goes on recurring. Mrs Bradley is able to distinguish between moral and technical guilt; she is an authority on extenuating circumstances and doesn't hesitate to rely on her own judgement, which often causes her to act subversively. In a number of cases the fatal blow is struck by a person whom Mrs Bradley exonerates from blame—*The Mystery of a Butcher's Shop* (1930), *The Saltmarsh Murders* (1934), and the much later *Gory Dew* (1971), for example. In *Speedy Death* (1929) Mrs Bradley *is* the person who has killed for the best of reasons ('. . . Jolly sporting,' another character remarks; 'she took a big risk for other people's sake') and this gives her a fellow-feeling for others whose motives will bear examination, or whose guilt is only relative. Mrs Bradley, of course, is both logical and humane; but the idea of justifiable homicide is a dangerous one which needs to be handled with great care. However, it seems clear that Gladys Mitchell's objective was simply to ridicule the thriller-writers' tendency to avoid moral complications by making their villains always perfectly villainous. Another of her targets in this instance was the ultimate denouement—the moment of high drama when the detective is exposed as the criminal—although Mrs Bradley's part is only that of the Second Murderer. Her confession marks the start, not the end, of a long career (written up in fifty-eight novels to date).

In fact, *Speedy Death*, which turns on an issue of transvestism never quite presented with sufficient aplomb ('Rather bad luck to find out that the chap you are engaged to is a woman, what?'), was something of a false start for Mrs Bradley. The detective's method and manner are far more successful in *The Mystery of a Butcher's Shop*, when she is under no obligation to bear the knife herself. In fact it is wielded with devilish skill by a person who makes no practical distinction between animal and human remains. The disappearance of Rupert Sethleigh is followed by the appearance, in a butcher's shop, of human joints correctly disposed on hooks ('An 'orrible sight it must have been!'). The skull of the unfortunate fellow later turns up on a beach, and is handed over to a bishop who presents it to the Culminster Museum in the mistaken belief that it is an object of some antiquity. The narrative operates partly in the area of black humour, where the first thing to be repudiated is always the conventional viewpoint. In fact the 'orrible details of the murder are not in the least revolting; this is due to the cheerful detachment of the author's tone. Mrs Bradley, who is one of the wittiest detectives in the genre, takes everything in her stride and keeps her self-possession even when she is confronted with startling news (conveyed in this instance by an Irish housemaid):

'. . . Sure, and there's poor Mr Savile from the Cottage on the Hill does be hanging by his braces from the woodshed door entirely.'

'I'm glad it's entirely,' said Mrs Bradley calmly . . . 'I am bored to death by mere limbs and joints . . .'

Mrs Bradley is already a distinguished professional woman when she first appears: a psychoanalyst, author of abstruse articles and books, holder of honorary degrees from every university except Tokyo, reader of modern poetry and possessor of a mind as cultivated and acute as Lord Peter Wimsey's or Philo Vance's. She is twice-widowed* and the mother of at

---

* In one book at least (*Lament for Leto*, 1970) three husbands are mentioned; this is one of the small inconsistencies that often occur in a long series.

least one son (in later stories she has two), the celebrated barrister Ferdinand Lestrange. She is also a woman of peculiar appearance, extravagant in manner and taste; at the age of fifty-seven her outward aspect puts one acquaintance in mind of the reconstruction of a pterodactyl he has seen in a German museum. But in spite of the lurid and unbecoming garments which she affects, Mrs Bradley is always stylish, high-powered and confident; this is in complete contrast to Miss Marple and Miss Silver who are modest, inconspicuous and deferential ladies.

The future Dame Beatrice, too, is always in control; she has no need to rely on the goodwill of her associates at Scotland Yard. She never gossips with servants or befriends distressed ladies on trains and buses. She doesn't resort to feminine subterfuge, but keeps her wits about her. Among her physical advantages is an iron grip. She is not accorded special narrative treatment on account of her sex; her qualities might be transferred to a male detective without loss of credibility. Allowing for the edge of fantasy, a prerequisite of the genre, she exemplifies a type of professionalism which transcends sexual distinctions. She is different from Miss Marple and Miss Silver in another important respect: her intelligence is shown in operation, not merely stated, and her opinions are always interesting and valuable, which makes an unexpected bonus for the reader.

Mrs Bradley is outside the conventions of her own time without being either a crank or a fanatic. Her views are rational and enlightened. Before 1930 she is 'extraordinarily well-versed' in the arguments in favour of birth control, and at roughly the same date she considers the Catechism immoral. 'But what's her objection?' someone asks.

'. . . The bit about your betters. She says the village children are led to believe it means the squire and the people who go fox-hunting and the factory-owners who pay women about half what they would pay men for doing exactly the same work.'
'Oh, I see.'
'And the bit about our station in life. She says it's retrogressive to teach children ideas like that. They just think it means never try to get on and do anything with your life . . .'
(*The Mystery of a Butcher's Shop*)

Nevertheless, Mrs Bradley is happy to contribute £500 to the Church Restoration Fund.

It is startling to find genuinely comic detective fiction with serious undertones (only Anthony Berkeley achieved comparable effects from the elaboration of a satiric impulse within a classic structure); but it is even more unusual when it defies many of the inherently conservative values of the genre without sacrificing the ceremony of the final disclosure, or leaving the reader with a feeling that the rules have been broken. The adulterous liaison, for instance, which more conservative authors use as a measure of radical depravity (one example is the guilty couple in Agatha Christie's *Murder at the Vicarage*) is presented sympathetically in *Death at the Opera* (1934) and evoked with a rare lyrical grace in *Sunset Over Soho*. Mrs Bradley herself is not above leaping into bed with a young man when it is convenient to do so, though her behaviour there is perfectly circumspect: 'Nothing disturbed the rest of either sleeper. At half-past six Bassin awoke, raised himself slightly and put an arm, son-like, over his sleeping companion.' It is a unique position for an elderly woman detective. In a more general sense, the complexity and ambiguity in human morals and compulsions which Gladys Mitchell, as a serious novelist, finds it impossible to disregard, are expressed in the elaborate narrative twists and sub-plots.

Later in the series Mrs Bradley tackles crime in her official capacity as Psychiatric Consultant to the Home Office, but in the first few novels she is an amateur criminologist. It is necessary to the author's purpose that her detective should be both flamboyant and idiosyncratic, but she never descends to caricature (unlike Nigel Morland, for example, whose slapstick detective Mrs Pym is an official at Scotland Yard: see Chapter V). Among Mrs Bradley's assets is a sense of humour—a characteristic first-degree murderers do not have: '. . . Lack of humour means lack of balance. Lack of balance implies mental instability. Mental instability is, logically, madness. All murders are committed by lunatics. I am referring to premeditated murders, of course . . .'

The truth of this observation is borne out by the behaviour of the villain in *The Saltmarsh Murders*, whose motive stems from an acute distaste for sexual immorality; the first victim is a servant who has just given birth to an illegitimate child. 'As though there were not mystery enough surrounding that poor girl, the next thing we heard was that she had been strangled at some time between nine o'clock and ten thirty on the night of the Bank Holiday.' This is a rather casual way to announce a murder but it is typical of the blithe, sympathetic but un-involved tone of the narrator, Noel Wells, a young curate whom Mrs Bradley values precisely because of the straightforward quality of his observations: he 'has a head like a turnip. I do not think the Bar suffered any great loss when he went into the Church.' In a later novel (*Printer's Error*, 1939) he remarks incautiously that his mind is a blank: 'Mrs Bradley would not, for reasons of kindness, have chosen this way of expressing a known fact, but as it had been so expressed, she accepted it with a cackle of appreciation.' Noel Wells's feeling for Mrs Bradley undergoes a number of changes from distaste to admiration; at one point (in *Death at the Opera*) his faculty for stating the obvious leads him to classify the detective as 'an old woman with the outward appearance of a macaw, the mind of a psycho-analyst and the morals . . . of a tiger-shark'. As he is just about to project himself, on Mrs Bradley's behalf, into the clutches of a madman who specializes in drowning his victims in seawater baths, his critical outburst is not excessive. It is merely the out-come of a moment of pique. Once the danger is over he is able to take a mildly humorous view of the episode: 'You can imagine with what pleasure I watched the evil fellow carrying about a hundred pailfuls of water up to the house.'

Saltmarsh is the setting for Noel Wells's first unfortunate curacy, where the vicar turns out to be an adulterer and his wife a murderess. Mrs Coutts's derangement is plain from the start: she harps obsessively on the unrestrained behaviour of the villagers at the annual Bank Holiday fête: 'The village will get itself a name like Sodom and Gomorrah if things are allowed to go on unchecked.' The method used to apply a check is somewhat drastic. The death of the vicarage servant Meg Tosstick is followed by the disappearance of an actress named Cora McCanley whose morals were a source of affront to the abominable Mrs Coutts. There is some monkeying about with burial arrangements to confuse the issue: the body of one young woman turns up in the coffin of the other, to the mysti-fication of everyone except Mrs Bradley who recognizes criminal maladjustment when she sees it. Mrs Coutts is down in the psychiatrist's notebook as 'a bad case of sadism plus inverted nymphomania'.

A subsidiary character in the novel is an author who deals in pornography as a sideline, evoking pompous distaste in Noel Wells, who cannot go along with Mrs Bradley's liberal opinion that 'it is not filthy postcards and erotic literature that enslave mankind, but the little insidious vices, treachery, malice, envy, jealousy and greed, covetousness, slandering, sentimentality and self-deception'. Only an unusually progressive and perceptive list of vices could include the last two.

Mrs Bradley's experience—unlike Miss Marple's—is wide, and her personal characteristics range from the unorthodox ('extraordinary pot-house accomplishments') to the conservative ('an old-fashioned precision of speech'). The young curate gets 'no repose in her company. I like old women to be soothing'; certainly she has many habits calculated to disconcert the unwary and the timid. It is her job to note reactions and estimate their significance. She doesn't hesitate to poke people in the ribs in the interest of science. When she meets with superficial lunacy she is able to deal with it. Mrs Gatty, who is batty— 'Hoots at one, and compares one with the beasts of the field'— is momentarily indecisive when it comes to finding a suitable object of comparison for the elderly detective: 'Serpent, or is it crocodile? Serpent, or is it crocodile?' she mutters nervously. The splendid Mrs Bradley is not at all put out, and responds briskly, 'Crocodile, I think. I am generally considered to be definitely saurian in type.' ('Mrs Croc' is her accepted nickname in later stories.) She sees at once that there is nothing the matter with Mrs Gatty but a thwarted craving for the limelight, and effects a cure simply by putting her in a play at the village hall.

A more eccentric, stylish and sinister version of the mad vicar's wife appears in *The Rising of the Moon* (1945). (The word lunatic comes from *luna*, as we are reminded in another novel, the 1977 *Fault in the Structure*.) Mrs Septima Cockerton is an antique dealer who holds strong views on the degenerate behaviour of young women: ' "Girls, Mr Innes," she pronounced, "are hussies and will-o'-the-wisps. Trust them less than the serpent that bites the dust, or the adder sunning itself on the open heath. Their appearance is deceptive; their beauty a snare . . ." ' The setting is a small town, dusty and stagnant;

the narrator, 'Mr Innes', is a thirteen-year-old boy; and the murders are performed in a fashion that causes panic-stricken whispers about Jack the Ripper. A frightful old rag-and-bone man falls under suspicion but the real fiend is Mrs Cockerton, who marries this character towards the end of the novel and then proceeds to boil him in a copper boiler. This is what comes of a fanatical aversion from sexual misbehaviour in others.

Death at the Opera is another of Gladys Mitchell's tongue-in-cheek mysteries, but in structure at least it conforms to an orthodox pattern. A peculiarly inoffensive arithmetic mistress is drowned in a wash-hand basin minutes before she is due on stage to play the part of Katisha in an end-of-term production of *The Mikado*. The school, co-educational and progressive, provides the standard closed community whose members can all be furnished with a motive of sorts. The plot is complicated by the fact that the victim, Miss Calma Ferris, has come briefly in contact with a known murderer addicted to drowning. Mrs Bradley tackles the case with gusto, eliminating one suspect after another until she arrives at the culprit after prolonged cogitation. 'I congratulate you,' she writes to the murderer, who has acted from a kind of misdirected perfectionism: she is a very old actress who cannot bear to see Miss Ferris travesty the character of Katisha. Mrs Bradley can only applaud a murder which is nothing but a gesture of artistic revulsion. Gladys Mitchell has simply pushed one aspect of the detective story—motive—to an extreme, just as she dealt with another—disposal of the corpse—in *The Mystery of a Butcher's Shop*.

Many of Gladys Mitchell's early novels occupy a dangerous area between spoof and classic detective fiction; this makes for originality but requires a high degree of narrative assurance and control. Of course they are not uniformly successful. There was a period in the 1940s when contrivance, absurdity and carelessness supervened. Instead of the effective combination of precision and intricacy we find gratuitous convolution. Plots thicken to the point of impenetrability. *Hangman's Curfew* (1941) and *Death and the Maiden* (1947) are probably the most extreme examples of the author's tendency to resort too blatantly to the bizarre and the inconsequential. The former is set in Scotland; and indeed it seems the author cannot send her characters across the borders of that country without involving them in an imbroglio of impossible dimensions. 'Everything in this little adventure seems more than a little odd,' Dame Beatrice remarks justly in a later Scottish novel (*My Bones Will Keep*, 1962). Only in *Winking at the Brim* (1974) is Scotland evoked without loss of humour and proportion.

The curate Noel Wells is a parody of the 'Boswell, Captain Hastings, Doctor Watson' figure, and he disappears from the series when Mrs Bradley acquires a more subtle, credible and original sidekick. Laura Menzies is a student at the training college where the detective has taken a temporary post in order to investigate the disappearance of the Warden after an end-of-term dance (*Laurels are Poison*, 1942). Amazonian Laura (the adjective is Gladys Mitchell's) is an athletic young lady who is always plunging naked into cold water. Moreover, she is intelligent and intrepid and is possessed of an irrepressible sense of fun. 'Action! Give me action!' is Laura's cry; and it persists even when she has turned into a married lady of many years' standing and the mother—somewhat reluctantly—of two children. '. . . If there's going to be any fun I'm all for being in the thick of it. None of this women and children business with me!' Laura declares in *The Dancing Druids* (1948), and she remains undismayed in the face of rough treatment: 'Half-stunned, she scrambled up again, however, and, with a last effort, leapt upon Miss Cornflake and proceeded to choke her with the towel.'

Laura gives up her teaching career to become Mrs Bradley's secretary and assistant: 'I am her dogsbody. I type, drive the car, chase away unwelcome visitors, answer letters, look up references, bark, balance lumps of sugar on my nose, jump through hoops at the word of command and sometimes join Dame B. in pastoral dances by the lee light of the moon.' The last is a joking reference to Mrs Bradley's interest in witchcraft which remains academic since she has not the least need to invoke supernatural aid. 'When one hears certain facts, one is apt to draw certain conclusions': this, coupled with the psychiatrist's awareness of the power of suggestion, is the simple basis of the process of investigation.

The presentation of Mrs Bradley becomes less exuberant and quirky in the course of the series; the detective is toned down but not diminished, as she abandons the extravagant gesture for a smoother kind of omniscience. An increasing note of mellowness is sounded, but Dame Beatrice remains uninterested in the central concept of propriety and seemliness which activated other women investigators. The moral schema can still accommodate an act of murder which goes unpunished: this is due solely to the detective's heroic disregard for the conventional viewpoint. She has the courage not to insist on convictions.

In the last year of the 1970s, Dame Beatrice has stumbled into a nest of vipers (in a novel of that title) from which she emerges characteristically unbitten. It is fifty years since 'the most out-of-place member of a house party' took it upon herself to move to the centre of the action, a position she has never relinquished. The detective has always, with distinction, been a law unto herself:

'Honest to God?' [asks Noel Wells, seeking reassurance].
    'I am not accustomed to refer my integrity to the Almighty,' said Mrs Bradley solemnly.

X

HOME SLEUTHS

The Wives of Some Famous Detectives

Oh like enough 'tis blood, my dear,
For when the knife has slit
The throat across from ear to ear
'Twill bleed because of it.
A. E. Housman, 'A Shropshire Lad'

'A LOVE STORY with detective interruptions' is the explicit subtitle which Dorothy L. Sayers appended to her last novel, *Busman's Honeymoon* (1937); the ultimate triumph of Lord Peter Wimsey is in the sphere of romance. The capitulation of dogged, self-reliant Harriet Vane is nothing if not complete—'my lord', she calls him, without irony, in a willing gesture of deference. No wonder the author's dedication solicits indulgence: 'If there is but a ha'porth of detection to an intolerable deal of saccharine, let the occasion be the excuse.'

A honeymoon complicated by the discovery of a corpse in the cellar seems like a variation on the old theme of the inexperienced couple beset by domestic troubles. The subject can only be treated facetiously: whenever Wimsey attempts to express his deepest feelings he is interrupted by a suspect in distress, a conscientious policeman or an ingratiating reporter. His temper suffers in the end: 'I knew I should make a bloody fool of myself,' he grunts, like an embarrassed schoolboy. Harriet's purpose in this book is to keep him cheerful and reassured. It's a curious reversal, after the perseverance and effort of Wimsey, and Harriet's resistance to his proposals of marriage. Moods, temperament and bitterness are only to be expected in a woman who has been acquitted on a charge of murder and consequently placed under an obligation to the detective who established the real facts of the case: the primary emotion Harriet experiences in relation to Wimsey is gratitude, and it begins to corrode all her other feelings.

Strong Poison (1930) is the novel in which the detective novelist Harriet Vane is accused of having poisoned her lover. It's obvious to Wimsey, when he sees her across a crowded court-room, that she has done no such thing. 'The girl's innocent,' he declares, at the same time deciding to marry her: it is one of those sudden moments of destiny which often occur in light fiction. A hung jury and an adjournment give him a month to uncover the true criminal. An obvious suspect exists, and he is guilty; there is nothing devious about the plot except the murderer's method; he has accustomed his system to arsenic so that he may share, without ill effect, the lethal supper prepared for his victim. The spectacular plight of Harriet and the impression she makes on Wimsey are the most important aspects of the book. From the start, the heroine is presented as a woman of courage and integrity, but it isn't until a later novel (*Have His Carcase*, 1932) that she is able to progress to the role of second-in-command.

Harriet is acquitted, goes on a walking tour to recuperate from the experience, and stumbles straight away on a rather beastly corpse on the seashore. It is a young man with his throat slit. She keeps her head, notes the position of the body and even has the presence of mind to photograph it from several angles. This turns out to be fortunate, since it is washed away before help can be summoned. 'You must produce the body . . .' is the subtitle for *Have His Carcase*; and indeed it turns up half-way through the novel in an even more distressing state. Harriet, who, in the interests of justice, has gritted her teeth and gone through the pockets of the corpse, finds that she herself is an object of suspicion in the eyes of the police. But Wimsey comes pelting down from London to offer protection which she is obliged to accept, with a fairly bad grace: '. . . Do you think it makes matters any more agreeable to know that it is only the patronage of Lord Peter Wimsey that prevents men like Umpelty from being openly hostile?' she storms. (It's a pity that the name of the policeman brings a note of farce into the outburst.) Wimsey, 'with a grey face', gets up and looks out of the window. We are given plenty of hints about the strength of purpose which enables him to resume a bantering manner.

Fortunately the book contains only one scene of this kind, which is included to remind the reader of the delicate relations between Harriet and Peter. Harriet does her bit in contributing to the solution of the crime, at one point getting herself up in a slinky dress and ringlets to disarm a suspect, and then shrieking when he makes a move to kiss her. It's not altogether to her credit that she is able to assume a flirtatious manner when she is *not* an actress; but her motive is above reproach and the object of her attentions is a coarse individual not in the least equipped to tell the difference between attraction and aversion. He is later taken to task by Lord Peter Wimsey, who advises him to speak of Miss Vane in a proper way, 'and spare me the boring nuisance of pushing your teeth out at the back of your neck'.

Wimsey in love is a sorry figure, hedged in by emotional constraints, his advantages of no account, his absurdities underlined and his author's want of detachment badly in view. Dorothy L. Sayers created a fantasy figure and then proceeded to lumber him with real emotions which no reader can take seriously. Wimsey represents suavity, accomplishment and elegance pushed to an extreme: he is an English aristocrat in the mould of Arthur Augustus D'Arcy of the Fourth Form at St Jim's, complete with eyeglass and drawl. D'Arcy's creator Charles Hamilton (who wrote the famous 'Greyfriars' and 'St Jim's' stories in the pre-war papers, the *Magnet* and the *Gem*) has contributed other details to the detective's manner: the expression 'all serene', meaning roughly 'don't worry about it', is a characteristic phrase of Hamilton's schoolboys; and Wimsey's description of the judge presiding over Harriet Vane's trial—'a beast, but a just beast'—was originally applied to the master of the Remove at Greyfriars. Bunter is a name which does just as well for a ponderous manservant as a fat schoolboy, but it is a name not at all common in fiction.

The Hamilton–Wodehouse mode of humorous writing is perfectly suited to all brands of light fiction, and these were natural influences for a detective writer. Wimsey is a perfectly satisfactory and entertaining character in the context of the detective story. He's liable to ridicule, of course, for his absurd turns of speech, his assumptions about the ways of foreigners and menials, his lordly, humorous relationship with his servant Bunter. All these traits have been pointed out and decried, but they are merely mannerisms of the time, and rarely have a seriously damaging effect on the mechanics of detecting, the twists and shifts of plot. At her best, in *The Nine Tailors*, *Murder Must Advertise* and *Five Red Herrings*, for example, Dorothy Sayers displays a truly remarkable feeling for the complicating factor, the obfuscating ingredient. Her stories are constructed in layers, unlike the jigsaw pieces of Agatha Christie. At intervals in the narrative a whole set of circumstances bearing on the climactic event is uncovered. Detecting is really a process of excavation, of digging deep. Both Sayers and Christie are middlebrow writers, of course, well within the bestseller tradition with its aversion from the untoward, in any critical sense. But Sayers gets a couple of degrees closer to serious fiction; in one book at least (*Gaudy Night*: see below) an authentic moral difficulty is postulated and explored. Her imagination was nourished on the works of certain classical authors whom she often quotes, not always felicitously. We are never too far from bathos when a really profound piece of writing is used as a measure for the profundity of Lord Peter.

Sayers is happiest with the Wimsey–Vane relationship when she can bring out its jolly aspect: in the parody of a music hall dialogue, for instance, which is inserted in the middle of *Have His Carcase*:

Harriet: A boot! I've found a boot!

Peter: Alas! Alas! What boots it to repeat.

Harriet: Hobnailed and frightfully ancient.

Peter: Only one boot!

Harriet: Yes; if it had been two boots it might mark the place where the murderer started to paddle.

Peter: One foot on sea and one on shore. The tide has risen and fallen several times since then. It isn't a good boot.

Harriet: No, it's a bad boot.

Harriet has strayed into the tradition of sturdy, devoted girls who relish nothing more than the practical side of an investigation. They bound along in old skirts and ankle socks, displaying an endearing athleticism. It's an aberration, of course, for she is really a complex and intelligent woman who comes into her own in an appropriate setting: an Oxford college where her talents are recognized and applauded.

It seems clear that *Gaudy Night* (1935) was inspired at least partly by nostalgia, a disabling pressure which signifies retreat —and indeed Sayers's Oxford is an impossible place, mellowed into unreality. In spite of this, however, the novel has many merits: it's an excellent detective story, although it lacks a corpse; it raises a number of interesting social issues; and it places Harriet Vane at the centre of the action in a way that contributes substance to her character. Once she's removed from the melodrama of the courtroom and the embarrassment of Lord Peter's attentions, she begins to evolve a style of her own. We know, of course, that she's meant to stand in for her creator in a very basic way; it is not only the common profession that unifies them. Harriet is the spokesman for the author's views, and in *Gaudy Night* one of the underlying topics for consideration is the effects, real and apocryphal, of sexual deprivation on the female psyche.

The setting is a women's college, Shrewsbury (Somerville), afflicted with an outbreak of anonymous letters and obscene graffiti. Harriet takes up residence at the college, at the request of the Dean, in order to conduct an investigation into the causes of the disturbance. She has observed Wimsey's methods and knows how to set the work in motion, although she points out that the college would be better served by a professional, and recommends Miss Climpson, one of Lord Peter's assistants. However, Miss Climpson is not available and neither is Lord Peter, at least for two-thirds of the book, and Harriet is forced to exercise her own powers of observation and deduction. She's successful, but only up to a point; having created her detective-hero, Dorothy Sayers is obliged to reserve the moment of triumph for him. Wimsey, who appears in person on page 292, has only to read Harriet's notes to arrive at the identity of the culprit.

Two kinds of waste are deplored in the book: the waste of training and intelligence when a scholar becomes a farmer's wife and does the milking herself; and the waste of emotional feeling which is denied an outlet. It wasn't usual, in the 1930s, to combine an academic career with family life, and Harriet is well aware of the grounds for castigating female celibacy, in the popular view: ' "Starved appetites and suppressed impulses"—"unwholesome atmosphere"—she could think of whole sets of epithets, ready-minted for circulation.' These are the terms of the quasi-psychological objection to certain advantages gained in the social field, hardly more cogent than the argument against women's education put forward by a nineteenth-century reactionary: 'The health of women cannot stand much evening reading.' It is obvious that unexpressed sexual feeling is going to be a burden to its subject, but no more troublesome than intellectual energies repressed out of existence. It doesn't seem unduly radical to suggest that *all* one's capacities should be used to the greatest possible extent, but for Sayers's 'learned and cloistered women' (Harriet's phrase) the choice is restricted to an either/or proposition: a life of intellectual or biological fulfilment, each quality precluding the other. The age demanded that the female scholar should accept celibacy as a social or moral necessity, and suffer the ensuing frustrations.

It is a matter of common observation that any enclosed group is liable to be affected by illogical antipathies and tensions; but only women are subject to the consequent charge of natural instability. There are moments in *Gaudy Night* when it seems as if the author's purpose is to add to the literature of discouragement, to contribute another warning about the dangers inherent in female academic life. The acts which disrupt the air of serenity in her women's college are spiteful, vengeful, lunatic, petty and squalid. But Sayers is merely trailing the red herrings which are the detective writer's stock-in-trade. She cannot afford to adopt a standpoint which will give away her own attitude, and thereby make it easy for the reader to spot the criminal. There are narrative speculations about the effects of frustration, but underlying these is a more liberal and progressive ethic which even extends to the characterization of Lord Peter. When he writes to Harriet, 'Disagreeableness and danger will not turn you back, and God forbid they should,' he is treating her as an equal, and it's from this point that her determination to resist his advances begins to weaken. He has surprised her by avoiding 'the normal male reaction'—'if only I could be there to protect you'. In fact, as she realizes later, he is about 'as protective as a can-opener'. This is progress of a kind, for a young man who stated in 1928 (*The Unpleasantness at the Bellona Club*) with typical facetiousness: '. . . Women are funny. They don't seem to care half so much about a man's being honest and faithful . . . as for their opening doors and saying "thank you". I've noticed it lots of times.'

Gaudy Night is an unusual detective story in which the identity of the culprit is a matter of sociological significance, not just the bare solution to a puzzle. In fact, the disturber of the peace is not a dishevelled scholar with cap and gown awry, driven round the bend by too much study and unnatural seclusion, but a college scout, a wife and mother demented by the pressure of a tremendous grievance, a hatred of all intellectual women and one in particular, who happens to have taken up a post at the college. There are clues to Annie Wilson's state of mind, and she makes no secret of her views on the proper function of women. When Harriet meets her in the street with her little girls, and makes a polite enquiry about the children's ambitions, 'I hope they'll be good girls, madam, and good wives and mothers—that's what I'll bring them up to be,' Annie replies.

> 'I want to ride a motor-cycle when I'm bigger,' said Beatrice, shaking her curls assertively.
> 'Oh, no, darling. What things they say, don't they, madam?'
> 'Yes, I do,' said Beatrice. 'I'm going to have a motor-cycle and keep a garage.'
> 'Nonsense,' said her mother, a little sharply. 'You mustn't talk so. That's a boy's job.'
> 'But lots of girls do boys' jobs nowadays,' said Harriet.
> 'But they ought not, madam. It isn't fair. The boys have hard enough work to get jobs of their own. Please don't put such things into her head, madam. You'll never get a husband, Beatrice, if you mess about in a garage, getting all ugly and dirty.'

Annie is a landlady's daughter who married out of her class: her husband was an Oxford historian, and it's his death that she is out to avenge. He killed himself after it was discovered that he had withheld evidence which invalidated the basic contention in his professorial thesis; the person responsible for showing him up was a Miss de Vine, at present working at Shrewsbury College. It is not senseless spite that motivates Annie, but spite with a purpose: to incriminate Miss de Vine, and by extension to discredit the entire system of women's colleges. A powerful anti-feminist motive lies at the back of the disturbances at Shrewsbury.

Annie is allowed to state her case—' "Nobody shall be accused in this College," said the Warden, "without a hearing . . ." '—and the high-principled women of the Senior Common Room are subjected to abuse:

'. . . You killed him and you didn't care. I say you murdered him. What had he done to you? What harm had he done to anybody? He only wanted to live and be happy. You took the bread out of his mouth and flung his children and me out to starve. What did it matter to you? You had no children. You hadn't a man to care about. . . . He told a lie about somebody who was dead and dust hundreds of years ago. Nobody was the worse for that. Was a dirty bit of paper more important than all our lives and happiness? You broke him and killed him—all for nothing. Do you think that's a woman's job?'

'Most unhappily,' said Miss de Vine, 'it was my job.'

This is the crux of the matter: professional integrity. Naturally it's beyond the comprehension of a person like Annie, with her narrow and pragmatic outlook. But injustice, for Annie, has a different meaning, with its own validity. Her husband's suicide is a disproportionate event in the normal line of consequences following on an act. She cannot be blamed for failing to value an abstract concept beyond her own comfort and the gratification of female instincts. She can only resent what has happened, without understanding. In her own view she may stand for affection, loyalty, proper feeling. She's wrong, of course, as the venomous nature of her actions indicates; and not the least of her confusions is the whole case she builds up from the irrelevant fact that her husband's adversary is a woman. The conflict is not between men and womanly women, on the one side, and unnatural women, on the other, as Annie is apt to suppose, but between different ethical systems, not of equal weight. There is a fundamental requirement which Annie has overlooked—'Honesty', as Katherine Mansfield wrote, '. . . is the one thing one seems to prize beyond life, love, death, everything. It alone remaineth.'

There is a point in *Busman's Honeymoon* when it appears that Harriet is going to be swayed by personal feeling just as irrational as Annie's, if less profound. A betrayal of trust is involved; information which she has received in confidence ('that poor little woman and her pathetic love-affair') is no more to Wimsey than a fact which may have a bearing on the case in hand. 'One can't suppress evidence, Harriet. You said to me, "carry on".' She experiences revulsion but overcomes it:

her business, and Wimsey's, is the pursuit of truth—an entity which is nearly always clear-cut and recognizable, in the context of detective fiction. It is just a matter of the identity of the criminal. Sayers, at least in *Gaudy Night*, begins to look beyond this to a more complex ethical structure in which values and virtues are not absolutely fixed. The process is not carried very far but the grounds for debate and conjecture are at least acknowledged. Only a very unconventional sleuth like Mrs Bradley (see Chapter IX) can tamper with evidence, once she has gauged the precise moral significance of each fact, in order to achieve an outcome which is desirable and just, whether or not it is strictly in accordance with the moral line indicated by the bare sequence of events.

Harriet Vane is most satisfactory as a character when she has an active function within the plot. She is gifted with initiative and common sense, she lacks effete mannerisms and therefore she has worn somewhat better than Wimsey, who is very much a figure of the period between the wars. She would have made an excellent detective—but when Dorothy Sayers created a female subordinate sleuth, a paid assistant for Lord Peter, she turned out a traditional spinster figure, another shrewd old lady with a disarming manner. Miss Katherine Climpson is just as refined and fluttery as Miss Marple (whom she preceded by three years), and equally alert to the uses of gossip. She is a woman 'of the class unkindly known as "superfluous",' saved by Lord Peter from a fate worse than detecting and placed in charge of an establishment which passes for a typing bureau, though its real purpose is the investigation of fraud. All Miss Climpson's employees are single women who would otherwise have lacked a profitable and interesting occupation. Naturally the business is financed by Wimsey who refers to it in moments of levity as 'my Cattery'.

Detecting at this level is a fantasy occupation which contributes purpose and glamour to the lives of uncherished women. Sayers is making out a case for women's right to work, a proposition which she strenuously approved: 'Every woman is a human being—one cannot repeat that too often—and a human being *must* have an occupation if he or she is not to become a nuisance to the world' (*Unpopular Opinions*, 1946); and it's natural, within the context of her chosen genre, that she should create a whole bevy of female investigators to endorse this view. We can't complain if she's traded a little on the familiar devices of popular fiction: the thrill, for the reader, in the awareness of a clandestine operation, the fascinating discrepancy between appearance and fact.

If Harriet Vane's emotions, with regard to Wimsey, were confused by a distorting sense of gratitude, it was partly because the detective's belief in her innocence was absolute from the start. It might have worked to his advantage if he had placed himself in the wrong by conceding the possibility of Harriet's guilt. The mistake was not made by two of Wimsey's near-contemporaries, Nigel Strangeways and Roderick Alleyn, who found their future wives among a number of suspects assembled on the scene of a murder.

'The trouble was that, if one took each aspect of the crimes separately, one found it attaching itself most easily to some aspect of Georgia Cavendish.' This disturbing reflection belongs to Nigel Strangeways, hero of fifteen detective novels written by the poet Cecil Day Lewis under the pseudonym of Nicholas Blake; the book is *Thou Shell of Death* (1936). Georgia, a celebrated traveller and explorer, has arrived on the spot in suitably flamboyant fashion: 'An ancient two-seater was approaching up the drive, with bits of luggage tied on to every available part of the bodywork. A lady was driving it, a green parrot perched on her shoulder, and a huge bloodhound sitting up beside her.'

Georgia is charming, with her pretty monkey face and her bright clothes; she is innocent of the crimes, of course, though she does have a certain amount of guilty knowledge which affects her actions. In her personal life she is like Harriet Vane in only one respect, the fact that she has been someone else's mistress before she becomes the wife of the detective. However, she also is the heroine of a single book in the series, which is not really a detective story but a high-class, quasi-political thriller, *The Smiler with the Knife* (1939). The title is a quotation from Chaucer's 'Knight's Tale', and the book is about the dangers of élitism: what is being threatened is the principle of democracy in English life. Instead of social malaise, uncertainty, and the disintegration of values so apparent to left-wing radicals of the 1930s, which provide distinctive undercurrents in realistic fiction, we find the summation of these forces represented in a single somewhat dramatic concept: conspiracy. An organiza-

tion which calls itself the English Banner is fostering an outbreak of revolution which will place a dictator in control of the
country's affairs. 'Do you believe in aristocracy, the rule
and government of the Superior Person?' initiates are asked. It
is all exceedingly cranky and distasteful, an inversion of the
idea of truly heroic leadership—'the strange new healer'—
mooted by Day Lewis himself in *The Magnetic Mountain* (1932).
It is remarkable, in *The Smiler with the Knife*, how easily the
author has adapted the mood of patriotism and resolution,
which used to be generated in archaic thrillers by the need to
oppose the activities of socialists and anarchists, to suit the
topical, liberal repudiation of the extreme right. Even the
terms in which the ultimate appeal is couched—'I'm asking you
to do it for England'—look back to a period when the well-
bred Englishman was characterized by a posture of understated
sincerity.

The subject of the appeal is Georgia. Sir John Strangeways,
uncle of Nicholas Blake's debonair detective, reminds her of
the Fascist doctrine on the position of women: '... You know
what the other side says—"Woman is for the recreation of the
warrior"—"Woman's place is in the kitchen"—all the
rest of that Neanderthal tommyrot...' This is splendid,
but unfortunately on the same page we find Georgia going
off for a walk to consider the proposition that has been put
to her:

> ... She believed that in the last resort decisions should be
> made—where women are concerned, at least—by the instinct.
> Intelligence could and should provide the material, set out
> fairly the pros and cons; but something deeper than intelli-
> gence must make the choice, ratify and execute the decision.

There is something a little somnambulistic and absurd in the
image of a person acting in response to promptings from an
unspecified inner core, but it's a recurrent notion in the series.
In another book the author credits one of his characters with 'a
first-rate *feminine* intelligence', and adds: 'her instinct was
sharpened to a razor-edge.'

Nigel Strangeways, for all his detecting ability and experience
of the particular, is prone to make unaccountable generaliza-
tions on the subject of women. They—all of them—have

such a temperamental attitude towards truth. Opportunist, rather. The truth is made for woman, not woman for the truth. One wouldn't mind that, if only they didn't make it so infernally difficult for men to be truthful with *them*; one's always being tempted to soften or sweeten or pare down or exaggerate the facts for them, so as to satisfy their vanity or avoid wounding their quivering sensibilities or bolster up their perpetually crumbling egos. Yet they're hard as nails too . . . (*The Dreadful Hollow*, 1953)

A somewhat querulous and vindictive note has got into this remarkable summing-up of feminine tendencies: we're reminded that even Patricia Wentworth, a writer greatly inferior to Nicholas Blake in almost every respect, had the common sense to observe, in connection with the theory of intellectual distinctions between the sexes, 'each human being presents an individual problem'.

When Georgia Strangeways is not the central character she remains very much on the periphery of her husband's investigations; if she does help, it is generally by accident: 'Georgia unwittingly laid her finger on another of the scattered pieces of the puzzle.' Nigel accepts without question her judgement of character since this ability, we may suppose, is based on nebulous and infallible inner feelings. But he doesn't often enlist her help. We might wonder why she is given the centre of the stage, even in a solitary novel; but the reason soon becomes plain. Georgia's task is to identify the proposed dictator—the leader of the English Banner movement—and ingratiate herself with him, even if it means responding to his advances. It's not exactly an honourable part to play, and therefore it has to fall to Georgia's lot; *Nigel* can hardly be expected to cultivate a chap's friendship only to turn on him at an appropriate moment. Georgia can, because she is not inhibited by a predetermined code of conduct, and because she knows what is at stake: 'the safety of a civilization'.

There is a subsidiary male character in the book who undertakes precisely this form of emotional deception, and a nasty business he finds it, conducive to revulsion and humiliation at every turn. He is the one casualty on the side of the heroes, when he gives up his life in an exuberant gesture of patriotism and expiation. 'He'd take it standing up, not like those quitters grovelling against the wall over there.' It's a true 'Sons of Old England' exit. But Georgia never experiences the least distaste for her own actions: why should she, since the man she's deluding represents a principle of plain evil? Even when she blinds Lord Chilton Canteloe by flinging the contents of a fire bucket in his face, the mood of the narrative compels us to applaud her initiative. It's all tremendous fun for the reader, first-rate entertainment; excitement builds up as Georgia takes off recklessly in a stolen car: 'She was out in the open now against her enemies, England's enemies.'

From this point on the gender of Nicholas Blake's protagonist becomes irrelevant: Georgia is just a person on the run, in possession of secret plans, pursued by disciples of Chilton Canteloe who are out to get her. 'The intellectual's day-dream of action' is a phrase used by Samuel Hynes in *The Auden Generation*, in connection with a more exalted work by Day Lewis, but it can be applied equally to the events which make up *The Smiler with the Knife*. Georgia, dodging around Manchester with her life in danger, finds her way into a department store where she dons the uniform of a Father Christmas. Shortly afterwards there's a dashing ride in a pantechnicon, when her ability to shoot straight comes in handy. Evasion, capture and rescue are the ingredients of the final section of the book. Georgia has her moment of triumph, before she's wiped out altogether (off-stage) when the ambulance she is driving in the London blitz is hit by a bomb.

It is not clear why Georgia Strangeways was removed from the series; her successor, Clare Massinger, contributes nothing extra in the way of active participation. There's an episode in *The Whisper in the Gloom* (1953) which sounds a slight echo of the part played by Georgia in the earlier thriller, when Clare spends an evening in the company of a suspect, to keep him occupied while Nigel searches his flat. Her feelings while she performs this task are not completely under control: 'Her relief, as time went by and he made no pass at her, was not unmixed with pique. Woman-like, she contrived to blame Nigel for this: how dare he throw her into this man's arms?' It's the adjective 'woman-like' which produces an irritating effect in the reader; *anyone* might experience an access of resentment in the situation. But Clare is generally a well-balanced and amenable young lady, with a proper occupation of her own which lets her out of the necessity to become the detective's wife.

She is a sculptor, a fact that underlines the detective writers' tendency to provide for the hero a woman distinguished in her own right. Harriet Vane is a celebrated author; Georgia Strangeways is a famous explorer; Agatha Troy, who captivates the aristocratic inspector created by Ngaio Marsh, is a painter who moves in an atmosphere of artists' smocks, brushes, turpentine, urgency and utter dedication. She's brilliant, of course; and she is another of those interesting women who are not beautiful in appearance (like Harriet and Georgia), but possessed of a far more subtle and impressive quality of style. People gifted with straightforward beauty are all too often lumbered with a balancing weakness of spirit or intellect. In *Artists in Crime* (1938) the victim and the murderer are a couple of squabbling, vicious beauties, but before the identity of the latter is established a rather tense investigation has to be carried out.

Roderick Alleyn is the fastidious policeman whose affection for the painter Troy (she is always known by her surname) seems unlikely to prosper in the circumstances. 'You can hardly expect me to be genial when you are about to hunt through my under-garments for incriminating letters,' Troy remarks, and who can blame her? Alleyn's is not a romantic or an agreeable occupation at this level, but he tackles it with a kind of stoical resoluteness which overrides mere personal scruples and hesitations. 'An odious trade . . . a filthy degrading job,' he is heard to mutter through gritted teeth. He is poking about in Troy's drawers at the time.

Troy remains abrupt and aloof for some time, but gradually Alleyn's natural delicacy and his higher motives are impressed upon her. A rather bleak regard for justice enables him to handle the low aspects of the business without undue reluctance. His association with crime, however, continues to cause friction and embarrassment, even when he and Troy are married. He prefers to keep his job and his home life apart ('Troy in one compartment; the detection of crime in another'); but Troy, in the usual way of detectives' wives, stumbles upon a murder or two herself. In *Final Curtain* (1947) she is engaged to paint a portrait of a flamboyant old actor who promptly bows out for the last time: '. . . a severe attack of gastro-enteritis . . .

brought on by his indiscretions at dinner' is the first diagnosis, but in fact a more sinister agency has been at work. The old man's histrionic relatives draw suspicion on themselves, one after the other. 'I don't know whether I've conveyed the general dottiness of that monstrous house,' says Troy, when her husband asks for an account of the events preceding Sir Henry Ancred's death. 'I mean, the queer little things that turned up. Like the book on embalming . . . and the missing rat bane.'

Troy, in fact, has done nothing at the time but proclaim the innocence of a child (Patricia Kentish, known as Panty because her knickers keep falling down) wrongly suspected of malicious damage to Troy's painting. Something in the child's manner has alerted the artist to the fact that Panty, for once, is not to blame; and in the same way she can tell that there is something queer about the atmosphere at Ancreton. There's one vital piece of information which she stores subconsciously and retrieves at a dramatic moment, but otherwise there is no overlap between her role in the narrative and Alleyn's.

At one point the detective is overcome once again by a sense of the social drawbacks in his calling:

'What a job!' Alleyn said suddenly.
'Ours, Sir?'
'Yes, ours. Walking down a country lane with a dead cat in a boot-box and working out the procedure for disentombing the body of an old man.'

Indeed it is some time before Troy is able to convince him that she has swallowed the job and its implications, including the fact that the end of detecting is execution. 'We've got into a muddle about me and your job,' she tells him firmly. It is after all a sensible relationship.

The couple produce a son, Ricky, and some time later the little family is caught up in a rather unsavoury affair in the Maritime Alps. *Spinsters in Jeopardy* (1954), like the earlier *Death in Ecstasy* (1936), is based on the very dubious activities of a group of pseudo-mystics. Into their clutches falls an unfortunate lady who is taken ill on a train; it is to be given out that she has died, so that a body on the premises may be accounted for. (The lady's ludicrously appropriate name is Miss Truebody.) A whole segment of the mystery is clarified when Troy spots a photograph in a newspaper; but this is a piece of luck, not deduction. In fact, Troy's function in this story is to offer moral encouragement to the merely misguided among the cult members. It isn't until *Clutch of Constables* (1968) that she's placed once more in a unique position to observe the prelude to a murder.

'Outlandish, ludicrous and extremely unpalatable', is Alleyn's view of the notion that policemen's wives should be involved to any great extent in their husband's work; but *Clutch of Constables* provides another occasion when he's glad to accept Troy's help. She has a good visual memory and can even recall the number of a passing motor-bicycle when she has to. Besides, she has had strange fellow-passengers on a short cruise she's just completed, among them a famous criminal known as the Jampot, as yet unidentified. Troy is the focus of interest for most of the novel, as she hobnobs cheerfully with murderers, forgers and impostors on the interesting waterways cruise, advertised not unreasonably as a surreal experience: 'For Five Days You Step Out Of Time'. 'I can *not* get rid of the feeling that I'm involved in some kind of performance,' Troy writes to her husband. She isn't wrong.

In fact, it's the successful performance that interests Ngaio Marsh, and her novels transcribe nothing so drab as a note of reality; she has evolved in her own field an ingenious type of play-acting. Her characters are all people who go in for exaggerated behaviour. Troy, Alleyn, all of them, are characterized to an impossible degree. Whether it's a bogus clergyman, an impresario, an affected actress or a diabolical doctor, the objective is to express to the fullest extent the qualities suggested by the stereotype. It's carried out with assurance and humour, and this is why it usually comes off; but there is an unmistakable touch of motley about the whole exercise. And since it *is* the stereotype that furnishes the basic material, the novels perpetuate many assumptions about feminine behaviour. ' "Quick! Quick! Quick!" she cried babyishly. "Sonia wants a d'ink" ' —this is the young gold-digger captivating a lecherous old man.

On the face of it, Amanda Fitton is the detective's wife who seems best fitted to enter into the spirit of the game herself; but in fact she plays very little active part after the first novel in which she appears, *Sweet Danger* (1933). Albert Campion, Margery Allingham's sleuth, who looks foolish but isn't, comes across Amanda while she is acting as miller of Pontisbright. She is seventeen at the time, red-haired, comely and emotionally uncomplicated. She is a competent electrician and mechanic— she goes on to design an aeroplane—engagingly candid and self-possessed, plucky and loyal in the usual way of a young person who is anxious to involve herself in the knockabout enterprise: 'I should like to point out that I would make a very good aide-de-camp.' Campion replies, 'Or lieut. . . . I often think that's what the poet meant when he said Orpheus and his lieut.'

Humorous understatement is the tone that Margery Allingham adopts to characterize the attachment between Campion and Amanda, but it's carried so far that it turns into comic reticence. 'Look here,' Amanda states while she's lying in bed recovering from a bullet wound acquired in the course of her activities as Campion's second-in-command, 'I shan't be ready for about six years yet. But then—well, I'd like to put you on the top of my list.' As a caricature of the English spirit this ranks with the fictional schoolgirl Jemima Carstairs's 'Oh, chin up, chin up! Chest out, old thing!'; but Campion's rejoinder takes us a stage further in the procedure of expressing affection without overdoing it: 'What's going to change you in six years, you rum little grig?' he wonders. It is a moment of tenderness.

The helping hand extended by Amanda ('By the way, before we get chatty, let's tie this fellow up. Amanda, the clothes line.') has matured somewhat by the time of their next encounter, in *The Fashion in Shrouds* (1938), but the girl remains 'as ever, the perfect gent'. The six-year period is up, and Amanda has come to claim her partner in adventure. 'Hello Orph. . . . the lieut. has come to report', is her cheerful greeting. Within a day or so, ostensibly to smooth over a moment of social embarrassment, she has announced to the company at large, with perfect aplomb, that she and Albert are engaged to be married; the fake engagement turns into the real thing when Campion realizes that he likes the position. In the meantime, a murder has taken place.

Sweet Danger is a detective fairy tale which ends with the noble family of Fitton restored to its birthright, Amanda transformed into the Lady Amanda and a villain named Savanake very properly passed through a mill wheel. *The Fashion in*

Shrouds is a fantasy of the *beau monde* with Campion's sister Val in the part of the worldly lady, the talented couturier, the social success with a true feminine heart. Of Val and her actress friend and adversary Georgia Wells, Margery Allingham notes:

> . . . They were two fine ladies of a fine modern world, in which their status had been raised until they stood as equals with their former protectors. Their several responsibilities were far heavier than most men's and their abilities greater. . . . They were both mistress and master, little Liliths, fragile but powerful in their way . . . and yet, since they had not relinquished their femininity, within them, touching the very core and fountain of their strength, was the dreadful primitive weakness of the female of any species.

There is something of an Edwardian flavour about this; but of course the preconceptions on which light fiction is founded are slow to change. In what is known derogatorily as the woman's story there is a moment of capitulation, a recognition of true values and deepest instincts, an overwhelming sense of the proper emotional arrangement. Here is Margery Allingham's version of it:

> 'I love you, Val. Will you marry me and give up to me your independence, the enthusiasm which you give your career, your time and your thought? . . . That is the offer. In return . . . I should assume full responsibility for you. I would pay your bills to any amount which my income might afford. I would make all decisions which were not directly in your province, although on the other hand I would like to feel that I might discuss everything with you if I wanted to; but only because I wanted to, mind you; not as your right. And until I died you would be the only woman. You would be my care, my mate as in plumber, my possession if you like. If you wanted your own way in everything you'd have to cheat it out of me, not demand it. . . . Will you do it?'
>
> 'Yes,' said Val so quickly that she startled herself.

We are in a world in which this detailed recipe for disaster is made to seem like an opening for emotional salvation. No matter that the speaker is the man who employs Amanda in a technical capacity: his own home life is going to be arranged according to the principles of Mrs Henry Wood. It's a common trick of anti-feminist writing to create successful, efficient women who are just waiting to be enclosed in a pair of protective arms, the ultimate retreat of those who have experienced one kind of freedom and found it unsettling. 'Love can really rot any woman up,' observes one of Margery Allingham's characters in the colloquial tone that is supposed to lighten the piece of age-old instinctive wisdom. It doesn't rot Amanda up, even when she's temporarily enamoured of a villain (in the 1941 imbroglio, *Traitor's Purse*), but Amanda is both sensible and fortunate, and the terms of her relationship with Campion have been set out early: 'You might consider me as a partner in the business later on.' When the forthright child has grown into a clear-sighted adult, 'I'll be happy to marry you if you care for the idea,' Campion offers. Truly, there is no unhappy excitement about the business, as an elderly lady friend of the detective remarks. The modern novelist can hardly avoid the subject of sex, but it's left to Amanda to bring up in characteristically throwaway manner. It is like the electric light supply, she claims ingenuously, 'not worth thinking about if yours is all right but embarrassingly inconvenient if there's anything wrong with it'. The simile isn't without an element of bathos. In fact, of the four relationships discussed in this chapter, Amanda's and Campion's is the only one entirely devoid of implicit erotic feeling—an effect of the jolly, romping, wholesome idiom into which the author falls. There is a moment in one of Margaret Drabble's novels when the heroine wonders 'What can it have been like, in bed with Mr Knightley?' With equal pertinence one can pose the question, 'What can it have been like, in bed with Mr Campion?' Alas, we shall never know.

Campion, the pale, astute young man in horn-rimmed glasses, is given a few things to say on the subject of women which have no particular value:

Most women ... muddled through to truth in the most dangerous and irritating fashion. All the same they were not quite so clever as they thought they were, which was as it should be, of course, but odd considering their remarkable penetration in most other practical matters.

It was astonishing how the simple, direct reactions of the ordinary male eluded them ...

It is astonishing how the simple, direct facts about individual characteristics, the dangers of generalization and complexity in social behaviour elude the popular novelist. However, Margery Allingham writes with gusto and inventiveness and these qualities help to mitigate the more banal assumptions in her novels; it is not until the 1950s that her style becomes impossibly mannered and strained.

The books could hardly be further in spirit from Dorothy L. Sayers's championing of women's right to work, or from the intellectual, left-wing undertones in the fiction of Nicholas Blake. Yet Allingham's narratives contain the class adulation of one ('Good class is attractive when it's genuine, isn't it?') and the bland, instinctive anti-feminism of the other. The 1930s, the period when each of these writers produced his or her most characteristic work, probably account for the qualities which the four detective novelists have in common. Active feminism was considered old hat and soon became a source of irritation to those preoccupied with more pressing issues like the war in Spain and threatening developments in Germany. It had acquired a ridiculous aspect, and so a fashionable author was forced to adopt a bantering tone on the subject, displaying at the same time an awareness of apparently fundamental traits and incapacities in each sex. But it was impossible to revert to the prewar system of restrictions in women's lives. Freedom and equality of opportunity were significant ideals, even if in practice, for women, the former boiled down to the freedom to attempt a rash incursion into the domain of business or industry. And the image of the proficient and distinguished woman retained an unmistakable quality of glamour, which may have had something to do with its comparative novelty. It's an interesting fact that none of these detectives' wives is a homebody, a nonentity, a doormat, a witless beauty, a wheedler or a domestic ornament. Each is treated seriously as an active partner, even if this attitude is contradicted by narrative implications elsewhere in the stories. We have only to think of the wife of Freeman Wills Crofts's Inspector French—Emily, who sits placidly at home and acts as nothing more distinctive than a sounding-board for her husband's ruminations—to see this as a progressive tendency.

XI

GUNS IN THEIR GARTERS

Spies and Special Agents from the Spanish Civil War to Détente

Ardena says in a cold sorta voice, 'Stay where you are . . . if anybody moves they get it!' She has pulled a gun outa her stockin' top. She is lookin' as cool as an iceberg.

Peter Cheyney, *You'd be Surprised*, 1940

BETWEEN THE WARS, slinky and seductive spies in the Olga Polowski/Mata Hari mould still cropped up in espionage stories. However, they were stereotyped to the point of anonymity, and it was only in the late 1930s, after the Spanish Civil War, that female spies began to assume the kind of realism already associated with many fictional sleuths. Spy fiction both furthered and frustrated the advance of the lady detective. In periods of war and international tension, when the primary aim of many women was gamely to do their bit, feminism was usually swept under the carpet, although some of its goals might be achieved as a by-product of women's patriotic endeavours. This kind of situation was accurately reflected in more serious books, and the female secret agent can be seen as a logical and specific development of the girl sleuth. However, in more bizarre, escapist stories, the actions of girl spies were so inflated and unrealistically represented that they gave rise to a new kind of woman detective—a cartoon combination of exaggerated know-how, toughness and sexuality.

In the early 1930s, the enemy against whom women spies directed their activities was usually a megalomaniac middle-eastern potentate or the ruthless dictator of an unspecified European state. In several thrillers by J. M. Walsh, girls rushed around in remote parts of the world working vigorously for British Intelligence, but his *Spies in Spain* (1937) has a realistic Civil War background. Rosalie and Isa, two girl spies, work with their husbands in an auxiliary capacity. They are almost as tough as the men, as they slog and scramble through mountainous country, overcoming adversaries by the use of guns as well as guile, but, disappointingly, they slip into the traditional attitude of many female sleuths and spies, and lean heavily on 'intuition':

> 'Terry'—for no apparent reason Rosalie dropped her voice a full octave—'something has gone wrong.'
> Terry glanced sharply at her. He had seen her in this mood before . . .
> 'Nonsense!' he exploded.
> 'It isn't nonsense,' she said gravely. 'I know. I'm feeling fey.'

It is true that hard-boiled masculine agents like Nick Carter or Deighton's Harry Palmer occasionally have weird hunches that pay off, but they are not noted for having feelings of feyness. These and other irrational impulses are reserved for female spies.

The bleak background of a country in the grip of civil war comes across well, and the refugees, informers and guerrillas encountered by Rosalie and Isa are slightly reminiscent of the strangely assorted group of partisans in *For Whom the Bell Tolls*. But unlike Hemingway, J. M. Walsh never gets down to the root of the conflict, and takes no sides. His British agents meet up with reasonable and fanatical supporters of both Government and rebel factions. It is naturally assumed, as the book is for British readers, that Britain's interests should be safeguarded, but despite occasional bluff and Buchanesque overtones there is little jingoism. It is in fact a degree of understatement in the face of powerful issues that makes *Spies in Spain* stand out from many of the stories about women spies or detectives which preceded it. However, the book brings to mind Robert Nye's comment on Len Deighton's espionage stories: 'You begin to see what is lacking . . . It is, putting it simply, a point of view.' Whether to create three-dimensional characters for both sides, or simply to provoke sympathy for the one by sacrificing the realism of the other, is always a problem for the authors of spy fiction, especially in peacetime when issues are not so clear-cut as in war.

Action and adventure rather than political realism provided the keynote of the long-running Sexton Blake saga (see Chapter IV), but shortly before the Second World War some of the

Blake authors went against the tide of popular fiction by high-lighting political tensions. Pierre Quiroule's Sexton Blake story 'The Hated Eight' (1938) makes no bones about the pernicious-ness of the policies of Hitler and Mussolini. 'King's Spy' Granite Grant, 'six-feet-something of brawn and muscle', works in partnership with 'Mademoiselle Julie' of the French Secret Service, who is impressive in a very different way from the heavyweight British agent. She is a 1930s embodiment of the untravelled Englishman's fantasy French girl. 'Chic . . . mercurial . . . witty, audacious' and of course sexually appeal-ing, she does everything with style, whether slipping a jewelled pistol into her smart handbag, or nipping around Paris in her little Peugeot coupé. Julie also has a red and black Daimler, a chauffeur called Alphonse, a giant Ethiopian manservant and a luxury apartment on the Rue de Ravenne. She is really la Comtesse de Joncfleur who has 'the glittering social life of the French capital . . . at her dainty feet' but, surprisingly, she has joined the Secret Service 'as a refuge from boredom'. Julie's fearfully feminine Frenchness is expressed in colourful, sensual terms. In between socializing and spying, she 'snuggles up on the divan' in her exotic, rose-damask room, 'with her slinky bronze-coloured head nestling against a crimson, diapered cushion'.

Julie and Granite Grant are not actually able to do much to contain the ambitions of Hitler and Mussolini, but with Sexton Blake's assistance they manage to break up a particularly unsavoury secret society whose aim is to organize 'wholesale sabotage in the event of an outbreak of war'. Julie's success as an espionage agent springs from her speedy physical reactions as much as her sleuthing ability. In *The Mystery of the Missing Envoy* (1939) she is shanghaied by a group of gunrunners. When one of them tries to make love to her, she smashes him sharply over the head with a bottle, leaps into the ship's dinghy and gets away. Generally speaking, if she gives her mind and energy to it, she is more than a match for most of her male adversaries. But girl spies in other story-papers of the period tended to be less adept. The *Modern Boy* ran a series by John Templer in 1938 about Sky-Detective Jaggers of the RAF. Maria Westernfeldt is a German who poses as an English girl and gets herself invited to the RAF depot ball. However, unlike Anna Lessing (see Chapter III) who claimed during the First

World War that more espionage could be done in one evening in the ballroom than on numerous field assignments, Maria found servicemen tougher nuts to crack than she anticipated. Her naïve approach probably gave the paper's boy readers a comfortable sense of superiority:

> 'The Merry Widow is my favourite tune,' said Jaggers. . . 'Shall we dance?' A slight frown passed over the girl's face. 'I'd rather not, if you don't mind,' she said. 'I'd much rather stay here and talk to you. Do tell me something about your work, it must be thrilling . . . tell me something about this gun—I'm interested. I find these things so romantic.'

It is not surprising that Jaggers quickly gets the measure of Maria, and she is soon shoved on to a plane bound for France, where she is wanted for questioning by the Sûreté.

Romanticization of the female spy during the Second World War is almost certainly at its most extreme in Denise Robins's picture of Tona, the twenty-year-old City typist heroine of *This One Night* (1942). Tona has 'a face like a flower' and, despite her foreign sounding name, is as English, reserved and unspoiled as they come. Nevertheless, soon after getting into the night train to Gardenia, a Balkan state to which she is travelling on business, Tona succumbs to the charms of Valentine, a man whom she meets in her compartment. He turns out to be the King of Gardenia and a passionate supporter of the Allied cause, which apparently puts his seduction of Tona on a moral footing. At that time Tona has no connection with espionage and her abandoned response does not suggest the calculating fibre of which a successful spy is likely to be made:

> . . . She was sealed fast in his arms. She had no resistance left. Her last vestige of control snapped and vanished when she felt his heart beat against her own . . . He was a wonderful, masterful lover. There could never have been, there could never again be such a lover . . . She was aghast at the relentlessness of such love. But she was no longer herself. She was his. All of her.

The Wagon Lit idyll is abruptly curtailed for the King by the call of duty and Tona, with only a 'scorching blush' (and pregnancy) to remind her of the 'heaven' revealed 'in the arms of a princely lover', soon finds herself alone and horribly vulnerable in Gardenia. Not surprisingly, typing as a career now seems a little insipid. She becomes a café dancer but is innocently caught up in Fascist activities and, clad only in a chiffon dance tunic and silver cloak, has to face a firing squad under the charge of espionage. It is all nastily confusing for Tona, but despite her dimness she manages to cheer wartime British readers by summoning up a suitably gritty, *Girl's Own Paper* spirit of defiance: 'She hung on to her courage desperately. She would show these foreigners how an English girl should die.' She doesn't, in fact, because she is suddenly rescued. Tona then becomes a British agent but, although hurled into desperate intrigues, her only real achievement is the provision of a sanctuary in her Norwood home for her royal lover when the Nazis drive him out of Gardenia. *This One Night*, as some of its audience might have suspected all along, then turns out to have little to do with espionage or detection, but a great deal to do with propaganda. The story ends with Valentine's rather unlikely statement: 'I never wanted to be a king. I wanted what I am going to have now, please God. An English home—an English wife—a son, whom [sic] I pray will be born on English soil.'

Helen MacInnes is more successful than Denise Robins in combining realism and romance in the spy story. Her first novel *Above Suspicion* was published in 1941, and it set the pattern for the rest of her thrillers, which have continued to appear during wartime, the Cold War and into Détente. Her central characters are not usually professional agents but highly intelligent amateurs; details of the background are closely observed, and suspense is highlighted and made bearable by touches of wry humour. *Above Suspicion* is memorable for its evocation of the mood in Britain during the lull before the storm of September 1939. Frances and Richard Myles plan a last peacetime holiday in Europe, but the innocent trip turns into a dangerous assignment when a friend in Intelligence seeks their assistance in locating the whereabouts of a vanished British agent. Frances typifies one kind of sleuthing spy—the ordinary girl reluctantly caught up in espionage. She has a natural antipathy towards the sensational, but occasionally catches herself indulging in melodramatic speculation, which is checked with characteristic self-awareness:

It was strange, she thought, how people seemed to change in a foreign train. More than half in this coach were English, but already they seemed so different . . . Nice beginning, indeed, when every stout Swiss commercial traveller seemed to be a member of the Ogpu or that pinched little governess looked like a German agent. I've seen too much Hitchcock lately, she thought; at this rate I'll be worse than useless.

Since the success of Agatha Christie's *Murder on the Orient Express* (1930) and Graham Greene's *Stamboul Train* (1932), transcontinental expresses have, of course, frequently provided suspense backgrounds for writers of spy stories as well as of detective fiction.

Frances soon adapts to the world of espionage. She learns when to put people off the scent by indulging in 'girlish gossip'; she knows too when to keep quiet and listen. Frances is the type of person who naturally attracts the confidences of others, but useful as she is in acquiring information, it is Richard who does most of the sifting and sleuthing necessary for the successful resolution of their mission. Like *The Lady Vanishes* and other suspense films of the 1930s, *Above Suspicion* conveys the flavour of the period through its incidental episodes—amusing vignettes of the English abroad avoiding their compatriots, and of British manners and breeding sustained in bizarre circumstances. However, the realistic portrayal of the wary, seedy atmosphere of international intrigue is often improbably softened in Helen MacInness's books by traditional romance. Torture and Gestapo grillings generally take place off-stage and are reported in retrospect, by which time the reader has the reassurance of knowing that the hero or heroine has survived. Her approach contrasts with the lurid cataloguing of violence in the sagas of Blaise, Bond and Lemmy Caution, and with the cynical indifference displayed by John Trevanium and other authors.

The woman spy featured in Helen MacInnes's second novel, *Assignment in Brittany* (1942), is very different in character from the likeable and unassuming Frances. Elise is a Nazi Fifth Columnist operating in France, who is not content to play a supportive role: she gives orders to men, whom she betrays if it is to her advantage. She is certainly not one of the author's usual innocents abroad, but when *Assignment in Brittany* appeared, of course, the stereotyping of Elise as a ruthless female quisling was acceptable.

In *The Black Baroness* (1940) Dennis Wheatley gives some macabre embellishments to the theme of women in the Fifth Column. Gregory Sallust, a glossy British agent, likes being 'a lone wolf' and working entirely outside the Secret Service. But there is one other agent with whom he does enjoy close professional—and personal—association. Erika, Countess von Osterborg, is German but an anti-Nazi whose peculiarly 'Aryan' appearance ('rich ripe golden' hair and eyes that are 'not china-blue but deep sapphire') enables her to penetrate an all-female and particularly effective Nazi spy-ring. This network of 'Ladies of the Golden Garter' (Gregory's nickname for them) is run with imaginative ruthlessness by a Frenchwoman named la Baronne de Porte. This 'Black Baroness' is, according to her own lights, a patriot; by linking her country with Nazi policies she hopes to save France from 'internal decadence'. Though condemning the Baroness's actions, Gregory sees her point about the decadence; indeed in his view the moral tone of most of the Allies seems flabbily unworthy of their association with Britain. He and Erika decide that the Baroness's death would be 'as great a victory as the destruction of a German Army corps'. However, when an opportunity arises for Gregory to annihilate her (almost half-way through this lengthy novel) 'somehow he could not do it'. There is no explanation for Gregory's vacillation, and certainly it seems to be an example of the kind of spinelessness that he usually condemns in others. Anyway, la Baronne Noire lives to fight on for the Fuehrer through another two hundred pages, and at the climax of the story both she and Erika are endeavouring to influence Leopold, King of the Belgians, in opposite directions:

> Erika smiled. 'Yes. I'm Leopold's new girl-friend.'
>
> Gregory made a grimace. 'I'm not at all certain that I like that. It's trying my patriotism a bit high.'
>
> 'You stupid darling!' Erika laughed. 'The poor man is much too occupied with events and overwrought by what has happened to his country to make love to anyone; but it seems that he likes blondes . . .'

But success in this instance goes to the brunette Baroness, and having brought down Norway, Holland and Belgium with her courtesan army she shoots off to Italy to persuade Mussolini 'to screw up his courage to the point of stabbing France in the back'. So it was a bad day for Britain and her allies when Gregory's chivalry—or indecision—prevented him from killing 'Hitler's great whore-mistress'. He comes off the worse in several meetings with this efficient organizer of espionage, and *The Black Baroness* suggests that women are rather better suited than men to the dubious business of spying.

Active agents are of course more attractive subjects for a great deal of espionage fiction than back-room girls, though these are sometimes convincingly portrayed. The most sardonically *un*realistic of them must surely be Trevanium's Felicity Arce, the grossly and symbolically named contact woman in *The Eiger Sanction* (1973). Miss Arce is instructed to pass to Jonathan Hemlock, the book's anti-hero, details of a political killing that he is to carry out. The only meeting between Felicity and Jonathan immediately erupts into a session of clinically efficient copulation—sex for Jonathan being 'simple, uncomplicated and . . . temporarily satisfying; like urination'—through which Felicity conducts the briefing of his assassination assignment to a background of orgasmic grunts and giggles.

From America, Mignon Eberhart's *The Man Next Door* (1944) provides an authentic view of how a young secretary might become involved in espionage activities. The office background carries conviction. In England, stories were appearing in books and women's magazines about sinister women spies operating in cosy village communities, or housewives in occupied Europe upsetting the Gestapo's grisly schemes. In fact, women who worked in offices, like Mignon Eberhart's heroine Maida Lovell, were rather more likely to have access to information that could be useful to either side. Maida is secretary to the head of a government aeronautical department in Washington. To save the man she loves from a trumped-up murder charge, she agrees to give confidential information to the enemy. *The Man Next Door* has all the twists and tricks of Mignon Eberhart's celebrated whodunnits: deductive logic is as integral to the plot as the espionage element. The author's strong feeling for place is used to reflect the drama of Maida's situation. For example, the reassuring atmosphere in one house—'the blended, clean fragrance of wax and potpourri and fresh air with a touch of wood smoke'—makes, by contrast, a sudden flash of fear that overtakes Maida particularly effective. Everyday settings appear in strange guises to set off a chilling mood or a questionable action; the unfamiliar bleakness of Maida's office, deserted at night, is an appropriate background for the furtive extraction of secret documents from files. The torments of the unwilling spy who has to work against the interests of her own country come over without hysteria or melodrama. There is, however, a moment when Maida finds herself assuming one of the classic postures of the fictional woman spy:

> She tore the paper from the typewriter and folded it up carefully and, after a moment's hesitation, slipped it into the soft, fragrant hollow under her brassiere; it would be safer there than in her handbag. With a kind of wry smile she remembered the old-fashioned novels . . .

A sleazier wartime mood is the keynote of several books written by Peter Cheyney in the 1940s. These relate the exploits of Lemmy Caution, the FBI G-man who is obsessed with 'dames' of all shapes, sizes and inclinations. Several of these, with exotic names like Ardena, Marceline, Edvanne, Juanella and Georgette, have 'stuck their necks into the espionage game'. The background to their actions is fairly realistic; there are 'guys makin' black market bargains, dames makin' guys an' other dames tryin' not to make mistakes', but despite Lemmy Caution's direct, first-person gangster-jargon narration, the stories are an almost unravellable tangle of side-switching and colourful sexual double-cross. The voluptuous females in the saga—'she heaves a sigh an' I can hear her brassiere strings creakin' with the strain'—are not the most highly organized of sleuths or spies, but they achieve a lot through their fast reactions: 'Ardena takes one look at him an' jumps over. She gives him a smack across the kisser that sounded like a whip cracking.' Towards the end of the war, Lemmy finds liberated France full of 'come-on girls' and racketeers, but he views the disruptive social aftermath of war with hard-boiled resignation.

For some authors, however, it provided unlikely but lush and romantic themes, such as redemption by love of a girl Communist spy. Pathetic German girls were likely recruits, at least in fiction, for Russian espionage. One of these is Lisel Orhler, the 'silver-haired' waif-heroine of Anne Duffield's *Beloved Enemy*

(1950). Clive Moray finds himself waylaid by Lisel in the rubble of Berlin at the end of the war. He is one of those utterly upright and unimaginative Englishmen who have no time or sympathy for foreigners even if they are half-starving. Lisel is under considerable pressure to serve the Communist powers, but Clive warms to her, and manages in the end to redirect her political sympathies. *Beloved Enemy* appeared at a time when the Russians had already slipped several rungs down the ladder of acceptability since the war years. This is illustrated by the attitude of Gloria Spence, a British girl—'utterly lovely, long-limbed, firm-breasted, beautifully tanned'—but, alas, bitchy. She takes every opportunity of being grotesquely rude to Lisel, that 'wretched little Hun governess', considering that all Germans are beyond the social pale, 'and as for Russians, I can't stick them at any price', she declares. (The Cold War permitted no compromise in this type of light fiction.) Like many novels that try to combine romance and espionage, *Beloved Enemy* creates an atmosphere so overblown and unreal that even the totalitarianism which it denounces loses its sting.

Through the influence of Eric Ambler and other writers of realistic spy stories, the highly-charged and escapist approach has recently given way to one of disillusioned resignation. Espionage agents are motivated by greed rather than patriotism, they are often insignificant or unpleasant, and spies who work for one side are as unsavoury as those working for the other. A more positive interpretation of realism in the spy novel is to introduce a degree of complexity into the characters of agents working for the Iron Curtain countries. These can be likeable or disagreeable, but they are not simply cyphers. Diana Winsor has created a sympathetic and distinctive Russian character in *The Death Convention* (1974). Dr Alexei Bransk is an elderly physicist whose defection to the West is not the result of ideological or monetary considerations—somewhere in England he has a daughter and grandchildren whom he wants to see. His defection is almost the result of a whim, but believable as a tired man's escape from the dreariness of the unsatisfying routine his life has become. There is a rapport between Alexei and Tavy Martin when they meet at a conference in Holland, and the girl helps the physicist to get political asylum. Tavy is attractive and engaging, a spy in the modern style, with a sense of humour and a lively interest in topical issues. She is, in a way, the nice girl next door who has gravitated from being something in the Civil Service to espionage.

In the United States, Tavy's equivalent is Selena Mead, whom Patricia McGerr created in 1964 in *Is There a Traitor in the House?* Selena's husband is killed during the course of an investigation for American Intelligence, and Selena finishes off his assignment. From then on she becomes part of 'Section Q'. Her sleuthing capacities are less sophisticated and sustained than those of Tavy Martin, however, and she rather overplays her hunches. Both Selena and Tavy are practical and quick-witted, but they are in no sense the inflated superwomen of the more fantastic extremes of spy fiction. Despite recent moves towards realism, some images of the female spy have in fact become more outlandish. Len Deighton's *Twinkle, Twinkle, Little Spy* (1977) throws up not one but two lesbian agents. Red Bancroft works for the CIA and Elena Katerina Bekuv is a high-ranking KGB officer. There are some intriguing ramifications of the problem of setting one lesbian spy to trap another— what happens if they fall in love? And of course there is the danger of losing an operative instead of gaining a defector. In the end, Red manages to persuade Elena Bekuv, who *has* fallen in love with her, to transfer her loyalties to the West; as Red puts it, 'If we all get out of this alive, she'll be a KGB target for ever and ever. And what have I given her in return— nothing but a good time in bed and a lot of worthless promises.' Girls, in fact, generally have such a tough time in espionage that one wonders why they get involved!

They play particularly unrewarding roles in several of the 'he-man' books. The luridness of Nick Carter's activities is generally summed up by the garish cover pictures of the paper-backs in which they now appear. (The authors are not named since the stories are supposed to have been written by Carter.) In *The Z Document* (1978) the period is Détente, and the enemy a paranoic individual with ambitions for world conquest. The cover girl wears nothing but a G-string and a very loosely meshed fishnet blouse. Her breasts are on view behind the large sub-machine gun that she somewhat awkwardly carries. This well-ventilated lady is presumably Jean Fellini, the CIA agent hired to share Nick Carter's Ethiopian assignment. As an agent, her function obviously is to obtain information as a result of sexual appeal rather than by observation and deduction. After Jean is attacked by an enemy spy, who is promptly knifed by Carter, she joins Nick in his room. She is not, as he expects, shivering with shock but is in an intense mood of a very different kind. Unzipping her slacks, she slings off the mesh shirt and is ready for the action that soon becomes very predictable in the Nick Carter context. With this strong taste for sex, and suitable apparatus for its fulfilment—Jean's 'shapely legs' and big bouncing breasts are referred to more than once—she works her way through several 'writhing and throbbing' sessions with Carter early on in the book. She also poses for a series of provocative nude photographs (the CIA demands nothing if not dedication from its female agents). However, Jean has one serious handicap—a complete lack of common sense. Fortunately she is not essential to the story, and is murdered soon after serving her purpose of titillating Carter's sexual appetite. She is in fact the aperitif to the stronger meat and drink of the Ethiopian girl who becomes Carter's next mistress.

Violence and sensual slickness also determine the predominant mood of the James Bond stories. After the banalities of Carter, however, Ian Fleming's succinct characterization strikes a satisfying note. Even the lusciousness of Bond's female sparring-partner spies becomes an acceptable combination of well-scrubbed niceness and seductive send-up. Generally speaking, whether American, British or Russian, these Tiffanys and Tatianas are almost as quick-thinking at the espionage game as Bond himself. Rosa Klebb, Bond's villainous Russian adversary, attempts to stab him with poisoned knitting needles, neatly reversing the meaning of those traditional symbols of female passivity. With the continuation of the stories by other authors after Fleming's death in 1964, some of the wit has been sustained but the backgrounds have become exaggerated, and the girls more brittle. They are more rushed and less discriminating about jumping into bed, whether in the interests of their countries or when following their own inclinations. In *The Spy Who Loved Me* (1977), Christopher Wood sets the tone by getting a man and a woman into bed together on the first page. However, a slight adjustment of roles occurs. A telephone call from the counter-espionage branch of the KGB halts the love-making session, but it is the girl, not the man, who is summoned to Moscow for an important assignment. She is

Major Anya Amatsova who, before long, joins forces with Bond and MI5 against a crazy but technologically brilliant enemy of Britain and Russia. Despite their professional alliance, it isn't until the end of the book that Anya's deep-rooted Marxist mistrust of bon viveur Bond and all that he stands for thaws sufficiently for her to allow him to become her lover.

Many trappings of the Bond adventures, including sartorial elegance, sexual panache and the souped-up gadgetry of spying, were taken up by Peter O'Donnell in his Modesty Blaise books. Modesty's exploits began in strip cartoons in the *Daily Express* in 1962, and have since been expanded in several books, starting with *Modesty Blaise* in 1965. In O'Donnell's sophisticated hedonism there is none of the tongue-in-cheek quality that relieves the '007' stories. Descriptions of Modesty's attractions are greatly overdone: she is actually far more attractive in the Jim Holdaway and Romero *Evening Standard* cartoons of recent years than in the books.

Modesty's refugee-to-riches progress must be one of the slickest and least credible Cinderella stories in recent fiction. Her transformation has come about not through the conventional process of captivating a Prince Charming but through her clever and calculated flirtation with crime. She takes up espionage comparatively late in her career, after 'retiring at twenty-six with well over half a million sterling' stashed safely away. But when boredom sets in for Modesty and Willie Garvin, her cockney sidekick, they are easily persuaded to undertake dangerous missions for British Intelligence. Modesty is very much the heroine—in fact, as Willie calls her, 'The Princess'—but the stories are told from the viewpoint of the male. Modesty is supposed to be a fearfully liberated woman but, alas for feminism, whenever she is eulogized it is as a sexual object. Everything external, from her coral red toenails to her high black chignon, is regularly inventoried and applauded, but even this most impressive of espionage agents has problems to overcome on account of her sex, as she explains when questioned about the type of gun she will use:

'The Colt 32.'
'From a shoulder holster?'
'No. They don't go with having breasts. I use a snap holster Willie designed, belted at the back of the hip . . .'

Peter O'Donnell's Modesty Blaise and Willie Garvin

But, generally speaking, her superb anatomy doesn't get too much in the way when she has to grapple with male adversaries. She disables these with well-placed kicks in the groin, or bashes from her kongo or yarvana-stick. She also has a nifty technique called The Nailer, which involves 'taking off her sweater and bra, and going into the room stripped to the waist ... The technique was guaranteed to nail a roomful of men, holding them frozen for at least two or three vital seconds.' And she has her own 'inner clock', a 'compass in her head', a proficiency at yoga that can seal her off from pain at any time, and a chignon and brassiere that are roomy enough to conceal kongos, coils of wire and cylinders of anaesthetized nose-plugs.

With Modesty and her 'Avengers'/'Angels' counterparts in television programmes, the female desperado in espionage has gone almost completely into fantasy. Compared with the super-women, a refreshing lady spy of the 1960s and 1970s is Dorothy Gilman's Mrs Emily Pollifax, a widow and grandmother from New Jersey. She is cast in the mould of the well-meaning, ostensibly muddling but actually extremely efficient elderly women sleuths of the 1930s. Of course, there has been some updating. Mrs Pollifax is interested in pretty hats and gardening, but her hobbies include yoga, karate, and the 'save our environment' campaign. She is altogether a surprising package, as the titles of some of her adventures indicate: *The Unexpected Mrs Pollifax* (1966), *The Amazing Mrs Pollifax* (1970), *The Elusive Mrs Pollifax* (1971) and so on. Mrs Pollifax has always nurtured a secret and apparently impossible ambition to become a spy, and she succeeds in doing so with considerable aplomb, when she virtually stumbles into her first CIA assignment. The assortment of bizarre characters who are her adversaries on various missions are rather too colourful to be convincing, and the torture techniques that she brushes aside would in real life have an effect on even so tenacious a female agent as Emily. But the stories are written with wit and originality. In the early novels, communist agents are easily suppressed, or else their better natures come to the fore. Later on, the mood of confidence has become muted, and Mrs Pollifax, like several other women agents, has to turn her attention towards deranged but powerful individuals rather than Iron Curtain agents.

Détente, however uneasy, now seems the established situation in popular spy fiction, even though the female agent is not always sure of her role in it. A stronger mood of ambivalence has been established by John Le Carré. The female spies in his stories are far removed from the quiet and cosy Mrs Pollifax, or the outlandish Modesty Blaise. Like his male agents, they are vehicles for the author's acute probing of complex intrigues at both national and personal levels. They are vividly characterized and never cyphers, and the fact of their being women is not used to obscure the wide variety of responses which influence their actions. The starkly authentic atmosphere of modern espionage and its potentially divided loyalties is well conveyed in the character of Elsa Fennan in *Call for the Dead* (1961). She and her husband, a British civil servant whom she married on her release from a concentration camp, are both East German agents; she connives at his murder because of her duty to her spymaster. Le Carré's realism, discernment and style have brought new dimensions to the role of women agents in espionage fiction since he has raised this genre to a new level of sophistication and credibility.

XII

'A CURIOUS CAREER FOR A WOMAN'?

The Lady Detective in Recent Fiction

> The snow is melting under the rain,
> The ways are full of mud;
> The cold has crept into my bones,
> And glides along my blood.
> > Sylvia Townsend Warner, 'The Image'

'A CURIOUS CAREER for a woman', states Lady Sharples, a character in Austin Lee's *Miss Hogg Flies High* (1958). She is referring to detecting, with the implication that violence and depravity ought to be repugnant to the feminine temperament. The phrase was later adapted to form the title of one of P. D. James's most celebrated novels, but by the time this was published (1972) the observation was more ironic than critical. When Miss Hogg first appeared on the scene, ideas of seemliness and unseemliness still held good.

Miss Hogg moves in ecclesiastical circles, investigating the backgrounds of dead deans and bogus bishops. She's a professional sleuth, and a forthright, sensible lady, but her personality is never impressed very strongly on the reader. She has made the usual smooth transition from instructing to detecting. 'Miss Hogg tramps along, guided by intuition and the horse sense she acquired when dealing with the fifth form of the county girls' school,' the blurb of one novel tells us; it's an adequate combination, in terms of the story, though we may find its implications contradictory. Horse sense and intuition are not compatible qualities, one steady and firm on the ground, the other coming out of the air to alight at random, like a dandelion seed. 'Inspired guessing', the heroine's own description of the detective's method, is possibly a more suitable term, if we take it that the inspiration is based on an apprehension of certain facts, however subconscious and dim. Guessing is roughly the same thing, however, which makes the phrase almost tautological. But it's the closest we can come to an explanation for Miss Hogg's conclusions.

Austin Lee's plots are both far-fetched and simple. 'The dean was murdered in Bishop Boumphrey's library. It seems he was hit on the head, and then pushed down the stairs' (*Miss Hogg and the Dead Dean*, 1958). The dean is a nasty old gentleman who fully deserves his indecorous exit; he has been using the parish registers to uncover shameful facts about his colleagues. Moreover, he has put out poisoned meat for a dog belonging to Miss Ermyntrude Bootle. No one regrets the dean's death, but his murderer is clearly an unbalanced person who cannot be left at large; Miss Hogg, a professional detective, is called in. Her first task is to eliminate from the list of suspects one Bernard Kott, son of the assassinated president of a country called Slavonia. This quasi-exotic touch immediately brings a stiffening, unnatural element into the narrative, as though the cast were suddenly turned into wooden figurines, like the toy soldiers who might defend the imaginary state. There are other suspects, some of them equally colourful, but the culprit is an archdeacon who goes by the name of Frognal-Tuke. Something scandalous about his birth is about to come to light. Miss Hogg has had her eye on him from the start: 'It may have been my Presbyterian blood coming out ... My forebears had a very low opinion of episcopal clergymen.'

Miss Bootle, whose dog was poisoned, is another suspect, but Miss Hogg doesn't for long waste time on *her*. The detective's reasoning is inconsequential, to say the least:

When Mrs Fairfax was killed, I crossed you off the list. Women very rarely murder other women ... Most crimes committed by women arise out of something intensely personal. The archdeacon was simply fighting to keep his prestige, though I suppose it might have involved his job as well.

Given such a clear division of motives, it is easy to determine a criminal's sex. Miss Hogg's sympathies are with her own, on the whole, though her feminism is just an endearing quirk which nobody takes seriously:

'It's all due to the idiotic taboos inflicted on us by men,' Miss Hogg said. 'Women never had a hand in making the laws. I must say I think most men who have been bumped off by women deserved it.'

'What about Lizzie Borden's father?' asked Parker. 'And I hope you don't hold a brief for Mary Blandy.'

'Of course there are exceptions,' said Miss Hogg airily . . . 'They were the victims of the economic circumstances of their time.'

In fact, there is a disinterested female murderer in *Miss Hogg Flies High*, but she is a horrid foreigner mixed up in a political intrigue: '. . . They were simply after the details of the latest ballistic missile. It was Madame de Valcours who jollied Tony into trying the aperitif port.' Poor Tony has ended up dead on the ante-room carpet: ' "Arsenic," said Hogg.' For the detective, from this point on, it is just one tight spot after another (' "Perhaps," he said, "you could explain what you were doing in Sir Hubert McFaddyn's potting-shed?" '). Finally she is found in a somewhat ignominious position ('this lady was tied up on one of the beds'), but not before she has put her finger on the murderers. ' "I think she egged you on," said Hogg, "and probably, like Lady Macbeth, handed you the cyanide." '

Miss Hogg, who is middle-aged, wears baggy tweeds and horn-rimmed spectacles, and refuses to tackle anything demeaning: '. . . You've no idea how many people come round wanting me to get them evidence for a divorce. And I simply will not peer through hotel bedroom keyholes, and eavesdrop under suburban windows.' This is not a suitable task for a lady, whatever one may feel about battery ('she was hit on the head in her sitting-room') or poisoning. Many people 'think adultery far worse than murder, as do most English juries', says another character in the series, echoing the point about social prejudices made years earlier, in a more serious context, by Tennyson Jesse (see page 102). It may seem that the detective is among them; but of course she is right to place prying into personal, sexual affairs on a different plane from ferreting out the truth about cold-blooded crime. Adultery is not 'worse' than murder, or only in the detective writer's terms: it is indisputably a subject less suitable for investigation. Miss Hogg is not being at all prissy when she expresses her aversion from this aspect of the private detective's trade; but of course it is easy to confuse genteel repugnance with a perfectly reasonable disinclination to poke one's nose into private matters. However, the latter is a luxury of feeling that the investigator, once she's placed in a situation of even superficial realism, cannot entertain. When P. D. James's heroine Cordelia Gray ends by accepting a divorce commission it is an indication of success, since it implies that she is going to keep her agency in business. It is just a job to be undertaken like any other; a person who finds the details obnoxious need not do it.

The stout unmarried lady detective usually conforms to a lesbian stereotype, whether this is acknowledged or not. In the Honourable Constance Morrison-Burke, heroine of a number of comic novels by Joyce Porter, the tendency is pronounced and overt. The Hon. Con is attracted to pretty young women, as a bull terrier might be to a butterfly, and she has about an equal chance of catching one. There is really no need for her domesticated chum Miss Jones to feel insecure. It is all very rumbustious and innocent, like the barging and charging in a game of hockey. The Hon. Con has too much energy and no finesse. The first title, *A Meddler and Her Murder* (1973), indicates at once that the detecting instinct is going to be shown up for what it basically is: nosiness and officiousness. But there is nothing unpleasant in these qualities, which are coloured by the jolly good humour of the author's tone. The Hon. Con's antics are meant to be endearing. Later titles in the series are artless and lumbering, like the heroine herself: *The Package Included Murder* (1975); *Who the Heck is Sylvia?* (1976); *The Cart Before the Crime* (1979).

The Hon. Con is noisy and dogged in her pursuit of the unlawful. Her objective is threefold: to uncover it, to get into the thick of it, and to put a stop to it; and Miss Jones is trailed along in her wake, uttering only hesitant protests: 'Well, I'm sure you're right, dear . . . but . . .' We're reminded of the *Knockout* version of Billy Bunter with his sidekick Jones Minor. The Hon. Con's usual custom is to cause disorder and get her facts all wrong, right up until the last minute when things start falling into place, perhaps as a result of all the weight that was thrown about. ' "Came to me in a flash!" the Hon. Con explained cheerfully. "As soon as I clapped eyes on Mrs Beamish lying there in her gore, something went click inside the old brain-box . . ." '

The Hon. Con, with her enthusiasm and tactlessness, her ability simply to exhaust her opponents, is a standard comic type which may occur in either sex. The funny female detective, however, is usually mannish and therefore scornful of men (' "Explain yourself," said Miss Hogg [to a police super-intendent] . . . "Nobody's tried to play a joke on you. Heaven knows I've been trying to get you to be sensible ever since we met." ') and until recently she was not classified in sexual terms at all. She simply wore trousers, or the next best thing, in order to prosper in a masculine profession. At the other extreme, of course, is the extra-feminine sleuth who owes her success to special familiarity with hat-pins and the behaviour of housemaids. In the Hon. Con, a product of the seventies, the sexual element is allowed in, only to be travestied. For all her leering at young girls, she is about as erotic as a suet pudding— and Miss Jones is a vicar's daughter who is easily shocked, to increase the novels' potential for humour. It's effective, but not very subtle—a long way from the teasing frivolity of Nancy Spain's stories, for instance (see Chapter V). No one actually makes physical overtures to the Hon. Con, and indeed, our sensibilities would be revolted if anyone did. The active lesbian detective needs a more sophisticated context, and one is provided by the American writer David Galloway in a single spoof novel, *Lamaar Ransome—Private Eye* (1979).

David Galloway's character is readymade and so is the setting (Hollywood in the 1940s); only the details need to be altered. One obvious difficulty—the role in the story of men attached to the sexually attractive women—is rendered in-effective by the heroine's sexual tastes. The initial trick, making the detective female, in this case will come off only if she's homosexual as well. Lamaar Ransome is tough, sardonic and glamorous. She is not a huge sour spider sitting behind a desk like Chandler's Anna Halsey; she's out there retrieving chopped-up bodies from left luggage compartments with the best of them. 'Me? I tried to pretend it was just another clearance sale at the friendly neighbourhood butcher's.' Her Mexican girl-friend is the pretty dimwit—a usual role—who falls into the clutches of a psychopath. Strands of hair, torn from Conchita's head, are found tied up on Lamaar's door-knocker, as a warning to the detective to lay off. She's not intimidated. 'The party's over, Riley. It's not just your movie that's being washed down the drain out there. It's your whole filthy racket.'

David Galloway has written a stylish pastiche; but occasion-ally, when the wisecracking stops, an unadulterated line from the old-style Hollywood thriller is allowed in: 'But really, my dear, I'd much rather talk about you ... After all, I scarcely know you, and yet destiny seems bent on bringing us together.' We know this is parody, but of what? It's not sharp or pointed enough to transcend the stilted note it sounds. The book is fast-moving and funny, but it is entirely outside the author's purpose to write about the woman detective as a credible figure, or even to bring out any of the traditional ideas inherent in the stereotype. Lamaar Ransome is really nothing more than Philip Marlowe in drag.

The English woman private detective was rarely a private eye: the term is quite unfitted to suggest the formal, sedate quality which English writers have used to counter the disarray of crime. The last thing she does is engage in repartee. The Scotland Yard employee is more likely to answer back, but she was not, on the whole, presented at the level of sophistication necessary to foster wit. She is more often rude than smart. The 'female busy' is not, in any case, a common character; and Mrs Pym, Lady Molly, Sally of Scotland Yard and others are used to gain somewhat unsubtle literary effects. By the early 1960s, however, the profession of policewoman was sufficiently ordinary to warrant moderately realistic treatment in fiction; instead of the comic female with the bullying manner we find a credible girl who suffers from menstrual cramps and, in her less confident moments, broods 'about all the women in Deerham Hills she had to protect'. The name of this unostentatious heroine is Charmian Daniels, and she first appeared in *Come Home and Be Killed* (Jennie Melville,* 1962). She is the product of a Scottish university and a working-class home and, in her twenties, has become a competent and respected detective constable; Deerham Hills is a new town in the Thames valley.

The style of the Charmian Daniels stories is rather jaunty and brisk ('Moreover it was a curious picture. Janet disappearing on the journey home, and Mrs Birley going off into the blue after a quiet domestic morning'), the murders are often quirky and the murderers' objectives idiosyncratic. Jennie Melville makes the most of sinister possibilities inherent in domestic closeness. A cloying manner is an obvious shield for vicious derangement. Mumsy and Janet are never the devoted

* Jennie Melville is the pseudonym of Gwendolyn Butler.

pair they seem. Janet, in this instance (*Come Home and Be Killed*) is a would-be murderess, and singularly inefficient: all three of her intended victims recover.

The process of elucidation moves backwards, towards the peculiar situation which is at the centre of the crime. In *Burning is a Substitute for Loving* (1963), the secrets of an odd little family are uncovered by Charmian. Harry Elder is a boy who lives with his aunt and uncle, Jess and Eli Nelson, and his grandfather, Mr Cobb. Mr Cobb has caused an explosion to occur at a lingerie shop belonging to his daughter, Harry's mother, killing the proprietor and two of her customers. He has taken this step to thwart an attempt by the boy's mother to reclaim the custody of her son. She is a Christian Scientist, and Harry's well-being depends upon a pill which he's obliged to swallow daily.

Harry's aunt, a kind-hearted woman, derives a curious satisfaction from her hobby of spotting cripples in the street: 'She saw them where no one else did. One of the high spots of her life had been a day at Brighton where she had seen thirteen lame and halt in one day. It was one of the nightmares of Harry's life that one day he would come in, with a sore foot or a blister, and the judgement would fall on him.' In fact it falls on Charmian Daniels as she hobbles along in fancy footwear: 'the silver shoes represented an attempt to re-establish herself as a woman.' It's a sign of the time that Charmian worries about preserving feminine qualities 'in a man's world', wondering whether 'in gaining success as a policewoman she would also lose all the qualities which made her worthwhile as a woman and a person'. The dichotomy between the last two groups is still pointed, though we might have supposed the one to be included in the other. Charmian is forced, in accordance with social pressures, to take a slightly defensive line about her profession; and sometimes she goes too far in her efforts to compensate for undue toughness in her image: 'Surely pink roses were wrong on a great big girl like her?' In fact, she has a style of her own, if only she could accept it; and it doesn't incorporate the frilly or the frivolous. She's a painstaking and efficient worker, relying on a 'massive memory, feeling for detail, and her patient measuring-up of one fact against another'.

Only once does she get off on the wrong tack, and personal

factors are involved in this case (*Murderers' Houses*, 1964). A man who preys on women, deluding them, defrauding them and then murdering them, is known to be at large in Deerham Hills; and Charmian is keeping a look-out for possible victims. One of these is a weak little woman who takes a lodger; in fact this lady is the criminal's wife (though this doesn't save her from being done in), and it is Charmian herself, the police-woman in charge of the case, who is the intended victim. The reversal of roles is handled with great care and conciseness. At one point the detective, neglecting nothing in her efforts to get on top of the problem, asks to be notified if an unlikely client should approach the town's leading hairdresser in search of an improvement in her appearance. Charmian proceeds to make an appointment for herself, a thing she's never done before, out of a vague wish to impress her new next-door neighbour, a man named Coniston. The significance of this act is not lost on the reader.

The lover/killer figure is a motif familiar to readers of Jennie Melville's thrillers, though in these it receives more romantic treatment. It represents a means to crystallize the erotic element in fear. The thrillers follow a pattern of their own: an ill-wished heroine is placed within the precincts of a lonely grange, an abandoned Victorian iron foundry or a house on an island. Someone means to do her harm, and someone else has nothing but her welfare at heart; and she cannot distinguish between the two. She may be, or imagine herself to be, in love with one or the other; and the central tension relates to whether or not the love-object is also the malefactor. Nothing in these stories is ordinary or straightforward, but usually the girl possesses sufficient grit to confront the unexplainable head-on. 'I was motivated now by a savage determination to get to the bottom of things.' (*Nuns' Castle*, 1974). At the bottom of things lies corruption, in its most romantic guise: the shrouded but unburied body of a young girl concealed in a tunnel. The killer often possesses that wayward, destructive charm which so fascinates the authors of romantic fiction.

Madness in the Charmian Daniels stories takes a more squalid, ludicrous or grotesque form. It is underhand and creeping, not invested with the glamour that attaches itself so readily to sophisticated wickedness. We are never too far from a spirit of drollery, a relish for the ironic and the unexpected.

There is little room in the books for ambiguity in motivation or in character—the latter, indeed, is often established succinctly by means of a half-mocking assessment, sometimes delivered in the subject's own words which are taken up by the author and repeated until the implications of the expression are embedded in the reader's mind. For instance, Charmian's subordinate and fellow-policewoman Chris lives 'a life and a half'. Charmian herself is ambitious and industrious, and she suffers morally for the lapse of judgement which afflicted her in relation to the man Coniston. Her suspicions are not aroused, she remains in a state of purposeless infatuation until the last moment and then she only gets herself out of a nasty spot by running pell-mell into the street: the episode reflects credit on no one. For a girl determined to prosper by her own efforts it's a chastening experience. But Charmian has yet to meet her proper partner, another member of the force; her marriage takes place in due course, and her reputation is soon restored.

Jennie Melville is often humorous and perceptive: in the new town, for example, she tells us, may be found the last heirs to a long tradition of eccentricity in the working classes:

> ... They were small craftsmen—cobblers, weavers, carpenters; behind them, generations of non-conformity— Lollards, Quietists, Levellers, Chartists, Socialists; their energies in the last generations turning from politics and religion into crankier channels; always conscious that they were not educated up to their capacities and yet over-estimating their own abilities ...

and the group may throw up criminals like Mr Cobb, whose motives are actually high-minded enough to stand examination. As a social observation this is pointed and informative, and it is also unusual in a narrative much taken up with flippancy and quick movement. The author's style is subject to variation in its effectiveness: at best it is economical, and also funny: '... Grace Chancey had been removed by Charmian from a local hotel, a doctor's surgery and the police station itself. At each of these places some unlucky man had been accused of hiding her sister from Grace.' But when the short sentence is used just to record insignificant actions it becomes tedious and juvenile: 'Dr Massingham came down in the lift and went into the reception room to see what had arrived for him. He was a plump, cheerful man. He had Charlie with him. They went inside the room, Charlie phlegmatic and Dr Massingham cheerful.'

The joking undertone keeps the reader from taking Charmian Daniels quite as seriously as she takes herself, but there is no attempt to ridicule her personality or her profession. One is strong and tough enough to withstand setbacks, and the other carries an authority of its own. Charmian is accorded the exact measure of approval due to professional competence. She's at the other end of the scale from the omniscient or inspired detective who flourished at the beginning of the century. She has no advantage in wealth or social position; but equally there is no obstacle in the way of promotion which her own cleverness and diligence may not rout. She's a scholarship girl who thrives on competition; and in this she is typical of the early postwar generation. Previously, women detectives were nearly always middle-class, well-educated, well-adjusted, socially adept and financially secure; these background qualities freed them from obvious disabilities which might have got in the way of their investigating. Exceptions were very highly coloured figures like the gypsy Hagar Stanley or freaks like Edgar Wallace's Mrs Ollorby. In general, working-class women were too busy working, or suffering hardship, to get involved in the affairs of others; and it would have stretched the reader's credibility too far if one had taken unaccountably to sleuthing. The profession requires also an authoritative manner and this, at the time, was not a usual attribute of the lower classes.

As a genre, the detective story was never noted for radicalism in its social views. Up until the 1950s, roughly, the quintessential woman detective was middle-aged and middle-class; and we find no notable difference in treatment between the amateur and the professional. Miss Silver, who is paid for her services, is not more advanced in outlook or behaviour than Miss Marple, who is not. The amateur and the private detective have more in common than either has with the policewoman, whose job, like that of the army woman, smacks of heartiness and officiousness. These characteristics it has inherited from the male branch of the profession, and they adhere to the job, of course, not to the individual who may legitimately confound every preconception about the business. In Charmian Daniels the qualities that make a policewoman are modified and made endearing: 'a slight physical clumsiness' instead of over-developed muscle; a sensible regard for the mechanics of law enforcement, never a bullying misuse of authority. If it's necessary to take action to prevent crime, girls like Charmian Daniels are as fitted as anyone to do it.

The privileged, cosseted amateur is definitely a character from the past, but several recent women detectives have jobs unconnected with police work. Their detecting is incidental to their actual occupations, but it ranks as detecting none the less. Like all those jolly girls from the children's papers, whose craving for adventure never went unsatisfied, the natural sleuth is always stumbling into crime. Tessa Crichton, for example, the actress-narrator in a series of novels by Anne Morice, has surrounded herself with many friends and acquaintances who harbour murderous impulses. Her old school friend, her god-mother's daughter, her secretary-assistant, a lady at whose house she attended children's parties ('dear old, conventional Helena'), the son of another old acquaintance all use drastic measures to rid themselves of a troublesome presence in their lives, and all are brought to justice by Tessa, in her cheerful, agreeable way. After the first book (*Death in the Grand Manor*, 1970) she's a policeman's wife, but this doesn't deter her from exercising her own talent for deduction. Her cases and those of her husband rarely overlap. There is nothing in the least formal, or forward, in Tessa's approach to murder; she's simply on the spot, familiar with the players in the drama, and possessed of luck and common sense in about equal measures. She can recognize criminal tendencies when she sees them in operation: 'People don't dress up as yobbos and crawl about under grandstands unless they are up to something shady.' Solutions and explanations float in the back of her mind, until something jerks them forward. Then the small inconsistencies begin to add up ('It is the only logical explanation for that mysterious affair with the goat'). Tessa is sometimes foolhardy enough to endanger her life (*Murder in Married Life*, 1971, for instance), but her own last-minute escapes don't trouble her any more than her friends' deaths ('. . . Poor old Julian . . . I believe . . . that he was actually trying to warn me about her, when he rang up, in his last throes'). 'Camilla may have been irritating, but she scarcely deserved that,' Tessa observes about a childhood acquaintance of her own who has been lured down to a river and held under until she drowns (*Scared to Death*, 1977).

It's a smart and sensible world that Tessa inhabits, a world of auditions, conferences at the Dorchester, inherited assets, dragon-nannies, horse-loving adolescents, stylish dressing in the bland manner of the 1960s. It has about as much substance as a lettuce leaf, and possesses the same kind of crispness and pleasant colour. It is arranged to accord with a very basic idea of glamour. London and the Home Counties are brought up to date, and lose their cosiness and crabbedness in the process. What they get instead is a *Homes and Gardens* gloss.

Everything about Tessa is unexceptionable, if we leave aside the company she keeps. Her nerve is good, her eye clear, her manner reassuring, her judgements sound ('I could never be friends with a murderer; not real friends like I am with Betty'). The interest she takes in people's business offends no one. Other detectives keep their suspects under surveillance; Tessa organizes luncheon appointments with hers. Her spirits are blithe and her personal characteristics subdued. She is not prone to suffer qualms of conscience, or stress of any kind. She is the well-behaved, impeccable Hastings figure made over as the detective; and sometimes her literary style is tinged with the kind of facetiousness we associate with the first-person narrative in light reading of a bygone era:

> . . . However, I did not allow myself to slide into the grip of mortal terror for more than a second or so, for common sense soon informed me that the noise did not emanate from Nannie's ghost tramping around the nursery, but from the aforementioned elements.

Tessa is calm and sensible, as befits the restorer of order; she has many strengths to draw on, including the staunch middle-class way of looking at things. It is a part of this to play down physical injury to oneself: 'Of course I'm all right' is the gruff response to the expression of concern delivered as one regains consciousness after being hit on the head by a miscreant. These are the very words of Jemima Shore, as she comes round after suffering an attack by a faceless nun, the Black Nun in person, no less, an apparition chilling to the blood of many schoolgirls at the Blessed Eleanor's Convent.

Debonair Jemima, a past pupil of the convent (though she's not a Catholic) and now a successful television interviewer and presenter of her own programme, is the heroine of two detective novels by Antonia Fraser. In *Quiet as a Nun* (1977) she is summoned to the school to investigate queer goings-on. A cry for help is sent out by her old headmistress Mother Ancilla, and soon Jemima is back in the world of bells, statues and rosary beads. It takes 'an outsider's eye to see clearly what perhaps we, so close to it all, have missed'. 'Jemima,' says Mother Ancilla, 'you've got to tell us. Why did she die?' 'She' is Rosabelle Powerstock, or Sister Miriam, who has starved to death in a ruined tower in the convent grounds (a prop straight out of the *Schoolgirls' Weekly*). There are political reasons for her death, as it turns out: she owns property, including the convent and its lands; and she has fallen under the influence of a person who holds fanatical views about the redistribution of wealth. The disrupter of the convent's peace is Alexander Skarbek who actually roams its corridors at night got up as the Black Nun, a legendary figure that proves convenient for his distorted purpose. At one point in the eventful narrative he traps Jemima in a crypt replete with the bones of nuns; it is a fearful spot, but the resolute investigator never loses heart. 'Come on, Jemima,' she rallies herself, with a cry from the hockey field.

One nun is Skarbek's accomplice, another is Jemima's rescuer on more than one occasion; the latter, the good but enigmatic figure, draws a small pistol from her habit to confound her Sister in Christ who is in the act of shoving a lethal pill down Jemima's throat. 'We must trust in God, Miss Shore,' says Sister Agnes, the imperturbable nun. No doubt she is referring to her fortuitous arrival.

Jemima's life is saved again, the mystery solved, the property justly disposed (it remains with the convent). Jemima the Protestant, the modern heroine, the independent woman with a married lover, can admire the nuns for the qualities of faith, order, composure and kindness which she sees in them. It's a romantic view.

When Jemima visits the Northern Highlands (*The Wild Island*, 1978) she is soon writing to Mother Agnes (promoted after the death of Mother Ancilla): 'I find myself in a very odd situation here.' She's not exaggerating: her host Charles

Beauregard has been found drowned shortly before she arrives, and she is surprised to hear him referred to as His Late Majesty King Charles Edward of Scotland; a crackpot royalist organization has the island in its grip. Jemima arrives in time for the funeral where she's told off publicly for failing to wear a hat ('Wummun . . . will you not cover your head decently in the House of God?'). Truly, the Beauregards are not an ordinary family. 'I'd do anything to be Queen,' declares Clementina, sister of the dead Charles. Delusions of majesty would appear to be catching. Clementina's uncle, Colonel Henry, provides a pair of arms for Jemima to fall into, when she needs to take time off from her ruminations. The islanders disapprove: '. . . You have now joined the ranks of his numerous wummin and strumpets,' she is told.

It is a new departure for the woman detective to sleep with a person who may be implicated in the curious events which make up the story. The traditional detective is quintessentially disinterested, outside the crucial imbroglio; she is never, like the heroine of a thriller, at once the object of persecution and the discoverer of its source. Colonel Henry Beauregard is attractive to Jemima ('Perhaps Highland lairds, like Scottish whisky, improved with age?'), and she is, after all, a sophisticated lady with no reason to forgo amorous satisfaction. It is only afterwards that she finds herself remembering a South American saying: 'First the horse, then the woman.' Can it be that the spruce colonel is *that* kind of man? Suave, ruthless, and contemptuous of his strumpets? The word implies that his behaviour is notorious. And indeed it is the root cause of the disturbances on the island, though he is not himself the guilty person: it is his mad wife Lady Edith who is a triple murderer. 'I'm going to shoot you like the other one,' she informs Jemima. In a moment of mismanagement, however, she shoots her husband instead as he barges in to save the incautious investigator.

Jemima, in fact, has done very little practical detecting in this novel, and her plea ('I'm a television reporter, not a detective') is not much of a defence from the reader's point of view. As a character, she is meant to stand for a fairly uncommon type: the harassed celebrity, continually at the mercy of those who attribute mysterious powers of judgement and action to the television performer. The title of her programme, 'Jemima

Shore—Investigator' (a parody of American 'private eye' jargon), is apt to be taken literally; though the subject of her weekly investigations is always a social question of great import. There is a double irony in the fact that the title has stuck to her, so that people always expect her to put their troubles right. She is willing to do her best; but the sheer magnitude and opacity of the mysteries facing an investigator on Eilean Fas (the Wild Island) are enough to stump anyone. In the end, nothing but curiosity, 'at once her best and her worst quality', drives Jemima on; and she fails to draw a logical conclusion from the facts as she observes them. Lady Edith's confession takes her by surprise.

The rules governing strict detective fiction have been relaxed, and increasing realism in one department is matched by increasing fantasy in another. The events described in both these novels are quite preposterous—convent life at its most unorthodox; Scottish nationalism gone haywire. Engagement with real social issues (schemes to provide housing for the poor and lunatic brands of nationalism do of course exist) actually lessens their credibility, since these are never treated seriously. But no miracles of elucidation are performed by the heroine; and in this respect at least she has moved closer to the plausible and unostentatious, qualities required of the modern, straightforward character. Indeed, the concept of the heroine has shifted from the extraordinary to the ordinary, at least in middlebrow fiction. *Apparent* ordinariness, which we find in the Miss Silver type of sleuth, won't do. Jemima Shore is really just the focus of interest in the books, not the powerful outsider who has got everything under control, the behaviour of other people as well as her own. She is as startled as anyone when the truth comes out, though she is quick to see how it makes sense of everything that had seemed puzzling.

There is no room for complication in Jemima's nature when incessant adventures are taking place around her; but, like Tessa Crichton's, her sanity is striking in the face of so much dottiness and criminal lunacy. The genre doesn't demand more than a clear outline for its central characters, about whom facts are presented plainly and without emotional fuss. Antonia Fraser has brought the Gothic mystery up to date, simply by transcribing its charnel atmosphere in very forthright terms. Her briskness, with its underlay of mild humour, works all the time to dispel the clouds of murk she's for ever summoning up, and the result is jolly and blithe in defiance of the subject, like 'The Mistletoe Bough'.

Jemima's behaviour on the Wild Island provides yet another instance of the modern writer's impulse to subvert the clichés of old-style mystery fiction: the 'other woman' in this case is also the nominal sleuth. However, Jemima has to acknowledge a measure of guilt when she considers the effect of her adultery on Lady Beauregard—and the voice of her conscience is the voice of that wise nun Mother Agnes. This is not an unusual role, at the present time or any other, for a nun in fiction: to stand for a kind of absolute propriety unattainable in real life, acting as a measure for the shortcomings of the unprofessed. (The bad nun of course is really horrid; but she is often someone who has joined the convent under false pretences.) The nun in her habit is an obvious symbol for virtue—and often it seems that she has attained, in her seclusion, a kind of divine wisdom which enables her to perceive the truth of any matter. It's a useful faculty in the field of detection, if it were not inappropriate for a holy sister to concern herself with any secular end. Several authors have tried to make their nuns detectives, by devising repeated situations in which the convent-bound heroine is able to draw conclusions about events which she has not herself witnessed. The nun becomes, not an armchair, for nuns don't loll, but a *pew* detective. (Sister Ursula, for example: see Chapter VII.) It is really the most extreme application of one formula for the detective story: the principle of the 'least likely person' as sleuth. Not only female, but cloistered as well . . . the reader's credibility is bound to fail.

The nun-detective deals in platitudes ('the outside world must be a very trying place to live in'), speaks with great sadness when the occasion demands it and twinkles sympathetically at the inspector in charge of the case she's just solved ('. . . amazing how much investigating one can do on the telephone'). This particular miracle-worker is named Mother Paul (June Wright, *Make-up for Murder*, 1966) and one of her assets as a detective is an ability to see things in people's eyes. (Not motes, but emotions.) Thriller, romance and magic tale have fused to produce a really mawkish result.

The nun may be supposed to possess absolute trust in a divine ordering of the world, and therefore in the proposition that wrongdoing cannot prosper. The moral element in detective fiction is given a boost, though it's translated into very palatable terms. Nuns' faith is always presented as an engaging quality. A nun on the loose is typically a cheery and proficient innocent, like the American author Dorothy Gilman's heroines in *A Nun in the Cupboard* (1975), whose unabashed belief in the supernatural is meant to be disarming. Dorothy Gilman has elected to emphasize the affinities between her religious sisters and a certain type of American flower-child that went in for mysticism and natural living; though her primary object is to write a thriller.

Sister John and Sister Hyacinth are the nuns, on leave from their convent, who have come to inspect a property mysteriously bequeathed to their Order. In the grounds they find a group of hippies, and in a cupboard indoors a man wounded in a shoot-out with a gang. It's an unusual situation, but the nuns are never at a loss to know how to act; they simply do whatever is right, speaking freely of miracles and marvelling at the injustices they find in the world. No one is unkind enough to question their faith, or their methods of putting things right, which are not based on discernment or authority but pay off none the less, in accordance with the scheme of values which attributes power to succeed to the wholehearted. The nun in detective fiction, for all her sprightly common sense, relies too heavily on divine intervention and naturally this reduces the proper logic of the story. On the ethical plane as well, it simplifies the concepts of virtue and villainy and this makes for childishness. There are in existence a number of good detective novels set in convents; but the nun herself makes an inappropriate heroine, at best complacent in her view of society, at worst symbolic of a kind of unreality which verges on sensationalism.

To return to the more moderate and intelligent story: the latest of the elderly spinster detectives is Miss Melinda Pink, JP, a creation of the journalist and mountaineer Gwen Moffat, whose tales of climbing are often centred on the discovery of a corpse in a crevice. Miss Pink, herself a climber, is attuned to danger and exertion and she can tell, by observing the antics of the people around her, who is in need of protecting and who is not, though sometimes her insight comes too late to be of any use to the victim, who is already decomposing on a rubbish heap, or going up in flames. People who get themselves murdered in the Miss Pink stories are often rash and sexually promiscuous women ('When Madge wanted a man, she took him without any thought at all for the consequences'). None of them is especially admirable or pleasant in character; but it might seem that an unduly harsh payment is being exacted for misbehaviour in one area. However, sexual indiscipline may stand for a more general selfishness and moral carelessness which justifies the bad end ('a whiff of putrefaction drifted past'). Miss Pink is sufficiently in touch with the notion of diminished responsibility to regard the murderer as a victim too, a victim of insufficient control and a fanatical view which can equate the death-blow with a blow struck for moral decency in a deteriorating world. It is, of course, a delusion familiar to the JP.

Miss Pink is quite without eccentricities of manner or appearance; her character is not built around a facile peculiarity, but is simply indicated in the way she responds to certain pressures. Unassuming competence is her principal trait. She is always ready for action in the open air, shinning up and down cliffs and plunging into cold water without hesitation, in spite of her age. We may infer that she is brave and wholesome, as befits an outdoor detective; and her straightforward view of life is never eroded by contemplation of the frivolous or the untoward. It is a point in her favour that the books are never disfigured by the arch tone which certain authors considered inseparable from the female sleuth. But it's possible that Gwen Moffat has gone too far in the other direction. Miss Pink's personality is almost too plain, too muted; and perhaps by way of compensation we sometimes find an excess of extroversion in the subsidiary characters. True, they're not allowed much room to expand (this is true of most detective fiction) so their distinguishing marks must be set out straight away.

Flamboyance in the detective, of course, is no longer acceptable as a substitute for serious characterization; nor is its inverse, mousiness, used to the fullest extent by Agatha Christie in her creation of Miss Marple, available to the present-day writer of crime stories. Its effects are played out. In the earliest phase of detective fiction, the atmosphere was often perilous and exotic, and the climax of the tale was marked by a grand gesture. Later, this gave way to an understated triumph for the detective at the moment of disclosure and arrest of the criminal; and technical ingenuity was at a premium. After 1930, the lady detective is no longer faultless in intellect and appearance (unless she's created by E. Phillips Oppenheim); she's just an ordinary person, often an aunt, gifted with uncommon powers of observation. In a sense, of course, this makes for subtlety; but the device, partly because of its initial effectiveness, quickly became a cliché of the genre.

The detective story is based on a clever presentation of exterior events, not on inner speculation or development; and this has usually kept it at a fairly undemanding level of composition. It deals in clear-cut issues and this diminishes its likelihood of encompassing moral ambiguity. It is a special form which imposes its own conventions and works within clearly marked limits, and it is not as such attractive to the serious novelist, the novelist who wishes to transcribe reality, the experimental or philosophical novelist or the ironist. It is a literary form which smacks more of entertainment than of depth in any of the usual departments of fiction (thank goodness, some might say).

Only at its most stylish and devious has it managed, without undue straining, to find a place for subtlety and humour (Gladys Mitchell, for our purposes, remains the prime example). But the woman detective at last, after her sentimental beginnings and her eccentric middle period, is becoming a character of real substance and efficacy. Cordelia Gray, for instance, heroine of a solitary novel by P. D. James (1972) whose title (*An Unsuitable Job for a Woman*) plays on everyone's most conservative feelings about the business, brings a new note of clarity and disabusement to the genre. The critical phrase is voiced three times like an incantation until the assumption is reversed. '. . . You can hardly keep the Agency going on your own. It isn't a suitable job for a woman,' says a carping barmaid whom Cordelia dislikes. 'No different from working behind a bar; you meet all kinds of people,' the girl retorts with spirit. The second reproving voice is foreign; it belongs to a lovely dimwit who is overheard to observe: 'It is not, I think, a suitable job for a woman.' Cordelia is ready, when a stranger whom she meets at a party begins to tell her: 'I should have thought that the job was—':

Cordelia finished the sentence for him.
'An unsuitable job for a woman?'

But the time has come for the platitude to be taken a stage further: 'Not at all. Entirely suitable I should have thought, requiring, I imagine, infinite curiosity, infinite pains, and a penchant for interfering with other people.' Suitable or unsuitable, the woman is wrong to do it; she is either repudiating her sex or fostering its unseemlier characteristics. All the varieties of disapproval aroused by the image of the female investigator are contained within these poles: but fortunately Cordelia herself is a character devised to refute the critics' unjust implications. The job is suitable, because she does it well; it is also painful, at times, because she takes no pleasure in the disagreeable facts she uncovers.

Cordelia Gray is exceptionally clear-eyed and courageous about her prospects for success, when she finds herself the surviving partner in a rundown detective agency whose founder has killed himself. She is strikingly devoid of hesitation, squeamishness or the power to dissemble. Her toughness of mind is never a formidable or an unlikeable quality. She has no preconceptions about the job or her own suitability for it: just a determination to do her best. She is capable of acting on her own judgement and lies to safeguard a more fundamental kind of truth, moral order or concept of justice—call it what you will. Her assets in the business lie simply in intelligence and a character not subject to vacillation or caprice. She is twenty-two years old and truly remarkable, steadfast as Gerda in 'The Snow Queen' and resourceful as Hop o' My Thumb.

Insecurity and danger are the central elements in Cordelia's life, and it is from her resolute facing of these that her quality derives. By her own choice, she is setting out on a hard course; she is even an orphan, like the sturdy heroine of an earlier type of fiction, and she is without emotional support in any department of her life. Sexual innocence, which she doesn't possess, is of course no longer demanded of a heroine and to suggest it would be a falsification; equally, its absence is not momentous or allied to drama in any sense. The virgin sleuth, with her coy acknowledgement of matters she wasn't supposed to know about but couldn't avoid in the course of detecting, has become an anachronism.

The professional and the amateur at their most accomplished and engaging, and most plausible in presentation, are embodied respectively in Cordelia Gray and in the American academic Kate Fansler, whose detecting is usually carried out in the precincts of a university or a high-class school. To date there are five Kate Fansler novels written by Amanda Cross (the pseudonym of Carolyn Heilbrun), beginning with *In the Last Analysis* (1964). Unlike Cordelia Gray, who is starting out, Amanda Cross's heroine is well on in life—established, gifted and civilized: impeccable, in other words, in position, ability and manner. She is a Professor of English at a well-known university and she embarks on detection for that most usual, most benign of reasons: to clear a friend, who also happens to have been her lover, from a serious charge. '. . . I am beginning to think that Alice was not in Wonderland after all; she was trying to solve a murder', Kate observes in a moment of perplexity; and indeed her investigations bring to light some incidents of a disconcerting oddity, including an impersonation and a murder in the past. Kate ponders on the facts and relates, as a story, the only solution that will fit them ('. . . Kate, all you've got is a fairy tale, beginning "Once upon a time" . . .'). But an inconsistency of literary taste confirms her theory: it is impossible that a man profoundly affected by a scene in D. H. Lawrence's *The Rainbow* should claim, some years later, to have read nothing by that author but *Lady Chatterley's Lover*. Clearly, a change of identity has taken place. Not since Nicholas Blake's *Thou Shell of Death* (1938), when a person who should know better appears to confuse Tourneur with Webster, has such a significant literary lapse occurred.

The habit of quotation and literary allusion, which might seem to smack of preciousness and affectation, is used in the Kate Fansler books in the way it should be: to foster style and wit. It is an enriching element. To see one thing continually in terms of another is not daunting, as it might have been, it is just clever: this is largely because of the cool manner in which the comparison is expressed. People who 'understand dishonesty but not the abandonment of surface rectitude' remind Kate of Mrs Patrick Campbell's view of the English: '. . . She said the English didn't care what people did as long as they didn't do it in the street and frighten the horses.' The state of coming up against a brick wall finds a perfect parallel in literary terms:

'. . . Kate, have you ever tried to explain *Ulysses* to a self-satisfied person whose idea of a great novelist was Lloyd Douglas?'

One of Kate's mysteries takes her back to her old school, the Theban, a progressive, upper-class establishment which 'imbued its students, despite their inevitable destiny of cotillions and debuts, with a tomboy, blue-stocking attitude which was never entirely eschewed'. We hardly expect to find the last two adjectives in such close alliance, but of course they represent traditions of female autonomy at different stages. 'A girl will always be a romp,' said Mary Wollstonecraft, herself a blue-stocking in the eyes of her contemporaries. The Theban also inculcates in its pupils respect for democracy, fastidiousness of mind and self-assurance, qualities exemplified in Kate. By the time of *The Theban Mysteries* (1971), however, Theban girls are wayward, opinionated, attend encounter groups to find release for their worst feelings and even get involved in the disposal of a corpse on the art room floor. Two guard dogs, accused of causing a heart attack in the dead woman, are finally cleared of blame. The Theban, with its strong traditions, endures.

Kate's effortless feminism sometimes finds expression in an impromptu compliment. 'Do you know what I like about you, Bill?' she asks, and goes on:

'. . . The fact that however much you stalk your prey, you do not class women with motor cars if they are attractive, and with eye-flies if they are not.'

'Eye-flies?'

'Well, something nasty. I was quoting Forster, who happened to be writing about India at the time, so it was eye-flies.'

It's a considered attitude, not a sudden response to a burning issue; but social forces have caught up with her. In *The Question of Max* (1976) Kate observes: 'All those women writers who've been ignored or forgotten for years are suddenly being rediscovered . . .'; and in fact this novel is based on an Oxford friendship between three women which loosely resembles the friendship of Vera Brittain and Winifred Holtby. However, only the information presented about the latter (Dorothy Whitmore in the book) accords in any sense with the biographical facts. Kate is actually caught off guard for a time in this adventure; a tale of illegitimacy and murder which she concocts *is* just a tale, though it suits the killer's purpose to go along with it. A well-bred, debonair and agreeable person is a fraud, and worse, and Kate ends by dodging bullets in an evergreen wood. This is what comes of acting (the phrase is spoken by Kate's husband) as 'a sort of over-age Nancy Drew . . .'

However, Amanda Cross's subject is more often the moral deadlock which results from the contemplation of 'conflicting demands with right on both sides'; the conflict 'between individual judgement and the conventions of society', as George Eliot has it, which goes back to the *Antigone* and shows how far we've progressed from the simple concepts of good and evil which mark the lesser detective story. 'In former days, everyone found the assumption of innocence so easy; today we find fatally easy the assumption of guilt,' Kate says. It's an acute social observation; and it prevents Kate from being able simply to get on with what she's doing, with an easy conscience ignoring the disorder around her: '. . . It's just no longer possible, not, at least, if you're the sort who listens and admits to being confused, which is something no one ever said of Nancy Drew . . .' The violent crime, the act of murder, is just a dramatic representation of nebulous social ills.

With the reference to Stratemeyer's heroine the wheel comes full circle: it is fitting that the most subtle of women detectives should acknowledge the most obvious, if only in an access of mock outrage and affront. The figure of the girl sleuth, which crystallizes spirit, optimism and adventurousness, is able to transcend its context: few people who remember Nancy Drew with affection and nostalgia remember also the poor literary quality of the stories in which she appeared—and indeed it is better that they should not. As a symbol, she is absorbed into the popular consciousness, like the Bad Boy or the Vamp. The female detective is no longer a product of wild originality or excessive characterization: these attributes have served their purpose. Realism, irony and moderation are the qualities demanded at the present time; but the real person is no less effective as a sleuth, as writers like Amanda Cross have shown. From the moment, however, when Mrs Paschal outraged convention by her choice of career, the theme and the character have interacted productively. Through all the changes in social attitudes, and through all her varied incarnations, the woman detective stands out as the most economical, the most striking and the most agreeable embodiment of two qualities often disallowed for women in the past: the power of action and practical intelligence.

SELECT BIBLIOGRAPHY

Haycraft, Howard, *Murder for Pleasure*, Peter Davies, London, 1942

Hubin, Allen J., *The Bibliography of Crime Fiction 1749–1975*, University of California Press, 1978

Mason, Bobbie Ann, *The Girl Sleuth*, The Feminist Press, New York, 1975

McCormick, Donald, *Who's Who in Spy Fiction*, Elm Tree Books, London, 1977

Quayle, Eric, *The Collector's Book of Detective Fiction*, Studio Vista, London, 1972

Queen, Ellery (ed.), *Ladies in Crime*, Faber & Faber, London, 1946

Routley, Eric, *The Puritan Pleasures of the Detective Story*, Victor Gollancz, London, 1972

Showalter, Elaine, *A Literature of Their Own*, Virago, London, 1977

Slung, Michele (ed.), *Crime on her Mind*, Michael Joseph, London, 1976

Symons, Julian, *Bloody Murder*, Faber & Faber, London, 1972

Watson, Colin, *Snobbery with Violence*, Eyre & Spottiswoode, London, 1971

INDEX

OXFORD

MORE OXFORD PAPERBACKS

Details of a selection of other books follow. A complete list of Oxford Paperbacks, including The World's Classics, Twentieth-Century Classics, OPUS, Past Masters, Oxford Authors, Oxford Shakespeare, and Oxford Paperback Reference, is available in the UK from the General Publicity Department, Oxford University Press (JH), Walton Street, Oxford, OX2 6DP.

In the USA, complete lists are available from the Paperbacks Marketing Manager, Oxford University Press, 200 Madison Avenue, New York, NY 10016.

Oxford Paperbacks are available from all good bookshops. In case of difficulty, customers in the UK can order direct from Oxford University Press Bookshop, 116 High Street, Oxford, Freepost, OX1 4BR, enclosing full payment. Please add 10% of published price for postage and packing.

DOMESTIC MANNERS OF THE AMERICANS

Fanny Trollope

Fanny Trollope (mother of the novelist) set out for America in 1827 and travelled widely through the country before returning to England, where, in an attempt to revive the family fortunes, she wrote this book which was an instant success, and with its bluff, often highly prejudiced, views of American life, provoked the United States to fury. This new edition of the most famous travel book of the Victorian age includes Mark Twain's essay on Mrs Trollope in which he comments: 'Of all those tourists I like Dame Trollope best . . . She knew her subject well, and she set if forth fairly and squarely . . . She did not gild us; and neither did she whitewash us.'

THE AUTOBIOGRAPHY OF A SUPER-TRAMP

W. H. Davies

Preface by George Bernard Shaw

This is the classic account of the poet W. H. Davies's adventures as a young man travelling around America and England at the turn of the century. His spare, evocative prose gives raw power to his experiences among tricksters, down-and-outs, and itinerant labourers, and makes the characters he encounters—New Haven Baldy, the Indian Kid, and Boozy Bob—unforgettable.

'Anyone reading this book will turn back to Davies's poems with renewed respect. Their lyrical fineness had been forged in a hard school, and the *Autobiography*, like *Amaryllis*, is the real thing.' Glen Cavaliero, *T.E.S.*

LATER DAYS

W. H. Davies

In this sequel to *The Autobiography of a Super-tramp*, Davies describes his early career as a writer, and his friendships with Hilaire Belloc, Edward Thomas, George Bernard Shaw, and other eminent literary figures of the period. He never lost his love of the open road, and he tells of his travels round England when, in his down-and-out years (and despite having only one leg), he went from village to village peddling lace, pins, and needles.

BAYONETS TO LHASA

W. H. Davies

Introduction by Brian Shaw

In modern times the isolation of Tibet first came to an end with the Younghusband Mission to Lhasa of 1903–4. Peter Fleming's account of this strange episode in British imperial history was first published in 1961. The expedition was conceived by Curzon as a move in the Great Game which Russia and England had been playing for years in Central Asia, reluctantly sanctioned by Balfour's Government, and carried out in the face of immense physical obstacles. It was led by Colonel Francis Younghusband, soldier, explorer, and mystic; and thanks to his patience, his force of character, and his flair, a treaty was signed and the foundations of Anglo-Tibetan friendship laid. Yet, despite Younghusband's heroic achievement, the episode was to end in this public censure.

THE SIEGE AT PEKING

Peter Fleming

Introduction by David Bonavia

Peter Fleming, brother of Ian—creator of James Bond—and the epitome of the enlightened English gentleman adventurer and explorer, was for many years the *Times* correspondent in China. His account of the Boxer Rebellion in 1900 is a brilliant work of historical journalism.

'provides a fascinating glimpse of the last days of the Mancho dynasty which ruled China from 1644 to 1911. Crisply written, meticulously researched. It is not hard to see why the Chinese have never been very keen on foreigners.' *Tribune*

THE TIBETAN BOOK OF THE DEAD

Edited by W. Y. Evans-Wentz

The Tibetan Book of the Dead—the *Bardo Thödol*—is unique among the sacred books of the world as a contribution to the science of death and of existence after death, and of rebirth. It is used in Tibet as a breviary, and is read or recited on the occasion of death, but it was originally conceived to serve as a guide not only for the dying and dead, but also for the living. For this revised and expanded third edition of Dr Evans-Wentz has written a new preface.

'Dr Evans-Wentz, who literally sat at the feet of the Tibetan lāma for years in order to acquire his wisdom . . . not only displays a deeply sympathetic interest in those esoteric doctrines, so characteristic of the genius of the East, but likewise possesses the rare faculty of making them more or less intelligible to the layman.' *Anthropology*